DEDICATIONS

This work is dedicated to my parents:
Leroy and Vallie Smith, Sr.

James R. Smith

To my sons:
Zachary, Alexander, and Radford

Ellen L. Walker

It Is Well With My Soul

When peace like a river attendeth my way,
When sorrows like sea billows roll;
Whatever my lot Thou hast taught me to say,
"It is well, it is well with my soul!"

It is well, (it is well),
With my soul, (with my soul)
It is well, it is well, with my soul.

Though Satan should buffet, though trials should come,
Let this blest assurance control,
That Christ hath regarded my helpless estate,
And hath shed His own blood for my soul.

My sin—oh, the bliss of this glorious thought!
My sin, not in part, but the whole,
Is nailed to the Cross, and I bear it no more,
Praise the Lord, praise the Lord, O my soul!

For me, be it Christ, be it Christ hence to live:
If Jordan above me shall roll,
No pang shall be mine, for in death as in life,
Thou wilt whisper Thy peace to my soul.

But Lord, 'tis for Thee, for Thy coming we wait,
The sky, not the grave, is our goal;
Oh, trump of the angel! Oh, voice of the Lord!
Blessed hope, blessed rest of my soul.

And Lord, haste the day when the faith shall be sight,
The clouds be rolled back as a scroll;
The trump shall resound, and the Lord shall descend,
Even so, it is well with my soul.

—Horatio Spafford, 1876

CONTENTS

Introduction

I met James Russell Smith on a Tuesday evening in early 1998 at Timothy Baptist Church in Athens, Georgia. It was my first choir rehearsal with the Athens Voices of Truth community choir. I had heard about the choir from one of its members, Stephanie Watson, a friend and colleague at UGA. She encouraged me to come to a rehearsal just to see what I thought. I was hesitant at first, as I didn't know anyone else in the choir and wasn't sure I would be welcome. But when I arrived, Stephanie greeted me in her usual gregarious way and introduced me to the director, Mr. Smith. He, too, was very welcoming and put me at ease. I was introduced to a couple of other members and was invited to sit with the sopranos. I hadn't expected to sing with them that evening, but Mr. Smith insisted.

Over the next two and a half years, I was a faithful choir member. I attended all rehearsals; participated in concerts and other performances; and helped with fundraising, organizing workshops, and creating programs for concerts and other events. At the time I joined the choir I was working full time as a graphic designer at the University of Georgia and raising three sons, ages 13, 9, and 2. I had very little free time, but singing with the Voices of Truth was pure joy and very special to me. I loved the music, I loved the joyfulness of the singing, and I loved Smitty (which he insisted we call him). Even when he was very hard on us and demanded nothing less than perfection, I appreciated his determination, commitment, energy, and even his exacting nature in the pursuit of getting the very best out of the choir.

Smitty had a toughness but also a very wry sense of humor. He was gregarious but could be very serious as well. As I got to know him, I began to hear small bits of his history. I sensed he had been through a lot in his life and I was curious to know more. After hearing a few stories, I remember thinking that I would love to record his life's journey. When I mentioned this to Smitty, he just laughed and said that no one wanted to hear about him. I disagreed, but at that point I could not promise if or when it would happen.

In 1999, I decided to pursue my graduate degree in design and create my own freelance graphic design business. During that year, I gradually realized I would not have the time to devote to rehearsals or performances with the choir, and I knew how Smitty felt about attendance. Choir members were expected to show up on time every week—or don't bother coming. It was a difficult decision to make, but in late 2000 I stopped being an active member of the Voices of Truth. I continued to help the choir with special projects, designing programs, booklets, and CD covers. I also attended their concerts and programs as often as I could.

The years rolled by and Smitty and I stayed in touch, even if there were long gaps between our chats. I never gave up on this project, but I still wasn't sure when or how it could be accomplished. Then, as the choir's 40th anniversary approached, he called me and asked if I could help with some of the preparations. I was happy he had called and happy to help. And then I realized that now was the time. I finally had the time to devote to this project. Even though I still work as a graphic designer, my children are grown and independent, and my time is much more my own. Thankfully, Smitty agreed to take on this project with me.

Smitty is a unique individual, but his story illuminates much more than one man's life. We often read and hear about the lives of famous Black Americans, and we praise their courage and success against all odds. Yet we hear little about the courage of "regular" Black Americans, those everyday heroes who faced the challenges of growing up poor in the Jim Crow South. It is vital, if we wish to understand our history, to document not only the stories of those who are prominent or powerful, but also the stories of people like Smitty—

hard-working, dedicated, compassionate, strong, serious, energetic, and steadfast citizens.

Smitty graduated from high school long before the schools in Athens were integrated. I knew he had stories to tell about what it was like growing up in the 1940s, 50s, and 60s. Smitty's life demonstrates the strength, creativity, and resilience necessary for an African American of his era to navigate the world with wisdom, courage, and integrity. I am grateful that Smitty was willing to share his story with me, and now with our readers. So here is his story. I hope it will be as uplifting, inspiring, and enlightening for you as it has been for me.

–Ellen L. Walker

Author's Note: Throughout this story I refer to Smitty by his given first name, "James," as this best represents who he was for much of his early life. Friends at Tuskegee began calling him "Smitty" and the nickname followed him back to Athens; he has been known as "Smitty" ever since. Since it seemed jarring to switch names in the middle of the story, I continue to call him "James." But because everyone now calls him Smitty, the stories in the testimonials all refer to him by this name. Additionally, James' wife Rosa is often called "Rose" by family and friends, as you will see in many of the testimonials.

Chapter 1

Athens, Georgia: 1941

April 28, 1941 was a mild spring day in Athens, Georgia. Like many spring days in Athens, this Monday started out cloudy and chilly, in the mid-40s, though the weather forecast predicted a high of 71 degrees by afternoon. It was the sort of day when mothers insisted their children wear jackets as they set out for school, though more likely than not those jackets would be dragging behind them as they walked home.

In a small house on Grove Street Extension at the edge of the Athens city limits, a very pregnant 20-year-old Vallie Christine Barnes Smith began this particular April day as she began every day, caring for her four-year-old son Joseph Lee and 16-month-old daughter Willie Mae. As she fixed breakfast for her family, she thought of the cleaning, cooking, gardening, and washing she needed to do. But what transpired on this day would be more eventful, as this was the day her third child, James Russell Smith, was born.

Local News

In 1941, Athens, like many medium-sized Southern cities, had a daily newspaper. The *Athens Banner-Herald* informed the community of local, national, and international events, usually spanning eight pages for the daily edition with an expanded 12-page version on Sundays. Of primary interest to its readers were decisions of the local government, notices of upcoming events, sports news, church announcements, the society page, sales ads, and activities at the University of Georgia. To a visitor reading the newspaper on this particular day, it would not be evident that 35% of Clarke County's residents at this time were African American. Most of the paper's offerings were intended for its white audience. Needless to say, this was not the full picture of life in Athens.

On the day James Russell Smith arrived in the world, the newspaper headlines were fairly mundane, reporting only a few noteworthy events. The U.S. was not yet directly involved in World War II, though it was fully engaged as an ally to Britain. An article titled, "Colonel Lindberg Resigns Reserve Commission in the U.S. Air Corps Today" led on the left side of the front page. Lindberg was adamantly opposed to U.S. involvement in the war, and when President Roosevelt publicly rebuked him, Lindberg resigned in protest. A shorter article, "Defense Efforts Hindered by Soft Coal Strike," followed. Several large-scale strikes in a variety of industries had occurred that year, driven primarily by demands for higher wages. The war in Europe required American resources long before the U.S. became actively involved, but while profits were soaring, salaries remained flat.

Another eye-catching front page *Banner-Herald* article proclaimed, "Swastika Flag Flying over Athens; Nazi Forces Pursue Retreating Britishers." But it was Athens, Greece, not Athens, Georgia, that was overrun by the Nazis. It would be just over seven months before the bombing of Pearl Harbor became the paper's major story, crowding out all other news for the foreseeable future.

On this spring day, the only major local news was an announcement of a concert to be held that evening in Mell Auditorium: "Capacity Crowd Expected to Jam Mell Auditorium Tonight for Rubinoff, Solis Concert." Mell Auditorium, located in the (white) Athens High School on Prince Avenue, often hosted such events for the community. The Board of Education claimed a portion of the revenue from ticket sales and facility rental fees for these programs.

Although by 1941 cotton was no longer "king" in Georgia, the price of cotton was still posted daily in the top left corner of the front page. Cotton prices were on the rise that year, recovering from the record lows recorded during the Depression in the previous decade. While Georgia farmers were planting fewer acres of cotton overall, however, it remained a staple of small landholders and tenant farmers. From 1930 to 1950 Athens was the second largest cotton market in the state of Georgia.

Farther down the front page was an article with the headline, "Negroes are Given 6 Months for Disorderly Conduct." The paper reported that three workers at Benson's Bakery in Athens attempted a "sit-down" strike for more pay. The article noted that one of the men made $2 a day, another $11 a week, and the third $12 a week. Although the men were merely sitting quietly at the bakery, they were quickly arrested, charged, tried, convicted, and jailed. The presiding judge chastised the men, asserting that they were earning more than an American solider at that time.

There was a grain of truth in the judge's statement, as some low-ranking soldiers with few years of service earned roughly the same as these men. But in general, soldiers in 1941 earned closer to an average of $60 a month, considerably more than the highest paid of the three workers. Moreover, the bakery employees probably worked much more than 40 hours per week and most likely seven days a week, and unlike the soldiers received no benefits, pension plan, or health care coverage. The federal minimum wage, enacted in 1938, was 30 cents an hour. However, it was not mandatory for states to follow this guideline, and Georgia did not.

The second page of the paper included a small announcement that day, a notice of Friendship Church's upcoming production of the play "Heavenbound." The announcement included an invitation to any "white friends who might like to attend," noting that seats were reserved for them. Also on page 2, a large display ad announced "National Baby Week" at the Gallant-Belk Co. store. Handmade infant gowns were 59 cents or two for a dollar and bassinets were $2.95 to $5.95. Boley's "ready-to-wear and millinery" store advertised a dress sale—$2.75 for one, two for $5.00. The three movie theaters in town were showing *Penny Serenade*, starring Cary Grant and Irene Dunn;

Victory, with Frederick March and Betty Field; and *Wild Man of Borneo*, featuring Frank Morgan and Billie Burke (of *The Wizard of Oz* fame).

The Seaboard Railroad Company's daily schedule also appeared in the paper, as passenger trains ran through Athens frequently at that time. On Sundays the paper featured a School News page that invited readers to "Follow Your Child's Story of His School Work." However, only the white schools' programs and grade-by-grade activities were listed. The church announcements, which also appeared on Sundays, listed only the services of the white churches.

Although not mentioned in the newspaper on this particular day, a major scandal that had erupted at the University of Georgia that year, known as "the Cocking affair," continued to reverberate throughout the Athens community. Eugene Talmadge, a lawyer, UGA Law School alumnus, and staunch segregationist, had just begun his third term as governor of Georgia. The conflict began when Walter Cocking, Dean of the College of Education, advocated for integrating Georgia's public schools, including UGA. Talmadge demanded that the Board of Regents fire Cocking, and the Regents complied. But as an unexpected—and unintended—consequence, UGA president Harmon Caldwell resigned in protest. To appease Caldwell, the Regents voted to reinstate Cocking, after which Talmadge used his political clout to remove the Board of Regents members who had voted in favor of Cocking's reinstatement. He then replaced them with new Board members who would follow his orders.

As a result of this controversy and its subsequent fallout, UGA briefly lost its accreditation, a consequence that was almost unthinkable for the state's flagship university. While these events represented a major crisis for the University at the time, they also constituted the first attempt in Georgia to recognize the Fourteenth Amendment in the arena of public education. Unfortunately, it would be another two decades before this acknowledgment came to fruition with the admission of Hamilton Holmes and Charlayne Hunter to UGA in 1961. It would not be until 1970 that the public schools in Athens and Clarke

County were fully integrated.

In 1940, of the 20,650 citizens living in Athens, approximately 65% were white and 35% were African American. An additional 7,748 people lived in Clarke County outside the city limits, representing roughly the same percentages. Jim Crow laws were present in all aspects of public and private life, and both city and county were deeply segregated in education, commerce, government representation, religious worship, and housing.

The separation of city and county governments resulted in separate school districts for the city of Athens and Clarke County. While the school districts merged in 1956, it was not until 1990, after four referendums, that the city and county governments would merge as well. James Smith grew up within the city limits, so much of the historical narrative surrounding his story is that of the city itself. Yet because the school district merger had a major impact on education in Athens in the years he attended public schools, some of that history influenced his life as well.

In 1941, Robert "Bob" McWhorter was the mayor of Athens. A UGA alumnus, a noted player and captain on both the UGA football and baseball teams, and a UGA law professor, McWhorter served as mayor from 1940 to 1947. One of the major projects Mayor McWhorter oversaw was the construction, under the auspices of the Works Project Administration, of a neo-classical U.S. Post Office on Hancock Avenue. The Downtown Post Office opened in 1941 and is still in use today.

In 1941, the Athens City School District Board of Education president was Dr. John G. Mell; the superintendent of schools was B. M. Grier. The segregated district schools consisted of four white (Barrow, Chase Street, College Avenue, and Oconee Street) and four Black (Reese Street, East Athens, West Broad, and Newtown) elementary schools; one white junior high school (Childs Street Junior High); one white (Athens High School) and one Black (Athens High and Industrial School) high school; and a white Vocational School. There was no Black junior high school during this time. Black students attended elementary school through seventh grade, then entered high school at AHIS. All of James' education in Athens, from 1947–1959, took place in a segregated system. However, many major changes occurred during these years, including the construction of new elementary and high schools and the consolidation of the city and county districts.

National Events: 1941

On the national political scene in 1941, Franklin Delano Roosevelt was beginning his third term as President. In December, in response to the attack on Pearl Harbor, Roosevelt would authorize the U.S. to enter the war in Europe and Japan, but he would not live to see the war's end. In the same year, FDR was responsible for initiating change at the federal level to limit discrimination. As the war in Europe intensified, the U.S. experienced an increasing demand for civil service workers at all levels. Roosevelt issued an executive order establishing the Fair Employment Practice Committee, which "affirmed a policy of full participation in the defense program by all persons, regardless of race, creed, color, or national origin." This order ultimately led to a policy of non-discrimination in awarding government contracts. And while most units of the armed forces remained segregated throughout the war, this was also the year that the U.S. Army established the African American Tuskegee Air Squadron, better known as the Tuskegee Airmen.

The new executive order stipulated that any company that had contracts with the federal government must comply with equal opportunity laws. Roosevelt intended to pave the way for African Americans to have more and better jobs in the buildup to war. As Athens became a hub of military training and education in Georgia, some local businesses and industries were directly affected by the law. As a result, better jobs would eventually become available to African Americans in the Athens community. The Fair Employment Practice law is credited with achieving measurable economic improvements for African American men in the 1940s by helping them obtain more skilled and higher paying positions in defense-related industries. However, Athens was still a Southern city and discrimination still prevailed in the overarching economic, social, and political climate.

In 1940, Congress passed a law declaring that all persons born in Puerto Rico as of January 13, 1941 were U.S. citizens by birth. Known as "The Nationality Act of 1940," the law went into effect in early 1941 and established Puerto Rico as part of the United States for citizenship purposes, thereby extending the protections of the Fourteenth Amendment to people born in Puerto Rico after this date. Perhaps not coincidentally, Congress approved this law just as it began to establish military bases on the Puerto Rican-owned islands of Culebra and Vieques.

In lighter news, 1941 was also the year Congress designated the fourth Thursday in November as Thanksgiving Day.

Also significant to the history of Athens, and the South more broadly, was the beginning of the Second Great Migration of African Americans in the early 1940s. The first wave of migration from the rural South began in 1910 as over one million African Americans fled sharecropping, Jim Crow, and an uncertain future to find work in factories in the North and West. The second wave of mass migration began in 1940, just after the Great Depression.

As the advent of federal work programs led to an expansion of jobs in factories, shipyards, and the defense industry, an additional five million African Americans moved out of the rural South to seek higher paying employment. In 1900, nearly 90% of African Americans in the U.S. lived in the South. By 1960, that figure had dropped to 60%. James' father was one of those who would benefit from the new law and its attendant programs, moving his family from Athens to Newport News, Virginia to work in the shipyards during the war.

In the early 1940s, African American men earned roughly half of what their white counterparts were earning, and African American women earned only one-third of the income earned by white women. In 1941, the average cost of a new house in the U.S. was $4,075. Annual average wages for all workers were $1,750. Gas cost 12 cents per gallon and the average price of a new car was $850. Bacon topped out at 59 cents per pound. Going to the movies cost a quarter.

In popular culture, two starkly different movies premiered in theaters in 1941: *Citizen Kane* and *Dumbo*. *Citizen Kane* initially received a tepid reception, but America LOVED *Dumbo* right from the start. Oddly, *Citizen Kane* has, since then, remained at or near the top of lists of the best movies of all time.

1941 was also the year M&Ms were invented, providing a way for soldiers to enjoy chocolate without it melting. During the war the candy was sold exclusively to the military. Notable births that year included Wilson Pickett, Chick Corea, David Ruffin, Joan Baez, Maurice White, Aaron Neville, Jesse Jackson, Stokely Carmichael, Otis Redding, Emmett Till, Paul Simon, Bob Dylan, and Chubby Checker. This was also the year Billie Holiday sang "God Bless the Child" to wide acclaim.

Histories of Athens

Several histories have been written of Athens, but most of these accounts focus on the more prominent (mostly white) citizens, the stately architecture, the Civil War, and detailed accounts of the growth and achievements of the University of Georgia (see Bibliography). One of the most comprehensive books about Athens' African American citizens was written by Michael L. Thurmond. *A Story Untold: Black Men and Women in Athens History*, initially published in 1978 and updated in 2019, provides a highly detailed, in-depth account of the history and accomplishments of African Americans in Athens up to that time. Thurmond's work provides a much more complete picture of the lives and experiences of Black Athenians than most other sources presented.

In addition, one other fascinating archival resource has documented the experiences of some lesser-known African American Southerners in the first half of the 20th century. During the Depression, the federal government funded a variety of programs to provide employment for those who were hit hardest by the Depression. One of these programs was the Federal Writers Project, part of the "New Deal" Works Progress Administration.

A notable component of this project was the Slave Narrative Collection. The federal government hired out-of-work writers to interview over 2,300 former slaves and record their stories. In 1939 several interviews were conducted with African American residents of Athens and surrounding Clarke County.

These archives offer a wealth of information about what life at that time was like for some Black residents. However, since their primary focus was on former slaves who were by then in their 70s or 80s, it was an incomplete picture. These stories also tended to be written in the vernacular and without commentary. This gave them immediacy, but also left out some of the details that would have made their portrayal of African American life in Athens at that time even more vivid and complete.

Beyond these resources, little information is available in libraries or archives that documents everyday life in African American communities in the mid-20th century South. It is my hope that James Smith's story will help add to this history.

James Russell Smith

It was into the context described above that James Russell Smith was born in 1941. The third of six children, James grew up in a completely segregated South. Yet with the love and support of his family and several other key individuals, he learned to thrive despite the obstacles, hardships, and challenges his environment presented. His life's achievements are noteworthy not because he made history in the usual way, but because he has been a dedicated and thoughtful citizen of his community through a challenging time in history. As an African American man growing up in the 20th century U.S., his story is unique, interesting, vivid, and vital to document and preserve.

James lived his life working hard at various jobs, raising a family, mentoring youth, encouraging those around him to do—and to be—their best, and being fully engaged in his church and his community. While still a young man, James found his passion in organizing and directing numerous choirs, including the Athens Voices of Truth. His music ministry now spans over 70 years. James put his trust in God and knew that one must create a life worth living; it is not simply handed to you. It is my hope that James' story and the recounting of his memories, experiences, and achievements will create a richer understanding of Athens history by providing a different picture of, and perspective on, life in the Classic City since the 1940s.

CHAPTER 2

Family Origins

James was born into a large extended family with numerous aunts, uncles, and cousins living nearby. James' father, Leroy Smith, Sr., was the oldest of seven children; born and raised in Oglethorpe County, he moved to Athens in his late 20s. James' mother, Vallie Christine Barnes, was born in Athens and grew up an only child just inside the city's eastern limits. While it is not known exactly how Vallie and Leroy, Sr. met, they married in Clarke County in 1939. James' maternal grandmother, Josephine Barnes, lived with the Smith family until she passed away in 1947. James knew his paternal grandmother, but both of his grandfathers died before he was born.

Leroy Smith, Sr.

Leroy Smith, Sr. was born in Oglethorpe County, Georgia on October 1, 1910 to Charlie and Betsy Smith. Little is known about Leroy, Sr.'s early life, but James does know that his father only attended school until the fourth grade. This was not unusual for African Americans living in very rural parts of Georgia at the time, as the children of farmers or sharecroppers were needed to help in the fields and in some instances, there were no schools nearby for Black children past the early elementary grades. James describes his father as a stern man who was something of a taskmaster. Leroy, Sr. could be personable, funny, and charismatic, but he also expected a lot from his children.

Leroy, Sr. believed in teaching his children the value of hard work. James recalls that by age six he and his siblings were expected to do chores around the house, with most outdoor tasks given to the boys and most inside chores assigned to the girls. The exception was that all the children worked in the cotton fields every summer for many years; the boys plowed, planted, and tended the crop and the girls joined them for the harvest.

James recalled,

> My father believed in what he believed in, and when he set his mind on something there was no changing it. He meant what he said. If you didn't do [what you were told] or respond when he told you [what to do], things just didn't go well for you. My brothers and I were shown and told how to do many things and we had to learn fast. He was a strict disciplinarian. You knew what to do and what not to do, whether in the home or away from home.

Leroy, Sr. was a private man who was not keen on his children participating in activities outside of school or church, but he did pay attention to their achievements and behavior at school. He would attend PTA meetings and teacher conferences to make sure the children were performing to the best of their abilities. Regarding their education, Leroy, Sr.'s primary directive to his children was, "Don't bring home any C's!"

Leroy, Sr. had numerous jobs over the course of his lifetime. He was always a farmer but throughout the 1940s and 50s he also worked as a truck driver and mechanic for various employers. In 1942, Leroy moved his family to Newport News, Virginia, where he worked in the shipyards for the next three years, returning to Athens at the end of the war. James is not sure how his father learned about the work available there. However, most likely the expansion of jobs in the defense industry, coupled with Presidential Executive Order 8802, passed in June 1941, which prohibited discrimination in hiring practices in those industries, allowed African Americans to work in defense-related jobs in greater numbers. Leroy, Sr. might have realized that moving his family to an area that had numerous defense-related employment

"Maybe this is what God intended for me."

Vallie lived with failing kidneys for the last 15 years of her life. James and his older sister Willie Mae took turns driving her to her frequent dialysis appointments. All of Vallie's children helped care for her as well as helping out financially. James' wife and children were also a great help and solace to her.

At one point Vallie thought she had qualified for a kidney transplant, but after the test results were reviewed, it was determined that the new kidney was not a good match. She was disappointed but accepted the news with grace. The only thing James remembers her ever "complaining" about were the dietary restrictions she had to follow due to her illness. She lamented that she could not eat some of her favorite foods. Vallie passed away in September 2003 at the age of 83.

Although James faced some challenging times while growing up, he stresses that there were just as many good and happy times. His large extended family was supportive and loving. He knows he was loved and appreciates all the sacrifices his parents made for their children to insure that they would have a good start in the world.

Grandmother Josephine

Some of James' earliest and fondest memories are of his maternal grandmother, Josephine Barnes. When the Smith family moved to Virginia, Josephine stayed in Athens, so James didn't really get to know her until they moved back. By then, James was almost four years old and unfortunately, she lived only another two years after their return. When the family moved back to their home at 283 Grove Street Extension, Josephine shared a bedroom with her grandchildren. James recalls Josephine's determination that all her grandchildren would succeed in the world, and her encouragement and insistence that he and his two older siblings, Joseph Lee and Willie Mae, "always give your best."

Aunts, Uncles, and Cousins

Although Leroy, Sr. and his siblings were raised in Oglethorpe County, they all eventually made their way to Clarke County and lived near one another. Leroy, Sr.'s six younger siblings, Rene, Hubert, Flora, Hoke, J.C., and Lois, all lived with their families within a small radius in East Athens. Hubert and J.C. lived on Branch Street, Rene and Flora lived on Arch Street, Hoke lived on Grove Street, and Lois lived on East Broad Street.

J.C. worked for years at Trussell Ford Company, a tractor distributor with offices on Clayton Street. Hoke worked at Empire State Chemical Company (the same company Vallie's father, Lucius Barnes, had worked for years before) and Hubert was a cement finisher. Lois' husband, Charlie Cooper, was a truck driver, and Flora's husband, Ollie Wade, worked for the F. S. Royster Guano Company, which used fish meal to make commercial fertilizer.

Rene eventually had four children, Flora had three children, J.C. had nine children, and Lois had one child. Both Hubert and Hoke married but had no children. With 17 cousins, the six Smith children had a built-in troop of playmates when the families got together.

Leroy, Sr. remained close to his siblings and the families spent a lot of time visiting one another. The cousins all had someone else in the family roughly their age and all the children attended East Athens Elementary School. J.C.'s oldest child, Fred, was one year younger than James so they became close, playing together at school and at their respective homes. James recalls frequent visits with his relatives. "We would go by their homes and there was plenty of talking and arguing. All of [Leroy, Sr.'s] siblings wanted to be right and it seemed to me that all of them knew everything."

James recalls his maternal grandmother's sister, Elizabeth Mc-Cambric, known as "Aunt Sis," with great fondness.

> She was a very sweet and kind lady. But we noticed when we visited that she did nearly everything while sitting. Whether cooking or washing, she would mostly be sitting. We learned later that she had been stung by yellow jackets when she was young and that affected her mobility.

Aunt Sis and her husband, Jerry McCambric, lived across the

street from James' family. Jerry also worked at Empire State Chemical Company. The McCambric home included their son Johnny, who was blind; their daughter Katie; Katie's husband, Will Davis; and Katie and Will's son Tommy, who was a few years younger than James. Katie never worked outside the home but after Jerry died, sometime between 1942 and 1947, she and Aunt Sis began taking in clothes to wash and iron. Katie's husband Will was a quiet man who worked as a gravedigger for Oconee Hill Cemetery for many years. James recalls that Katie was a funny lady and that for some reason, she wouldn't let Tommy start school until he was eight.

Brothers and Sisters

James is amazed and grateful that as of this writing, all of his siblings are still alive and well. James describes his experiences growing up with his brothers and sisters as "a little different than a lot of his peers," primarily due to the expectations of his parents that all the children work from a very young age and the fact that they had very little "free time." The Smith children supported each other and James speaks of each of his siblings with great love and respect. He feels blessed that they have one another and is proud of the lives they have all made. James is thankful that the Smith siblings are close and have supported one another through life's ups and downs.

Joseph Lee Smith, b. 2/2/1937

Joseph was a bright and determined child. As the eldest, he worked hard at everything: farming, school, and chores, among other responsibilities. He was a gifted student, skipping the first and fifth grades and graduating from Athens High and Industrial School, tied as the class salutatorian, at age 16. After graduation, Joseph moved to Atlanta to attend Morris Brown College. He later transferred to Morehouse College, where he completed his undergraduate degree. Joseph subsequently earned his master's degree in social work at Atlanta University, then settled in Baltimore, where he lives to this day. Over the years he worked for the City of Baltimore, AT&T, and Johns Hopkins University.

Willie Mae Smith, b. 12/31/1939

James' older sister Willie Mae was loyal and dependable, always taking care of everyone else. James describes her as the second mother in the family. A somewhat serious child, she was a good student who worked hard to please her parents.

After Willie Mae graduated from high school, she attended cosmetology school to learn a trade that would allow her to be independent. She worked in a salon on Hancock and later owned her own shop for many years. When she was employed for a time at Bellgrade Manufacturing Company and at Action, Inc., both in Athens, she continued to have clients come to her home to get their hair done. Willie Mae remained in the family home and took care of her mother until Vallie's death in 2003. She continues to be actively involved in the First A.M.E. Church, and is the only one of the children who is still a member.

Frank Richard Smith, b. 1/17/1945

Born during the war when the family lived in Newport News, Virginia, Frank was a free spirit from the beginning, always marching to the beat of his own drum. James recalls that Frank got into trouble with their father more often than the rest of the children, but that he also stood his ground more than the others. Like his siblings, Frank was a bright student who learned quickly. He was self-confident, a quality that helped him weather whatever came his way. Of all the siblings, Frank was the most likely to bend the rules regardless of the consequences, including missing the curfew imposed by his parents. James recalls Vallie observing, "the middle child is usually the most difficult." But Frank was a bold and determined child. After graduating from high school he attended brick mason school, and has had a successful career in the construction industry for years.

Christine Vallie Smith, b. 3/28/1947

James thinks Christine was their father's favorite. Christine had a lively personality and loved to talk. She was a sweet child, but James observes that she had a knack for getting Leroy, Jr. in trouble when it seemed expedient to divert scrutiny from herself. Christine was the first in the family to graduate from the newly-named Burney-Harris High School in Athens. She attended Morris Brown College and received her master's degree from Atlanta University. She taught in the Atlanta Public Schools for many years.

Leroy Smith, Jr., b. 6/26/1951

Leroy, Jr. had a slightly different experience than his siblings growing up, partly because he was the youngest and was cared for from a young age by Aunt Sis, spending a lot of quality time in her home. James believes that Aunt Sis shared with Leroy, Jr. what little was known about his parents' early years and the rest of the extended family. Perhaps as a result, Leroy, Jr. is deeply interested in family history and genealogy, recording details and archiving stories. Leroy, Jr. was very talented academically and a meticulous scholar, and James describes him as the most responsible of the siblings and an excellent businessman. Leroy, Jr. attended Morris Brown College, studied law at John Marshall University, and has enjoyed a long career in the legal profession.

The Smith Family c. 1994. From left to right: Joseph, Willie Mae, James, Leroy, Jr., Christine, Vallie, Frank.

Character is Key

James credits much of his work ethic and drive to his upbringing. He reflects that his experiences growing up also helped him decide what kind of parent he wanted to be and shaped his attitudes about raising his own two children. He often says how important it is for him to talk to his own children about everything, from family relationships to the challenges they may confront. Most importantly, he always lets them know that they are loved and how proud he is of them.

James knew early on that character was the key to making it in the world. Growing up, the Smith children learned "honesty, the right behavior, how to talk to one another, how to treat your brothers and sisters, and most of all how to respect and honor your parents." James' parents taught him the rewards of hard work, the importance of not giving up when things got challenging, and the value of doing what you could for your family each day.

James particularly attributes his ambition and drive to his mother, who knew that her children needed a good education to succeed in the world. Vallie pushed all her children, and all her grandchildren, to become better, to be more, and to do more. James recalls, "When the grandchildren went to her house, she was going to teach them something. You didn't just go to play."

Vallie taught James that "whatever you need to learn, learn it well. Whatever you have to do, do it well." James took this and all of Vallie's lessons to heart, and they have guided him throughout his life.

Chapter 3

Home on Grove Street Extension

When James was born, he lived with his parents, two older siblings, and grandmother Josephine Barnes at 175 Grove St. in Athens. Josephine and Vallie had lived in the house since at least the mid-1930s, after Vallie's father Lucius died. When James was one year old, his father moved the family to Newport News for the duration of the war.

When the Smith family returned to Athens in 1945, they lived with Josephine at 283 Grove Street Extension. This may have been the same house they lived in before the war, since the house number could have changed in the interim when additional houses were built on that road. Grove Street and Grove Street Extension were just inside the southeastern boundary of the city of Athens (see Map 1).

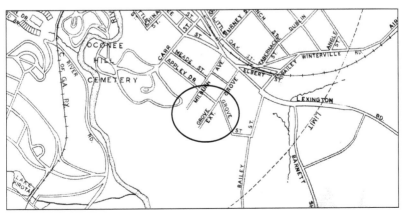

Map 1. Detail of Athens, 1949, showing Grove Street Extension.

Grove Street turned south off Oconee Street just after Winterville Road turned off on the opposite side, heading northeast. At the time, Grove Street made several left turns before merging with Bailey Street, which completed the loop to reconnect with Lexington Road. Most of the surrounding area was farmland and with the exception of Oak, Oconee, and Lexington Roads, the rest of the streets in the eastern part of the city were dirt roads. James recalls that when he and his siblings walked the two miles to East Athens Elementary School on Water Oak Street, none of the streets they traversed were paved.

Grove Street Extension headed straight south at the first bend of Grove Street and the Smith family home was the very last house on the left. The Extension was, and still is, a dead-end road, trailing off into the woods that cover the steep slope down to the North Oconee River. The Oconee Hill Cemetery was practically in their backyard.

The Smith Family House

The house at 283 Grove Street Extension was small, but cozy and well-tended. It was a modest one-story wood frame home with two small bedrooms, a sitting room, a kitchen, and a hallway. The hallway was partitioned off in the 1950s to create another bedroom. The house had no indoor plumbing, running water, or electricity until around 1954.

Leroy, Jr. in the Smith family home, c. late 1950s.

Water had to be fetched from the well in the backyard for cooking and washing, and the children did their homework in the evening by the light of a kerosene lamp.

The house's "bathroom" was an outhouse in the yard, and baths were taken in tin tubs with water heated on the stove. The house sat up above the ground on small posts, which helped keep it cooler, drier, and slightly less likely to be invaded by creatures large and small.

The furnishings were modest but comfortable, and sufficient for the growing family.

It is not as unusual as one might think that the Smith family home had no indoor plumbing at that time. While indoor plumbing made its debut in the 1840s, it was not the norm in new home construction until after 1925, even though blueprints for house floor plans that included bathrooms became readily available for purchase beginning around 1910. It took a while before consumers saw indoor plumbing as a necessity when building a new house. One enterprising company, Standard Sanitary Manufacturing, made porcelain toilets, sinks, and tubs as early as 1899 and advertised their wares in popular magazines of the day.

The 1940 U.S. Census was the first one to ask whether households had indoor plumbing, which was defined as a flushing toilet, a sink with a faucet, and a bathtub or shower. The Census data revealed that roughly half of U.S. homes had these amenities. Rural areas were even less likely to have indoor plumbing, and homes in rural areas of the South were among the last to be fitted with any type of plumbing.

The Smith house was heated by a wood-and-coal-burning stove in the sitting room. The walls were white-painted beadboard and the windows were hung with flowered curtains. At least one of the bedrooms was adorned with flowered wallpaper. The family slept in iron frame beds, sharing the space as siblings arrived. Meals were cooked on a wood-burning stove in the kitchen and the "ice box" was cooled by large blocks of ice the family would purchase. Inside the kitchen door was a place for buckets of well-drawn water.

Willie Mae in front of the Smith family home (to the right), c. late 1950s.

A long porch ran across the front of the house, and the yard was kept clear of most vegetation. Dirt yards were common and James remembers having to clear the tough Johnson grass with a sling blade. There was always a large woodpile stacked in the yard for use in cooking, heating, and to do the washing. It was James' and his brothers' job to keep the woodpile stocked. The large laundry washtubs and fire pit in the yard were used almost daily.

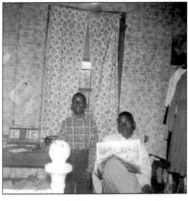

Leroy, Jr. and Frank in the Smith family home, February 1961.

In addition to the garden, which was planted with a wide variety of vegetables, a peach tree grew in the yard and the children would pick peaches as well as wild blackberries from the surrounding bushes. James doesn't remember eating a lot of fresh fruit unless it was in season or growing nearby. His family raised chickens for the eggs and meat. His mother canned any food from the garden they could not eat during the growing season and set it aside for the winter. Anything else the family needed was bought from the local A&P grocery store, located at East Broad and South Thomas Street across from the old Farmer's Hardware.

The remainder of the yard was taken up with a corral for the mule. James remembers many trials and tribulations with the creature, but it was a work animal and necessary for farming and pulling the wagon that carried loads of all sorts. James does not recall when his father bought his first Buick, but he has fond memories of being able to ride in the car as opposed to having to hitch up the mule to the wagon.

Neighborhood

The area historically known as "East Athens" long pre-dates what many residents think of when they talk about East Athens today. Old East Athens was predominantly African American and covered much of the eastern part of the city between the eastern city limits

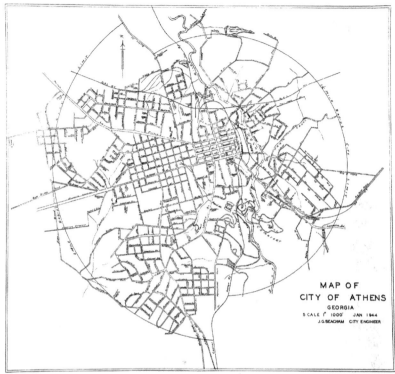

Map 2. Athens, GA, 1944. (Map courtesy of Hargrett Rare Book & Manuscript Library/University of Georgia Libraries.)

and the North Oconee River to the west (see Map 2). The eastern city limits roughly followed the path of what is now the eastern section of the Loop 10 bypass.

It is difficult to discern from the various maps of Athens over the years exactly which streets existed at any given point in time, especially near the city boundaries. City engineers recorded detailed information about electric lines, sewer and water mains, street lights, and streets to be paved. However, there were several areas close to the perimeter of the city that were the last to receive these services and were occasionally left off the maps. Some of these perimeter streets were also left out of many of the City Directories of the 1930s, 40s, and 50s. Grove Street Extension was one of these streets. Its existence comes and goes on the maps and its houses change address frequently, making the history of the neighborhood challenging to document with any confidence. Map 2, for example, does not show Grove Street Extension, although it most certainly existed by 1944.

Regardless, the Smith family has long and deep ties to this area. James' older sister, Willie Mae, still lives at 283 Grove Street Extension, where the family settled after the war. She and James had a new house built next to the old family house in the mid-1960s. They felt that building a new home for their parents equipped with all the modern conveniences was part of their duty as grown, working children. As soon as the new home was completed, they tore the old one down.

James remembers that in the 1940s when you turned from Oconee Street onto Grove Street, white families lived on the first leg of the street, until you reached Appley Drive (which can be seen on Map 1). There were no houses along Grove Street after it turned left at an oblique angle until it reached Bailey Street. Grove Street Extension and Bailey Street were occupied entirely by African American families.

This recollection is corroborated by the 1959 map entitled "Negro Settlement Areas in Athens, Georgia" (Map 3). Grove Street Extension and Bailey Street can be seen as shaded areas in the very southeastern quadrant of the map (within the circle). Bailey Street extended from Lexington Road due south from Oconee Street to the North Oconee River; everything to the east was farm fields and woods.

There are numerous reasons why the African American neighborhoods (settlements) were interspersed with white neighborhoods in Athens during this time. At the beginning of the 20th century, the population of Athens was roughly 10,000, equally split between Black and white residents. Many African Americans in Athens worked in white households as domestic labor, often living at the back of their employers' property or very close to it. Athens, unlike many Southern cities at the time, did not have any segregation ordinances that limited where African Americans could live and work. There was also a burgeoning Black middle class in Athens due to educational opportunities and the availability of work as teachers, in health care, or in business.

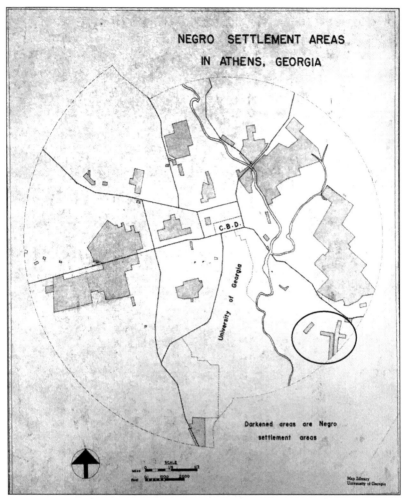

Map 3. Negro Settlement Areas in Athens, GA, 1959. Circled area shows Grove Street Extension and Bailey Street. (Map courtesy of Hargrett Rare Book & Manuscript Library/University of Georgia Libraries.)

In addition, after the boll weevil scourge (which arrived in Georgia in 1915), followed by the Great Depression, many Black families left farming or sharecropping and moved to the city for better paying jobs, often finding places to live close to other Black families who already lived in town. Athens was also still a fairly small city in the mid-century, with areas of undeveloped land within the city limits. This made it easier for African American families to just settle on "unused" land that was deemed undesirable due to its proximity to either a railroad, a flood plain, or industry. Many of these Black "settlements" flourished and became cities within the city, providing commerce, services, churches, and residences for African Americans during this time. Many of these communities were disrupted by the "urban renewal" of the 1960s, which will be covered in detail in Chapter 8 of this book.

Two white families owned the farmland on either side of Grove Street. The Seagraves owned the land on the inner part of the curve and the Birdsongs owned the land on the outer portion that stretched south to the river. Both families had addresses on Grove Street, the Seagraves starting in 1940 and the Birdsongs by 1949.

Many members of James' family on both his mother's and father's sides lived on Grove Street (or its Extension) at various times over the first half of the 20th century. James' maternal grandfather, Lucius Barnes, lived at 160 Grove Street as far back as 1909. At some point, Josephine's brother, Will Pope, began to purchase property in the area of Grove Street and what would become Grove Street Extension.

When Lucius married Josephine Pope in the late 1910s, the couple moved to 445 Oak Street. When Lucius died in the mid-1930s, Josephine moved back to 175 Grove Street with teenage Vallie. Jerry McCambric and Aunt Sis lived at 194 Grove beginning in 1923. Eventually other members of the Smith and Barnes families built homes there or moved to the area to settle.

It is difficult to discern how the house numbers were assigned in this area. It is also nearly impossible to determine whether families actually moved from one house to another or if the numbers were arbitrarily changed as more homes were built. James is sure the family lived in the same house for years, so he is baffled by the numerous address changes for family members. We can only speculate that as more homes were built along Grove Street and Grove Street Extension, the numbers of the houses were changed.

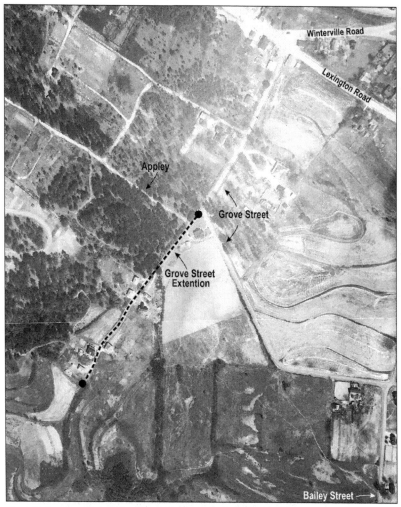

Aerial photograph showing Grove Street and Grove Street Extension, 1946.
(Photo courtesy of the Abrams Foundation.)

In 1937 the City Directory lists only four addresses on Grove Street. In 1938 the number jumps to eleven. This stays somewhat consistent over the next four years, but in 1942 it drops back down to only six households, possibly due to wartime migration such as James' family experienced.

By 1947, the listings for Grove Street had expanded once again to thirteen households, most of the families James remembers from his youth. By 1949 the Directory listed eighteen households on the street, including a rather large trailer park in the first block of Grove. However, while James grew up on Grove Street Extension, none of the City Directory listings from the 1940s or 50s identify Grove Street Extension as a separate street. It was not until 1962 that it was listed as such.

Given these inconsistencies, even if a family was listed in the City Directory as residing on Grove Street, they could well have lived on Grove Street Extension, further undermining any certainty about the exact location of some houses. An aerial photograph from 1946 shows several houses along the section of road known to be Grove Street Extension. Even today, while houses are numbered somewhat consecutively on Grove Street from Oconee to Appley, there are huge gaps in the numbering, and addresses begin in the 100s again for Grove Street Extension. The only convention that seems to hold up over time is that one side of the street has even numbered addresses and the other odd. Further confusing the history of this area is the fact that the bypass cut Grove Street in half, so that several Grove Street addresses are now outside the loop.

Thus, while one can research and locate addresses associated with particular individuals within the Athens city limits over time, historical sources do not always tell the complete story. It is difficult to determine with any certainty where houses were located and when they were included in the Directory, complicating accurate documentation.

Neighbors

In addition to several relatives living nearby, James also remembers other neighbors fondly. Grove Street Extension consisted of eight houses while James was growing up. His neighbors included Mrs. Della Cochran, Mr. and Mrs. Willie and Ruth Johnson, Mr. and Mrs. Barney Rucker, Mr. and Mrs. Guy and Mary Lou Rucker, and the Waymon Johnson family.

The Johnson household included Waymon Johnson, his wife Carrie, their daughter Hazel, their son James, and grandsons Sam and

Danny. Mr. Johnson always walked to and from his job at Hodgson
Oil Refining on Oconee Street near downtown Athens. (The build-
ing still stands and is now home to UGA offices). Carrie worked in
the homes of "well-to-do white folks" and also took in washing and
ironing. She was generous with whatever she had and often brought
James' sisters brand new dresses that her employers had given her.
What James remembers most vividly was that several members of the
Johnson family had beautiful singing voices.

One of James' fondest memories was the vocal music that filled
the evening air in his neighborhood:

> When Mr. Johnson got home from work he would sit
> on his porch and you could always hear him singing in a
> sonorous bass voice. Mrs. Carrie would be outside, going
> back and forth from the washtub to the wash pot, sing-
> ing all the while she worked. She did not sing formal-
> ly, but she had a beautiful soprano voice. Her daughter,
> Hazel, sang in church choirs and had an unusual voice as
> she could sing all four parts when needed–soprano, alto,
> tenor, or bass. Carrie's son, James would join in the sing-
> ing in his beautiful tenor.

James recalls that Hazel, her aunt, and another friend formed
a trio and would rehearse on the Johnsons' front porch. James recalls, "My, what a sound rang in the community. We as children were
amazed and loved those evenings."

CHAPTER 4

Daily Chores and Seasonal Work

James and his siblings awoke each morning to a long list of chores they needed to accomplish around the house. Some of the children's chores were seasonal but many were year-round, as they helped with daily tasks that kept the household running. Their days often began before dawn and lasted until long after dark. During the school year homework was an added task at the end of each day. It was not unusual for the children of farmers and others who lived in rural areas to do chores around the home, but the Smith children probably had a few more labor-intensive tasks than many of their peers.

School Days

Winter mornings started very early for the Smith family. One of the boys would rise before dawn and start a fire in the sitting room stove. This warmed the house just enough to motivate the rest of the household to get up and start their day. Once the fire was blazing, coal would be added, as it burned more slowly than wood and kept the house warm throughout the morning.

The children's next chore was to make a fire in the kitchen stove so their mother could cook breakfast, a hearty meal that fortified the children for their two-mile walk to East Athens Elementary School. If the water buckets by the door were empty, one of the children would go out to the well and lug the full bucket back inside. They also made sure the woodpile just inside the kitchen door was fully stocked.

When the children returned home from school, the boys would

stoke the fire in both the kitchen and the sitting room stoves, then head outside to finish the other chores that had to be done before supper and homework. Their last task on winter days was to build yet another fire in the open fireplace so the home would remain moderately warm throughout the night.

The Woodpile

Keeping the woodpile stocked was a major responsibility for the Smith brothers. Because their mother cooked over a wood stove and water must be heated for washing clothes and bathing throughout the year, this was not just a seasonal chore. It was an endless routine for James and his brothers from a very early age.

In the front of the Smith house was an abundance of unoccupied land with groves of trees. On the other side of these woods sat the Oconee Hill Cemetery. James recalls that the boys could watch the frequent funerals in the cemetery while they chopped and gathered wood. He describes the laborious work:

> In order to have enough wood for the various fires we built, we had to cut down trees, trim the limbs off of them, and cut them up in pieces small enough to fit in the stoves in the house. This work had to be done with a hand ax. We would gather up the wood, carry it to the house, and keep it in a pile for future use. We also stacked plenty in a corner of the house. The supply could not run out or we would be in serious trouble.

James and his younger brother Frank often worked together to gather wood. Frank has a vivid memory of an incident that occurred one day in the woods:

> We were gathering firewood in the woods one day and "somehow" the ax broke. When Deddy (this is what we called our father) found the ax and wanted to know who broke it, James and I both denied it. With no one else in the woods but the two of us, Deddy determined that it

was I who broke the ax. Because I kept denying that I did it, my daddy began whipping me. I finally gave up, and said I broke the ax. He whipped me some more for telling a lie. Of course, you know, I really did break the ax.

Washing Clothes

Washing was a major undertaking in the Smith household, since the family did not have indoor plumbing or gas appliances. This chore fell primarily to Vallie, who also took in washing for other households, but all the children were expected to learn and participate in this task. All of the washing took place in the yard. It was a long and tedious process, but one that Vallie taught all her children to do meticulously.

James has vivid memories of the process:

> To prepare for washing, first we had to separate the dark clothes from the white ones. Then we had to draw buckets of water from the well. This water was divided into the wash water and the water that had to be boiled over an open fire.
>
> In the first tub of water, we had a washboard where the clothes were scrubbed. Then more water had to be poured into a big black pot under which a fire was built. After the water began to boil, we placed the white clothes in the pot and let it boil for several minutes. Then we would take them out and place the clothes in a tub of waiting cold water. Then we had to squeeze them out piece by piece.
>
> Some clothes had to be starched before all were hung out to dry on a clothesline. After the clothes had dried in the sun, they were taken into the house. The ones that had been starched were sprinkled with cold water and rolled up for a while before they could be ironed.

Ironing was as much of a chore as the washing itself. Since the house had no electricity, the irons were heavy flat implements that had to be heated over smoldering coals. The family had two irons; the first would be set over the coals and when it was hot enough, it was taken up and the second one placed on the coals to warm while the first was used to iron. This way, no time was lost waiting for the iron to heat. Care had to be taken that the irons did not become too hot or sooty from the coals or the entire wash process would have to be repeated.

James reported, "As a boy, ironing my shirts and jeans was a chore I looked forward to. My mother always told me, 'You iron your clothes better than all the rest of the children.'" To this day, James continues to live up to his mother's praise. He has always paid meticulous attention to detail, whether in the work he does or the clothes he wears, which undoubtedly would make his mother proud.

James still does his own washing and ironing, as he has a particular way he likes things done and believes it is just better to do them himself. James and his siblings were taught to be clean, no matter the circumstances. His mother was known to say, "You may get sick away from home, so even if your clothes are ragged or torn, always make sure they are clean."

Caring for Livestock

Leroy, Sr. owned a mule for much of James' childhood. It was a beast of burden, pulling various loads in the wagon and toiling in the fields, and so was necessary to the family's livelihood. However, James described the tending of this animal as:

> a depressing situation at times. Sometimes, the mule would break out of the fence and roam through the neighborhood and woods. We had to corral him and put him back in his pen. Then the fence had to be repaired and we hoped that this wouldn't happen again, in the same week at least.

Not only was the mule used in farming, but it also had another distinctive chore for James' family and the neighbors. When it rained, their dirt road turned into mud that was very difficult to drive through. When a car trying to navigate the mud got stuck, James and his brothers would hitch the mule to the car and the boys would "urge the mule to pull the car out of the mired condition."

At the other extreme, James recalls that often during the hot summer months the dirt road became dry and dusty. Their neighbor Mrs. Mary Lou did not want the dust to soil the clothing she had just washed and hung on the line, so she would carefully water the street to keep the dust from blowing into her yard.

James' family raised chickens to provide eggs and meat for the family's consumption. Killing a chicken for a meal was a particularly onerous chore. When his mother wanted to serve chicken for dinner, James remembers having to wring a chicken's neck and he and his siblings would watch the poor creature run around the yard until it fell over dead. They would then pluck it free of feathers before taking it in to be cooked.

James never thought of the chickens or the mule as "pets" but as necessary farm animals. His family did not have any domestic pets, such as a cat or dog. He is not sure why, but keeping up with the live-stock was enough of a chore as far as he was concerned.

Other Daily Chores

When the Smith children were growing up, their father worked as a mechanic for various employers. It is not certain how he received training, but he was especially adept at fixing any kind of motor. Eventually Leroy, Sr. purchased the first of his many beloved Buicks. The Smith sons quickly learned to help their father with repairs and routine maintenance. James recalls,

> After we finished our schoolwork, it was our responsibil-
> ity to come outside and assist. One of the main chores
> was to hold a light so that he could see to work under the
> car at night. Another chore was to help bleed the brakes
> [purging the brake lines of any air bubbles].

Frank recalled the period when the Buick and the mule overlapped in service to the family:

> On very cold mornings when our Deddy's 1949 Dynaflow Buick wouldn't crank, Deddy would call on James to hitch the mule to the car and pull it out of the driveway. Once in the street we would push the car down the hill so it would crank. Deddy told James to drive the mule and he told me to whip the mule's butt to make him pull the car.

Having to work in the cotton fields every summer, the boys were delighted when their father eventually purchased a tractor. Over a period of years, the tractor helped to retire the need for the mule. The tractor changed but did not decrease the boys' chores, as it had several different attachments for various farming tasks. The boys had to learn how to hitch the different rakes and harrows to the tractor and how to fix them when they broke.

The Smith boys were also responsible for keeping the yard clean. Maintaining the dirt yard required keeping the area closest to the house clear of grass. The tough Johnson grass grew in tall and thick; the boys would cut it with a swing blade and feed the cuttings to the mule.

The Smith children all helped with chores around the house, including cleaning, washing dishes, and sewing. Vallie believed it was important for all her children to learn to prepare meals, so even the boys were taught to cook and bake. James enjoyed cooking and baking in particular. He is thankful he had this early instruction, as competency in all these tasks has proven to be advantageous throughout his life.

The Vegetable Gardens

Every spring, the Smith family planted a big vegetable garden on the land next to their house. This was one of many gardens the Smith children helped tend. Leroy, Sr. was notorious for planting gardens wherever he saw a piece of land lying fallow. Sometimes these garden plots would be next to a neighbor's house where Leroy, Sr. would be compensated for his labor through a share of the harvest. Ever the astute opportunist, he would also plant gardens on vacant land that the owners just didn't use. James especially remembers the years of planting acres of watermelons on a neighboring piece of property off of Grove Street.

Wherever the gardens were, the process was the same:

> The land had to be prepared for planting. First it had to be plowed, then leveled off, and then the grass had to be raked off. Holes had to be dug to set out the sweet potato plants and collard plants. We planted corn, potatoes, peanuts, watermelon, peas, beans, and any other vegetable available.

> We picked the crops as they ripened and dug up the potatoes and peanuts. The peanuts, still on their vines, were laid on top of the barn so they could dry out before removing them from the vines. When dry, they were placed in containers for shelling and eating. After all the items were gathered, my father would keep some and sell some to different neighbors or homeowners.

The Cotton Fields

For most of James' childhood, he and his siblings planted and worked a cotton field outside the city limits. Their mode of transportation for the nearly five-mile journey was a wagon drawn by the mule.

> Somehow my father made connections with a land owner who wanted someone to use his acreage to grow cotton. This property was located far from our home, way over on the west side of town, miles from Grove Street, near where Timothy Road is now. There were acres and acres of farmland there. This was where my brothers and I farmed each summer.

Most of the farming was performed by the Smith boys and the mule. Their father still had his day job as either a mechanic or truck driver, but at the beginning of the growing season he would get the children started. Once they were established in the work, the children would hitch up the mule and wagon and head to the fields every day during the summer. Leroy, Sr. would come by the field in the evening at the end of his regular workday and check on their progress.

> Our usual day during this time was to get up early, get dressed, and eat breakfast that my mother always prepared. My mother would also prepare a sack lunch for each of us and then we would head out to the barn. In the barn, we gathered the mule, harnessed it, led him to the wagon, hitched him up, and began the long trek to Timothy Road.
>
> Traveling in the spring and summer, the five-mile journey began on Grove Street and took us along Appley Drive, Poplar Street, Oconee Street, Ingram Street, Campus Drive [behind Sanford Stadium], Milledge Extension, Highway 441 [Macon Highway], and finally to the farm on Timothy Road. We worked all morning, took a lunch break, fed the mule, and then went back to work until around 5 in the evening. Then we had to travel back over the same long route home. Once home, we had to unhitch the mule, feed and water him, and then draw water for use in the house. We had to make sure there was sufficient wood in the kitchen for cooking before we even thought about our own hunger and exhaustion.

Vallie would prepare the family's supper, which James remembers as always hearty and delicious. James' favorite foods growing up were collards, butter beans, cornbread, his mother's delicious pound cake . . . and especially fatback. When James told me about this favorite food, he described it in mouthwatering detail. I could tell he could almost taste it, all these years later. Soon after dinner, the boys headed to bed.

They repeated this routine, day after day, from May to September. Frank tells the story of his first time in the fields.

> On the first day of my job hoeing cotton, I hoed half a row. My brother James told me, "Deddy ain't going for that." Keep in mind the actual size of the rows were about a half of a mile. James was right. Sure enough my daddy whipped my butt. The next day I hoed a row and a half.

James notes, "The end of the farming season came when we had to chop and pick the cotton by hand and plow the field. At that time, both boys and girls would pick the cotton, so my sisters joined us." After the harvest, Leroy, Sr. would take the cotton to be baled and sold. Farmers were paid by the weight of their bales. James is not sure what arrangement his father had with the landowner, but assumes it was a sharecropping agreement in which the proceeds were split between the men. James and his brothers consistently farmed cotton on the same plot of land until 1958.

School started again in early September, but the Smith children could not attend until they had completed the cotton harvest. James recalls that they always started school as much as a month after the school year had commenced. Their teachers and their parents insisted that the children make up all the work they had missed, knowing they were all bright and capable and could quickly catch up. However, for a while, this added to their daily work at home, as they studied by oil lamp well past dark. Their mother would help them with their studies in the evenings when needed, exhorting them to work carefully, read critically, and go above and beyond what their teachers expected of them.

James reflected,

> As children, we didn't really understand why we had to go through all this to make a living. However, my father did and we had to obey. We also knew that we always had plenty; we never went hungry. We were poor but it didn't bother us. We were taught to accept what God had blessed us with and to be content and work hard.

CHAPTER 5

Elementary School: 1947-1954

Preparing for School

James' grandmother Josephine wanted him to be able to write the letters of the alphabet before he began formal schooling. At the time there were no kindergartens for African American children, so school would begin for him in the first grade, when he was six years old. Josephine began working with him at home, putting the pencil in his right hand. After numerous attempts at instruction and practice, however, James had made little progress. Somehow Josephine realized that James might make more gains if she let him work with his left hand. Once she placed the pencil in his left hand, his writing skills took off.

Josephine worked diligently with James and he credits her with saving him some struggles once he started school, both by helping him learn to write and by recognizing that he was left-handed. Sadly, the summer before James started first grade, Josephine suffered a stroke in their shared bedroom and passed away before reaching the hospital. James is sure that although she didn't live to see the full fruits of her labors, she was proud of him.

This chapter will focus on James' childhood experience in the public elementary schools of Athens and in his church. In the following chapter I will explore the broader historical context of this critical and transitional time in the Athens City School District.

Athens City School District

On October 15, 1885, the city of Athens chartered a public school district. Its mission was "to establish a system of public schools in the city of Athens, Georgia and provide for the maintenance and support of the same, to provide for the issuance of bonds of said city for the purpose of building school houses and for other purposes." Section Seven of the charter identifies for whom this district was created. "Be it further enacted, that provision shall be made under this act for the education of all the children, both of the white and colored races, but separate schools shall be provided for white and colored children."

James attended segregated schools for the entirety of his public education in Athens. It was a time of great change in education both locally and nationally, especially for African American children. The mood of the country was changing as the stirrings of the Civil Rights Movement included demands by African Americans that their children be provided the same educational opportunities, facilities, and resources as white children.

The doctrine of "separate but equal" had never been accurate or acceptable. When the Supreme Court handed down its 1954 *Brown v. Board of Education* decision, Athens, like many other Southern cities, saw the writing on the wall. Yet—also like many of its Southern neighbors—the school district was exceedingly slow to acknowledge or respond to either the letter or the spirit of this momentous decision. However, the Athens public schools could not escape some of the challenges, controversies, and upheaval that confronted many school districts during this period. The merger of the Clarke County School District with the City of Athens School District in 1956 further exacerbated the unease of this time.

Some of the changes that Athens and Clarke County eventually instituted were not widely embraced by either the African American community or the white community. Long before the public schools were fully integrated, the merger of the two districts took jobs from many African American teachers, as most of the rural Black schools were closed. The merger imposed very long bus rides on mostly Black children, who were coming from rural parts of the county. While the merger may have provided the county's children with a more comprehensive and consistent education, it did not necessarily create equality or equity. The physical condition of and resources available to the African American schools were still far inferior to those of the white schools.

East Athens Elementary School

When the Athens City School District was chartered in 1885, there were three elementary schools for white students and only one for African American students. The African American school was located at the corner of Baxter and South Pope Streets. When it became clear that the district would need to build new schools to accommodate the growing population of children who wanted to take advantage of a free public education, the Board of Education renovated and expanded the Baxter Street School for white children and built two other schools for Black students.

Thus, in the spring of 1892, East Athens Elementary and West Athens Elementary (known today as West Broad School, which still exists at 1573 West Broad Street and is part of the Clarke County School District) opened their doors to African American students in Athens. Students who lived east of Lumpkin Street went to East Athens, and those who lived west of Lumpkin Street went to West Athens. These schools housed the first through seventh grades.

When James began his formal education in 1947 as a first grader at East Athens Elementary School, it was one of the oldest schools in the city. By this time there were four elementary schools for African American children: East Athens, West Athens, Newtown, and Reese Street schools.

East Athens Elementary School was located on the block bounded by Water Oak, Odd, Griffeth, and Strickland Avenues in the far northeastern part of the city. All of these streets were unpaved and the northeast corner of this rectangular block was transected by a railroad track. The school was a two-story wood frame structure with four

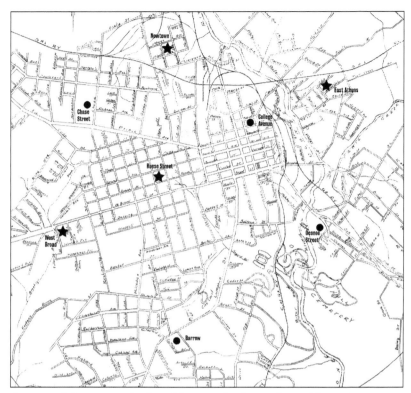

Location of elementary schools in Athens, 1947. Stars indicate African American schools; dots indicate white schools.

classrooms on each floor. Heated with coal stoves, it had no running water or electricity. The toilets were outside and James remembers that there were eight "stalls" for over 300 children.

In 1947, there were no buses for Black children living within the city limits, so the Smith children walked the two miles to and from school each day. James remembers the walk along Grove to Lexington, to Poplar, then left on Mulberry. Turning left again, they crossed the North Oconee River on Broad Street and walked a short distance to First Street. Turning right, they walked all the way up First past Moreland Avenue until they reached Water Oak Street.

Their route home often varied, but they consistently took the same route to school to make sure they arrived on time. James doesn't remember exactly how long it took to walk to school, but a two-mile walk for a six-year-old could not have been quick or easy. Arriving at school, the children would play outside until the bell rang.

All of James' elementary school teachers were women. He remembers all of them as demanding and strict, but he also felt that they cared deeply about the welfare of their students and were dedicated to helping every child succeed.

The principal of East Athens Elementary was Mrs. Jessie McWhorter, who had been teaching in the district for some time. It was not unusual for principals of African American elementary schools to continue to teach while also serving as head of the school. Mrs. McWhorter was James' first grade teacher. In 1947 she earned $1,800 per year. This was equal to 64% of the salary of white elementary school principals, who earned $2,805 per year. This disparity in pay would remain an issue until the 1952-53 school year, when teacher salaries were finally equalized. Salaries after this time were based on number of years of college, the type of teaching certificate the teacher held, and years of classroom experience.

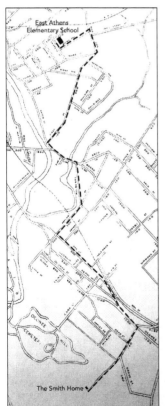

James' second grade teacher was Mrs. Mary H. Harris. James recalls that she was very strict, and also very determined that all her students would learn everything she taught from the curriculum and accomplish the goals she set for them. James said he was afraid of his first- and second-grade teachers but reported that his third-grade teacher, Mrs. Elisa Nolan-Stanton, was more affable while still maintaining very high standards for her students.

The Smith children's route to school.

James notes that if he had to pick

his favorite grade and teacher, it would be fourth grade and his teacher Mrs. Ruth Davis-Hawk. James describes her as an extraordinary teacher who went the extra mile, literally and figuratively, in taking the time to nurture her students. Mrs. Davis-Hawk insisted that her students use "proper" English and taught them to write well and spell correctly.

When it came time for the district spelling bee, Mrs. Davis-Hawk was determined that her students would participate, even though it meant a long walk across town.

> I can remember Mrs. Hawk walking from our elementary school on the east side all the way to the Reese Street School to enter my classmate Hattie Wilker and me in a spelling bee competition with the other Black elementary schools in the district. Hattie won the contest and I came in second place! Hattie Wilker went on to become the valedictorian of our high school class.

James' last year in the old East Athens Elementary School was fifth grade with his teacher Mrs. Addie Brantley. He recalls the students being excited that the following year they would be going to a newly built school. The Smith children were especially happy because it was a bit closer to their home.

A New East Athens Elementary School and the Black Mammy Memorial Institute

In the summer of 1949, the Athens City Board of Education appointed a committee to select an architect and a site for a proposed new school to replace the aging and crowded East Athens Elementary School. By October the Board agreed to hire William J. J. Chase as the architect for the school. Mr. Chase was one of the most prominent architects in Georgia. His Atlanta firm designed numerous state courthouses, hospitals, schools, and jails throughout Georgia. Over the course of his career he designed over 100 schools in the state. The Athens Board of Education had also recently hired Mr. Chase's firm to design the new (white) Athens High School.

At the November 23, 1949 meeting of the Board of Education, board member Mr. Broadus Coile announced that he had researched the ownership of the land known as the Black Mammy Memorial Institute in the First Ward as a possible site for the new African American elementary school. Mr. Coile discovered that the property had been deeded to the city in 1941 by the remaining trustees for the Black Mammy Memorial Institute. At the time of the transfer, the trustees specified that the land must be used to provide a playground for African American children who lived in the area. The Board of Education decided to approach the city about deeding the property to the BOE as a possible site for the new East Athens Elementary School.

Samuel F. Harris

The Black Mammy Memorial Institute

Samuel F. Harris was the superintendent (principal) of the African American Athens High and Industrial School in the early years of the 20th century. Classically educated, he was determined that Black Athenians be offered the same quality of academic training he had received. However, he watched as the Black schools of Athens became increasingly crowded, dilapidated, and underfunded.

In pondering ways to increase support and funding for African American education in Athens and expand educational opportunities for all Black students, Harris decided to create an institute focused on practical training in the domestic arts and farming. He recognized that not everyone had the ability or desire to enter teaching or other professional fields and that existing educational options were too limited to develop the full range of talents and skills in the Black community. Thus, in 1910 Harris founded the Black Mammy Memorial Institute.

Numerous sources, including a dissertation by Monica Knight, report that Harris made a strategic choice to name his school the Black Mammy Memorial Institute. Aware that he needed the white establishment's financial support both to build the school and to provide ongoing funding, Harris drew upon the nostalgia many white Southerners felt toward their Black nannies. It was common practice for white families to hire Black women to help raise their children; thus the image of the kind, nurturing, dutiful, loyal Black mammy evoked sympathy and fondness among the white community. This non-threatening name portrayed the school as lifting African Americans out of dire poverty and dependence by training them to excel in precisely those skills that would benefit white America. This was a model of "improvement" that the white community could support.

In an article in *Good Housekeeping Magazine,* author Riley M. Fletcher Berry lauded Mr. Harris and his school, stating that he would provide the country with "the opportunity for securing real American and nearly perfect servants." Ms. Berry asserts that the school's principal objective was "the practical training of plain, everyday workers for the house and the field" and that Harris believed in providing "training in the simple work for which the negro [sic] is as a rule best adapted." She also writes that while emerging Black leaders and academic institutions were doing a good job of educating African Americans for the professions, there remained a need to train "the women as cooks, maids, seamstresses and laundresses, the men as agricultural and trade laborers" (562).

However, Harris' actual motivations and beliefs were perhaps much more complicated than Berry's article portrayed. It is difficult to know for certain whether his genuine goals and views on the education of African Americans were exactly as he presented to the public. Knight suggests that Harris may have determined that the most effective way to increase funding and support for educating African Americans was to make that education less threatening. Whether or not Harris believed in African Americans' capacity to excel in leadership and professional roles, he certainly believed that the time had not yet arrived to provide a strictly academic course of study for Black Athenians.

That an educated Black man at the turn of the 20th century might have held this view is not as surprising as one might think. Other prominent African Americans of the time, including Booker T. Washington, voiced similar views. Despite founding Tuskegee Institute, Washington believed African Americans needed "practical" training before academic instruction if they were to be accepted as equal citizens. Washington worried that educating and promoting Black scholars and professionals too quickly would upset Southern sensibilities and prompt a backlash that would undermine the gains African Americans were slowly making.

Harris also may have felt that a more "realistic" form of training was needed "to bridge the chasm so long and dangerously widening between the two races." He also believed that while there was nothing wrong with the hundreds of academically focused schools for Blacks that were established in the U.S. following the Civil War, these schools were mostly of Northern invention and relied on the financial support of (mainly white) moneyed individuals in the more affluent parts of the country (Berry 563).

Although Harris wrote and spoke as if he genuinely believed that many Black people lacked the capacity to benefit from higher education, it is possible that this, too, was a strategic stance adopted to gain the support of white Athenians. Harris knew that to establish his Institute he would need the assistance and financial support of white citizens, "who have heretofore failed to find stimulating interest in the cause of the colored people." He assembled a board of advisors (12 white men) and a board of directors (nine Black men) from among Athens' business and community leaders to assist in this endeavor.

Encouraged by Harris, the advisors and directors sought to raise funds to purchase property on the eastern edge of the city of Athens. Harris dreamed of having an actual building to house his school and even had plans drawn up for his "Memorial Hall." Though he eventually raised sufficient funds to purchase several acres of land within the far northeastern boundary of the city, the building never came to fruition.

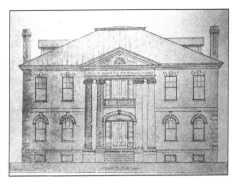

Architectural rendering of Memorial Hall.

Though the physical Institute was never built, Harris continued to offer domestic and agricultural classes to teenagers and adults at Athens High and Industrial School as part of his Institute's night school for several years. There is little detailed information about the Institute, as Harris was able to establish the curriculum and hold evening classes at AHIS without the oversight of the local school board. It is possible that once these courses were available, there was no great demand to build a separate structure.

In her dissertation, Knight also suggests that perhaps Harris' goal of providing practical training in place of an academically focused education did not sit well with Athens' growing Black middle class, who wanted the same educational opportunities offered to all citizens regardless of race. It seemed limiting, and to some degrading, to suggest that the vast majority of Blacks were not fit to be leaders or professionals. Knight speculates that Harris' goal all along was to draw white Athenians' attention to the deplorable conditions in the Black public schools. Harris may have hoped that if he could offer the white community an acceptable way to support the education of Black children and adults by focusing on non-academic training, this would open the door to convincing the school board to improve the conditions in the other Black schools as well.

It is difficult to determine exactly what happened to the Black Mammy Memorial Institute. Most historians and academics agree that as an idea and an institution, it slowly faded into Athens history. By 1913 it was no longer mentioned in publications. The property the Institute had purchased was eventually turned over to the city to be used as a recreation area for Athens' Black citizens. It was this property that the Athens Board of Education procured from the city to build the new East Athens Elementary Colored School, and which is now the Miriam Moore Community Service Center on McKinley Drive.

A New East Athens Elementary Colored School

At the April 12, 1950 meeting of the Athens Board of Education, the Black Mammy Memorial Institute property was duly deeded to the Board. The Board paid $1,000 for 10 acres of land on the far eastern edge of the city. At the same April meeting the BOE decided to name the new school, "East Athens Elementary Colored School."

Now that it owned the property, the Board of Education sought to acquire additional land to accommodate the size of school they wanted to build. An adjacent landowner, Mr. F. H. Mendenhall, whose property lay between the Black Mammy property and Peter Street, offered to sell 16 acres to the Board for $100/acre. The BOE ultimately purchased 10 acres of Mr. Mendenhall's land to expand the plat for the school.

Ironically, Samuel Harris had been the principal of the old East Athens Elementary Colored School in the early years of the 20th century, before moving on to become principal of Athens High and Industrial School. Thus while Harris never saw his Institute building become a reality, the new East Athens Elementary Colored School was built on land he had helped procure some decades before.

By September 1950, G. M. Caskey and Son were awarded the contract to build the new East Athens Elementary Colored School for the sum of $140,673. At its December meeting the BOE requested that the mayor and city council extend Vine Street across Trail Creek, so students would not have to go down to the Athens Manufacturing Company property and cross the creek to reach the new school. However, a bridge over Trail Creek does not appear on maps of Athens until 1955, when a footbridge is shown crossing the creek at Moreland Avenue.

As construction on the new school moved forward, the Board of Education began discussing the need to sell the old East Athens

School property as soon as the new school was completed. At the Board's July 26, 1951 meeting, the members agreed that they would offer it for sale and ask for bids. However, when the first round of bids came in the BOE rejected all the offers, as they were far below what the Board had hoped to procure.

Shortly thereafter, a delegation from an African American church in East Athens (the minutes did not specify which church) asked if the BOE would give the church a price on this property and then give them time to raise the money. The BOE did not reject this offer outright, but rather than give the church a price they decided to re-advertise the property, asking for bids that were no less than $4,000. By March 1953, the highest offer the Board had received was $1,500.

The board decided once again to advertise the property for sale and to accept the $1,500 bid if they received no higher offer. By February 1954 the Board still had not sold the property, and in June they decided to hold an auction. On July 8, 1954, a Mr. Clarence Fulcher was the winning bidder, purchasing the old East Athens School property for $1,800. This ended the Athens City Board of Education's ownership of that historic piece of property.

By the time James entered sixth grade in the fall of 1952, the new school had been completed. The new building was a vast improvement over the previous school, and James and his peers were delighted to have a new facility with all the "modern" conveniences. James' teacher that year was Mrs. Thelma Hurley. James completed his elementary school education the following year with his seventh grade teacher, Mrs. Anna Furr.

The old 1892 East Athens Elementary School was torn down and there are now several houses on the block where the school once stood. The 1952 East Athens Elementary School building still exists but is no longer a school. It is now the Miriam Moore Community Service Center on McKinley Drive.

Education is a Priority and a Joy

Reflecting on his attitude toward education in his youth, James observed:

> Learning has always been a priority for me. In elementary school, I was eager to learn. Reading, writing, spelling, and English were my favorite subjects. I loved spelling. To be able to spell all types of words was very rewarding. When called upon to read aloud, I would respond with what I know now as vigor. I wanted my teacher to hear me read and to see my writing. However, I did not like mathematics, nor did I care for geography. I had to really press to make passing grades in those subjects.

One of James' other favorite subjects at school was music, especially singing in the choir. He remembers that East Athens Elementary School had a wonderful choir, directed by Ms. Daisy Lee Shaw, which competed every year with the other African American elementary school choirs in the district. James also knew the West Broad School choir director, Ms. Maudestine Burton, an extremely talented pianist who played at James' church on Sundays. In fact, both Ms. Shaw and Ms. Burton were members of First A.M.E. Church.

James recalls that Ms. Shaw was the only African American musician in Athens who knew how to play a pipe organ. She played at Ebenezer Baptist Church, which was the only Black church in the city to have one. (James laments that at some point the church sold the organ.) However, it was Ms. Burton's West Broad choir that won the school choir competition nearly every year. Occasionally another school would win, but West Broad was like a powerhouse sports team that has the best players, trains with the most rigor, exhibits the most discipline, and nearly always comes out on top.

James also participated in plays and operettas in elementary school, and he loved these performances. In addition, there were various types of assemblies during the year in which each grade would perform or give presentations for the school. James was never shy about participating in these events.

James had many good friends during his elementary school years, including Waymon Sims, Joe McCurry, Lamar Robinson, Carlton Cobb, and Dewey Sims. He never went to their houses to play, partly because his parents didn't believe in their children visiting other people's houses, and partly because all the Smith children had chores to do when they got home. But the friends played with one another at school and walked to and from school together, picking up and dropping each other off as they went. The Smith children were among those who had the farthest to go, so this constituted a large part of their social lives.

Books and the Dunbar Branch Library

James remembers that each classroom at East Athens Elementary School had a decent supply of books. He was not sure if they were donated, purchased by the district, or contributed by his teachers from their personal collections. But he felt they were sufficient for the students' needs at the time. He does not recall ever going to the Athens Public Library while in elementary school, but he knew a library existed somewhere in downtown Athens. He does remember the "Black library" he visited while in high school. He thought that at one point it might have been in Dr. Donarell Green's offices on West Hancock. He also recalls that Ms. Arabella Murray worked there and eventually moved to the main public library.

The Athens Women's Club is credited with establishing the first public library in Athens in 1936, which catered to white patrons only. A separate library branch existed for African Americans in Athens from 1942 to 1972. It was named the Dunbar Branch Library after African American poet, novelist, and playwright Paul Laurence Dunbar. Located inside the old Knox Institute Building (then Athens High and Industrial School) at Reese and Pope, it served all Black county residents and was one of only thirteen public libraries for African Americans in the state.

The funds that supplied and maintained this library initially came from the Works Progress Administration (WPA). However, when the WPA withdrew funding for both the white and Black libraries in 1944, the library system as a whole went through a rocky period. Fortunately, the state and some local governments in Georgia recognized the need to help sustain the public library system. In 1947 the first bond issue was put before the residents of Athens to determine whether the citizens were willing to continue to support a public library. The bond issue passed and the main (white) branch of the Athens Regional Library System opened at the

Paul Laurence Dunbar, 1905.

corner of Hancock and College Avenues. Now supported with local funds, the public library system in Athens could expand its services.

The Athens library had a bookmobile that had served white schools in the outlying areas of Oglethorpe, Oconee, and Athens for several years, but had not served any of the Black schools. After funding was secured by the bond issue, the main library began delivering boxes of books to the Black schools of Athens in 1948. This is probably how James' school acquired many of the books he remembers in his classrooms. It is likely that these books were either duplicates from the main library or were considered in poor condition and therefore deemed donatable to the Black schools. While teachers at the white schools in Athens and surrounding counties were allowed to check out books from the bookmobile, it was not until much later that the bookmobile began allowing teachers at the Black schools to check out books for use in their classrooms.

The Dunbar Branch continued to operate throughout James' years in school, moving several times as it expanded its services, collection, staff, and programs, including creating Vacation Reading Clubs. In 1957, the library moved to the Home Economics Building of the old Athens High and Industrial School complex on Reese Street.

However, by this time a new Black high school had been completed on Dearing Extension and the buildings that formerly housed the high school were in deplorable condition. Additionally, the Board of Education was preparing to sell most of these properties, as the city and county school districts had recently merged. So in 1962 the Dunbar Branch moved again to 196 E. Washington Street in downtown Athens.

The Dunbar Branch Library's final move was to the second floor of Dr. Green's offices on West Hancock, where it was housed from 1965 to 1972. The branch ended its tenure as a separate entity when it merged with the Athens-Clarke County Library in its new building on West Dougherty Street (now government offices).

A Typical Day at School

James and his siblings were in the habit of arriving early at school. Their school day began with a devotion and prayer, followed by the Pledge of Allegiance. Classes in language arts (English, reading, writing, spelling); social studies (geography, history, citizenship, health, science, and nature study); fine arts (music, drama, drawing, and painting); arithmetic; and physical education followed throughout the day. At lunchtime, the children had a brief outside recess before resuming their studies.

When they went outside for recess, the boys had to play on one side of the schoolyard and the girls on the other. Two of the students' favorite games at the time were hide-and-seek and hopscotch. James also recalls that some students liked to play baseball, basketball, or football, but James very seldom participated "because my ability to coordinate the activity was weak." James did not see himself as very athletic, although he was certainly fit and strong due to all the physical labor he performed at home.

James remembers getting in trouble at school only once, when he threw a shoe at a girl in sixth grade. When asked why he would do such a thing, he explained to his teacher, "Because she threw her shoe at me first." He doesn't remember whether the girl got in trouble as well, or what punishment he received as a result, but the incident remains very vivid to him to this day. James did not like to be in the wrong nor to have attention drawn to him for this reason.

The classrooms at James' school were simple but sufficiently equipped with blackboards, crayons, pencils, paper, and books. Students sat at individual desks to do their work. Most of the classes were crowded, however, and it was not unusual to have over 40 students in one classroom.

Sunday School at First A.M.E. Church

Vallie Smith and her children attended First A.M.E. Church, the second African American Church in Athens, founded in 1866. It still exists on the corner of Hull and Dougherty Streets in downtown Athens. Vallie herself was raised in this church and it was there that she walked every Sunday with her children in tow.

First A.M.E. Church, Athens, Georgia.

Church was an important part of James' life from a very early age. James recalls:

> Getting up early on Sunday, eating a good breakfast, getting dressed, and preparing to take the long walk to worship were non-negotiable. It was my mother's desire that we attend every Sunday. She was a strong woman and persevered. She knew the struggles of life but never complained in our presence. We knew by the example that she set that we as children had to work hard and continue to persevere.

At the Smith household, preparations for church began on Saturday night. Every child took a bath in a large #2 tin tub (holding roughly fifteen gallons of water) and laid out their best clothes for the next day. Rising early Sunday morning, they would dress, eat breakfast, and walk the two miles to church. Everyone attended Sunday School, then gathered in the sanctuary for the main service.

James remembers dreading the walk home, especially when it was blistering hot and humid and they were in their dress clothes. At home after church, the Smith children were allowed to play, and James remembers the tricycle and red wagon they would use to pull each other around in the yard. Of course, they still had the usual household upkeep tasks to do on Sunday, including drawing water, stoking the stoves, and washing dishes, but the children did get a bit of a respite from their chores.

James' first organized Sunday School class was the Beginners class with Ms. Rosa Bell Strickland. Ms. Strickland was an elementary school teacher in the county schools. She was proud, disciplined, and strict. "There was no unnecessary talking in her class," James recalls. The class was taught from Bible Sunday School cards, with scripture and a biblical picture on the front of each card and a spiritual message on the back.

James has particularly fond and lasting memories of the Strickland family. Over the years, Ms. Rosa Bell Strickland and her mother, Mrs. Sarah Strickland, took the Smith children under their wing. Ms. Rosa Bell became the godmother for James' younger sister Christine and his youngest brother, Leroy, Jr. James describes Ms. Rosa Bell as "faithful in this role, providing many resources for them." He recalls:

> Mrs. Sarah Strickland, Ms. Rosa Bell's mother, served as a second grandmother to us. The spirit of this lady was huge. She had a very sweet manner with deep, deep wisdom. At her home there were always some delicious baked goods to eat or to carry home.
>
> When I visited the Strickland home on Hancock Avenue, they always had some chores for me to do. Just like a lot of families where there was no gas for heating, wood had to be cut or split for making fires. And since they did not have a man around the house, it fell to others to help with these chores. We were always happy to do so.

In my older years, it was my good fortune to pick up Mrs. Sarah Strickland for worship service each Sunday morning. It became my responsibility to get her there on time. However, because of swelling in her legs and feet, she moved slowly. After worship we would return with her daughter back home, talking about the worship we had experienced. You see, Ms. Rosa Bell walked to Sunday School every Sunday, rain or shine, cold or hot. Mrs. Sarah was a great encourager. She always complimented me on being a safe driver. Mrs. Sarah Strickland lived to be 101 years old. She was able to see me get married and attend the reception.

After the Beginners class, the children moved to the Primary class, then up through the ranks to the Senior class. During much of this time, students were taught from a *Sunday School Quarterly* that contained lessons for an entire quarter. They also memorized Bible verses that they would recite for their teachers the following Sunday. James' mother read the Bible to the children at home and made sure they had time to prepare for the next Sunday School class. James remembers many dedicated leaders and teachers at the church, including Mrs. Oree Favors, Mrs. Annie Hill, and Mrs. Minnie J. Diggs.

James oldest brother, Joseph; his older sister, Willie Mae; and his youngest brother, Leroy, Jr. still attend a Methodist church. James, Frank, and Christine attend Baptist churches.

Childhood Health

Over the course of James' elementary school years, all children were vaccinated at school for diphtheria, tetanus, and pertussis (DPT), smallpox, and polio. James reports that his family was relatively healthy and he doesn't recall any of the Smith children going to the hospital. If they did need a doctor they went to Dr. Andrew Jones or Dr. Donarell Green, African American physicians who served the Black community at that time. On rare occasions, they would go to Dr. Anthony H. Gallis, a Greek immigrant, whom James called "the specialist in everything." Dr. Guy Thomas was the family dentist whose office was in his home on Billups Street. The Smith family did not have health insurance so they always had to pay out of pocket for any medical and dental services.

James graduated from elementary school in the spring of 1954. That fall he would begin the eighth grade at Athens High and Industrial School. He was excited to be moving on to high school and happily anticipated it through the long, hot summer of 1954 as he toiled in the cotton fields with his siblings. Going to high school brought James one step closer to his goal of growing up, leaving home, and pursuing his dreams, wherever they might lead.

the chance to speak publicly. As president of the Speech Class, he never passed up an opportunity to read his work in front of an audience. In elementary school he would memorize a passage or poem to recite for assemblies, but now he could write and present his own words as well. His favorite subject was English; he delighted in reading and writing. James' least favorite subjects were chemistry and physics. Both classes were required, and while James liked and respected the teacher, Mr. E. T. Roberson, he could never generate any enthusiasm for the subject matter.

James and his siblings rarely participated in extracurricular activities. They were needed at home after school to do chores and watch the younger children. In addition, there were no school buses for African American students until 1958, nor was public transportation available. (Athens did not have a fully functioning public transportation system until 1976.)

When James turned 16 and learned to drive, a few of his classmates

JAMES R. SMITH IN MUSIC RECITAL

James Russell Smith was presented in a recital at the First A. M. E. Church October 5, 1958 at 5:00 P.M. He was accompanied by Miss Martha E. Swinton, who is the music instructor at the Athens High and Industrial School.

The program was as follows:

I Londonderry Air — Walter Goodell
   Break Bread — Spiritual
   Without A Song -- Vinvent Youman
   Bless This House — May H. Brahe
II Nobody Knows — Spiritual
   I'd Rather Have Jesus —
                George Beverly Shea
   My Desire — Thomas A. Dorsey

James is an active member of the First A. M. E. Church where he works cooperatively as assistant superintendant of the Sunday School, a member of the choir, and Usher Board.

He is a senior at the Athens High and Industrial School, advertising manager of the senior class.

After graduating from the said school, he plans to study toward the A.B. degree in the field of music at Morehouse College, Atlanta, Georgia.

had cars but none of James' close friends did. His father allowed him to drive the family car on occasion, but James remembers that if the family needed transportation when his father was not around for needs such as trips to the doctor or dentist, their only option was to take a taxi. He does not recall who operated the taxis, but said there were taxis that would carry African Americans.

James did not spend much time with friends after school. The Smith children were allowed to stay after school only for school-related activities, and they never went to local parks or other popular venues on the weekends. Walking to and from school with friends thus constituted a large part of their social lives. James' parents insisted that the children focus on school, church, work, and home.

Although James was nearly always a model student, he recalls one incident that was a minor blemish on his otherwise stellar record of good behavior at school. Perhaps for that reason, it remains vivid for him to this day.

> We had a social and educational group called the Tri-Hi-Y for boys. [The Tri-Hi-Y club, associated with the YMCA, promoted "high standards of moral character through improvement, brother/sisterhood, equality, and service in High Schools" for boys and girls.] One morning, while in Mrs. Carolyn Haye's eleventh grade math class, an announcement was made on the intercom system for all cheerleaders to report to the gym. Although we were not cheerleaders, some eight boys from Tri-Hi-Y got up and walked out of her class. Of course she reported us and we were suspended. We were told by the principal not to return to school until we were called. However, we returned back to school the next day.

James recalls that the parents of all the young men involved were informed of this incident, and while his parents were upset with him, they told him to go back to school regardless. They thought it was more important for him to return to school to show his commitment to his education than to wait for the school to call letting him know when his suspension had ended. James doesn't remember the exact nature of the reception the students received when they returned, but they were allowed back and the incident was forgotten. He says that to this day he really doesn't know why they did it: "It was just a spur-of-the-moment thing."

Classmates

When looking through his high school class pictures, James recalled many details of almost all of the students. He knew which subjects they were best at in high school, the sports they played, who their siblings were and whether they came from a large family, where they lived, where they went to church, where they went after graduation and which college they attended, what they did in their professional lives, who they married, and how many children they had. Many of his classmates either joined the military or became teachers, ministers, business executives, police officers, doctors, professors, or lawyers. James spoke with pride and admiration for all of them. One hundred fourteen students graduated in his class of 1959.

Joe McCurry

One of James' best friends was Joe McCurry, who also grew up on the east side of Athens. Joe also came from a rather large family, with four brothers and two sisters. James and Joe have been friends since the first grade and are still close. Often when James spoke of his life and his memories of childhood, he would pause and write himself a note, saying, "I'll have to ask Joe about that."

James recounts that of the 114 graduates in their high school class, there were fourteen honor graduates. Somehow he and Joe ended up as numbers thirteen and fourteen. They laugh about it to this day, joking that they were competing for those last two slots. Neither of them can remember who was in which position and it clearly does not matter to either. Joe entered the military after graduation, moved to the Midwest, and subsequently worked as an executive at Sears for many years. He is now back in Georgia and James revels in their frequent communication and visits.

Another good friend was Eugene Terrell. After graduating from AHIS, Eugene attended Albany State University. He later returned to Athens and taught at North Athens Elementary School on Barber Street. During this time, Eugene and James were roommates at the Kappa Alpha Psi House on Hancock. Tragically, Eugene was killed in

Eugene Terrell

Harry Tate

Marvin Billups, Jr.

Hattie Wilker

a car accident in the late 1960s. James named one of the first choirs he organized in honor of his friend. The E. L. Terrell Ensemble went on to have a long and successful musical life.

Two of James' other good friends, Harry Tate and Marvin Billups, Jr. both attended Tuskegee Institute after high school graduation. James described Harry as "a very smart guy" who may have tied with Chester Davenport or Charles Lester as salutatorian of their high school class. Harry, Marvin, and James remained friends long after high school and James remembers many long and vibrant discussions with them about work, goals, and life.

The valedictorian of James' graduating class was Hattie Wilker, the same Hattie who bested him in the spelling bee back in fourth grade. After graduation, she attended college and then taught English in North Carolina, eventually returning to Athens to teach at Clarke Central High School.

Another classmate, Donald Moon, was a Korean War veteran who became one of the first two African American policemen in Athens, along with his cousin, Archibald Killian. Officer Moon had served in the Athens Police Department for only 19 months when he was shot and killed by a 15-year-old while off duty. Officer Moon died in November 1963 and was survived by his daughter.

James says he did not have time for dating during high school, but he and his friend Audrey Milner teased each other a lot. They remained friends long after high school and James later became the godfather to Audrey's daughter.

Waymon Sims was the class president and played on the football team. James recalls him as

Donald Moon   *Audrey Milner*   *Waymon Sims*

a very popular young man who was part of a social group called the "Black Knights." James did not belong to this group and says that while there was some social stratification among the students in his class, he was not interested in joining any group that did not further his education.

James was aware of the ways in which students would group themselves socially as well as some subtle differences in how teachers would treat them. He perceived these distinctions to be based on the position a child's parents held in the African American community. He does not know whether the parents felt their children were treated differently, but James did notice that some students seemed to get more attention or extra consideration based on who their family was. James says this was notable only because all the families knew each other. The community was small enough that the children of doctors and lawyers were friends with the children of mechanics and farmers. Still, James recalls that even among the African American community some stratification and subtle favoritism existed based on class, profession, family, and even skin tone.

AHIS Faculty

James has distinct and fond memories of many of the AHIS faculty. While looking at the yearbook photos of his teachers, it was clear that his connections to them went beyond the high school walls. He knew them not only as teachers, but also as members of the community and part of the broader fabric of life in Athens.

James' favorite teachers, in addition to Rev. Billups and Ms.

Swinton, were Ms. Jewell McAdams (Math); Mrs. Ilene Nunnally (French), who is still alive as of this writing; and Mrs. Clara B. Smith (English). Mrs. Smith, his senior English teacher, organized and directed all the plays and operettas in which AHIS students performed. When asked why these teachers were his favorites, James pointed not just to how dedicated they were as teachers or how interesting their classes were, but also to his perception that they treated everyone fairly and equally.

Ms. Jewell McAdams

Mr. Marvin Billups, Sr., taught history and social studies. Though James never took any of his classes, his son, Marvin Jr., became one of James' best friends and also attended Tuskegee Institute after graduation. James remembers with great fondness Reverend J. H. Geer, who taught driver's ed. Rev. Geer would sit in front of the school every day and tell silly jokes as the students came in the front door.

Mrs. Ilene Nunnally

Rev. Robert B. Hawk taught history. His wife, Mrs. Ruth Hawk, was James' fourth grade teacher at East Athens Elementary. She moved to the high school after many years at East Athens. James thinks she may have been one of the first Black teachers to integrate Athens High School's faculty. Mr. Walter Allen was the high school band leader. James briefly played trombone but says he was not as dedicated to the instrument as he needed to be to continue.

Mrs. Clara B. Smith

Many of the teachers were also coaches, including Mr. James Holston, Mr. Walter Jackson, Mr. A. J. Robinson, Mr. James D. Crawford, and Mr. Eugene Holmes. James remembers that Mr. Holmes had to go to the white high school to borrow equipment for the AHIS football team, which lacked even the basics. He also had to ask the Board of Education if the AHIS football team could use

Mr. Marvin
Billups, Sr.

Mrs. Ruth Hawk

Mr. Walter Allen

the white high school field for their games, as AHIS had no field of its own.

As of this writing, James noted that Ms. Elizabeth King, who taught English, is still alive at over 100 years of age and lives in Athens. Music teacher Mrs. Mattie Joe Sims became a lifelong friend and played music for James' wedding. Mr. Howard B. Stroud taught at AHIS from 1956 until 1963 and was a longtime, dedicated educator in Athens. He went on to serve as assistant principal and then principal of Lyons Middle School.

Mr. Stroud rounded out his career in the school district as associate superintendent from 1982 to 1992. When the school district decided to begin naming schools after local educators, they renamed the elementary school on Fourth Street after him. Likewise, Ms. Annie M. Burney, another well-known and venerated educator in Athens, still taught algebra at AHIS in 1959. She had been the assistant principal of AHIS under Samuel F. Harris (who created the

Mrs. Mattie Joe
Sims

Mr. Howard B.
Stroud

Ms. Annie M.
Burney

Ms. Alice Wimberly   *Mr. H. T. Edwards*   *Mr. Farris Johnson, Sr.*

Black Mammy Memorial Institute) in the 1930s and briefly held the position of principal when Mr. Harris became ill. Ms. Burney taught in the school district for 42 years and would be honored with having the new African American high school named after her and her long-time principal, Mr. Harris, in 1964, just a year after her death.

Ms. Alice Wimberly, who taught physical education, was the daughter of Drs. Lace and Ida Mae Johnson Hiram, Athens' first African American dentists. Ms. Wimberly also attended First A.M.E. Church and when James served on the Junior Usher Board at the church, the group held meetings at her house. Mr. Paul Troutman was the industrial arts teacher, whom James recalls had only one leg. James didn't particularly like shop class, but he respected Mr. Troutman for his dedication and perseverance despite his disability.

James did not have much interaction with the AHIS principal, Mr. H. T. Edwards, but he notes that although Mr. Edwards was stern he always led with an even hand. Mr. Farris Johnson, Sr. was the assistant principal and also taught math. Mr. Johnson and James' mother had been classmates at AHIS many years before. His son, Farris Johnson, Jr., became one of James' close friends. Farris, Jr. went on to become a physician and is James' doctor to this day.

The Long Journey to a New AHIS Home

In the fall of 1956, James' sophomore year at AHIS, a new building for Athens' Black high school students opened its doors. This was also the year the city and county districts merged. While everyone was thrilled with the new facility, it did not come about without some controversy and missteps along the way. The system was still segregated at this time and the path to constructing the new building was long and winding. Discussion of the need for a new African American high school began in 1948, but it did not open until 1956. In the meantime, a new white high school had been proposed, funded, designed, and built between 1948 and 1952.

In 1948, when James was in second grade, the Board of Education (BOE) was beginning to acknowledge that the old Knox campus that housed AHIS was overcrowded, ill-equipped, and beyond repair, and that a new high school for Black students was needed. The African American community had been watching the plans and expenditures for the new white high school and began to ask when a new facility for Black high school students would be built.

In July 1949, several options were discussed at the Board of Education meeting for the location of a new AHIS. The Superintendent agreed to confer with city attorneys regarding the title to the "Negro Recreation Ground," also known as the "Negro Ball Park," which was located off Broad Street near what was then the western edge of the city. After discovering that this property was owned by the city, the BOE Building and Grounds Committee recommended using this site as a locus for the new Black high school.

The Board realized it would have to acquire additional acreage to provide sufficient space for the new building and grounds, which meant purchasing several adjacent homes and lots, mostly from African American residents. The Board discussed perhaps needing to condemn this additional land, as it anticipated difficulty in getting clear titles.

Mayor Jack R. Wells attended all BOE meetings as a representative of the City of Athens government, not just an observer but as an active member of the Board. The Mayor did not support condemning these properties, arguing that such an action would be costly and might not result in the best possible financial outcome for the Board. He suggested instead that the BOE let the Mayor and City Council handle the proceedings to acquire the land, as a "slum clearance project" was in the works and they might be able to acquire the plots with the aid of the federal government. He assured the BOE that in any case, the city would deed the approximately three acres of land that constituted the ballpark to the Board.

While these discussions continued during the next school year, much of the BOE's attention was on the construction of the new white Athens High School. During this time the African American community began to grow restless. By the spring of 1950, a group of (African American) "Interested Citizens" drew up a petition and presented it to the Board of Education. The petition outlined in great detail the disparities between the educational resources, teacher pay, facilities, and funding allocated to the white and Black schools of Athens.

While the Board did answer the petition, its response was woefully inadequate. Fearing litigation or findings of fault, however, the Superintendent asked the city attorney, James Barrow, for his opinion on the petition. Mr. Barrow straightforwardly and explicitly told the BOE that it was treading on thin ice by not employing more direct measures to ensure at least the appearance of equality between the schools for white and Black students. Thus, while the petition did not directly lead to an amelioration of these disparities, it did spur the Board to move forward on its promise of a new Black high school. (See Appendix 7 for the Interested Citizens of Athens' petition and the BOE's response.)

In July 1950, the Board formed a committee and authorized it to seek additional property to purchase for the new AHIS. By December the committee had identified a likely tract of land consisting of 11.4 acres (see the map below). The board unanimously approved the purchase of this property.

Although acquiring this land proved problematic, by June 1951 the BOE had finally reached agreements with several property owners. The BOE decided to make offers to the remaining property owners and give them a deadline to accept or reject them. If the property owners refused the offers, condemnation proceedings would begin immediately.

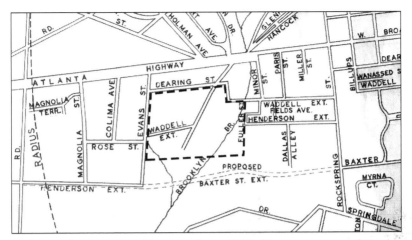

1949 map showing proposed location of new AHIS. (Base map courtesy of Hargrett Rare Book & Manuscript Library/University of Georgia Libraries.)

Condemnation of private property is complicated and time consuming. If a public entity (e.g., school system) wants to acquire land for any purpose, it must first offer the property owner a reasonable sum to purchase the parcel. There may or may not be several rounds of negotiations, but if the two parties cannot agree to an amount, the public entity has the remedy of "condemning" the property. As soon as this process is set in motion, an arbitrator is brought in to try to help the two parties agree to a price. If this effort fails, the issue goes before a judge and jury, who have the power to set a price.

Once the price is set, the property owner has no alternative but to accept it and relinquish the land. The problem with having the negotiations go this far is that often the public entity comes out worse than originally expected. Juries often gave the property owner more than the public entity had been offering, and the public entity also incurs court fees.

In May 1952 the BOE agreed that plans could be drawn up not only for the new AHIS but also for another new "Negro Elementary School." Reese Street School was in decline and it was thought to be more expensive to try to retrofit it than to build a new building with all the modern conveniences.

At this point in the state's history, the State Board of Education and State Building Authority had the means and authority to provide additional funds to construct a new school once the property had been acquired. The Athens School Board had to apply for this funding by presenting detailed plans and budgets. By June 1952, the Athens BOE had not yet applied to the state for funding for the new AHIS or for a new African American elementary school, as land had still not been completely secured for either project.

When the initial plans for the new AHIS were drawn up and shared with the public in March 1953, some African American leaders and citizens were upset that a gymnasium was not included. This was particularly distressing because the BOE had spent significant money on the new white Athens High School, which included not only a gymnasium but also a rifle range, tennis courts, and a graded football field with lights. And while Athens High School had only opened the previous fall, there were already plans in the works for additions and expansions to the campus.

A delegation of African American citizens met with Superintendent Ayers to discuss their concerns. Mr. Ayers disingenuously informed them that it was "the desire of the BOE to give them equal facilities but that funds coming from the State Building Authority did not permit building of the gymnasium" for AHIS. He also informed them that "the BOE does not have the money to be used for this purpose." Mr. Wolfe, a BOE member who was also present at the meeting, "pointed out to this group that when the building program is completed the Negro children will have complete new facilities with the exception of West Broad." It might be noted that when the new white Athens High School was completed, the total cost came to roughly $2 million, more than double the original estimate. When AHIS was eventually completed in 1956, the total cost was just under $400,000, belying the BOE's contention that the facilities were equal.

By April 1954 the new AHIS facility was finally approved and funded by the State Building Authority. At the BOE's April meeting, Mayor Wells made a motion to authorize Aeck Associates Architects to prepare working drawings for a new gymnasium for AHIS, even if current funding was not available. One year later, all the land had been acquired, the plans were approved, and ground had been broken for the new AHIS. However, it would be another three years before the school had its own gymnasium.

When the new Athens High and Industrial School opened in the fall of 1956, James was beginning his sophomore year of high school. The entire process began when he was in second grade. For the last three years of his education in Athens, James would finally reap the benefits of the long-awaited, modern, relatively well-equipped new school.

Merger of Athens City and Clarke County School Districts

In the same year the new AHIS opened, the city and county school districts merged. This process was every bit as long and complicated as the building of the new AHIS itself. The precipitating factor for the merger was that the county had very poor or no educational facilities for its African American students. The county district was constantly struggling not only to provide funding for the provision and upkeep of facilities, but also to hire qualified teachers and manage the logistics of busing children long distances.

While the county had five schools for white children (including a Demonstration School operated by the University of Georgia to train teachers) and thirteen for African American children, many of the schools for Black students were located on properties owned by rural African American churches and were in poor condition. Many had no running water, electricity, or basic supplies. The logistics of providing a quality education for the Black students of the county was proving increasingly challenging. In addition, the political and economic will for this endeavor was virtually non-existent.

Because the county had no public high school for African Americans, students who wanted a high school education attended either AHIS or Union Baptist Institute in Athens. Tuition was paid by the county school district for each of its African American high school students and the rates were negotiated each year. However, on

November 1, 1949, the State Department of Education sent a letter to the Clarke County School District stating unequivocally that no further public school funds could be paid to Union and instructing the district to terminate its agreement with Union immediately. Mr. William R. Coile, Clarke County School District Superintendent, was instructed to call Mr. Fred Ayers, the Athens City School District Superintendent, to inquire whether Athens would take all of their African American high school students.

This event set in motion consideration of a possible merger of the Athens City and Clarke County School Districts. However, it would be another two years before any serious discussions would begin. In the meantime, the county continued to send students to AHIS and pay their tuition. Students who wanted to attend Union had to pay their own way, and many did.

In March 1952, when Athens was in the early planning stages of building the new AHIS, Mr. Coile spoke with Mr. Ayers again. He proposed a long-term contract that would allow the county to send all of its African American high school students to the new school. They also discussed the possibility that the State Building Authority might provide money to the county BOE to help fund construction of the new AHIS.

By July 1952, both the Athens BOE and the Clarke BOE had approved a contract to construct a new AHIS that would serve all Black high school students in the county. This agreement seemed to be a win-win result for Athens, although it negatively impacted Union Baptist. When the new AHIS was completed in 1956 and the districts fully merged, Union was closed and the building demolished.

At the same time this contract was approved, the county schools received the results of a "Survey of School Properties" performed by a Reviewing Committee made up of representatives of other state school districts and state educational agencies in Georgia. The survey recommended a number of rather drastic measures to improve the quality of education for all students in the county. The report included the radical recommendation that **all** thirteen existing African

American school plant facilities "be abandoned at the earliest practical date" and that one elementary school "center" be built for all African American elementary school students in Clarke County in grades one through seven.

This survey and its recommendations spurred the county district to seriously consider a complete merger with the city district. On November 10, 1952, the city district received a letter from the county district asking if Athens would join them in commissioning a feasibility study on a possible merger. Both parties agreed that this study should begin immediately.

However, real progress on the merger was excruciatingly slow, to the extent that in the fall of 1954, the county moved forward with constructing its new elementary school center for African American students on county-owned property near the airport on Winterville Road. Mayor Wells expressed concern that this new school would be too near the city's East Athens Elementary School, which had just opened in 1952. When the merger was complete, the system would have two African American elementary schools barely one mile apart. Mayor Wells expressed his concerns again in January 1955, when he stated unequivocally that he thought the county was building its new Black elementary school in the wrong place. He asked that discussions be held to reconsider the location of the new county school.

However, such discussion never occurred. As a result, prior to the merger, Lyons Elementary School was built on Winterville Road near the airport, becoming the sole elementary school for the 481 African American students in the county at the time. As had been recommended, when it was completed, all other African American elementary schools in the county were closed.

Not until fall of 1954, when the League of Women Voters asked the school board to include the whole community in discussions about the consolidation, did the citizens of Athens and Clarke County become aware of a possible merger of the districts. As a result of these discussions, a proposition was placed on the ballot for the November 2, 1954 election. The proposition asked citizens of Athens and Clarke

Counties to "approve an amendment to the Constitution of the State of Georgia providing for a merger of the Athens City Schools and the Clarke County Schools."

The majority of Athens and Clarke County citizens voted in favor of this proposition, with 2,848 votes for the merger and only 241 against. Interestingly, the same ballot included another amendment to the state Constitution proposing to codify that "Separate schools shall be provided for the white and colored races." This initiative, a direct response to the Supreme Court's *Brown v. Board of Education* decision in May of that year, was an effort to thwart any attempts to desegregate the state's public schools.

The measure passed statewide by a fairly narrow margin: 210,478 for and 181,148 against. Clarke County (including the city of Athens), however, rejected the amendment by a vote of only 981 for and 2,629 against. While the amendment passed and became part of the state constitution, in 1968 the Supreme Court finally ordered states to unequivocally dismantle segregated school systems "root and branch," conveying clearly that federal law would always trump state law.

On Jan 19, 1955, an "act of merger" was finally approved by both BOEs to be presented to the legislature. By March 7, 1955, the legislature had approved the merger and the "enabling act" was signed by Governor Samuel Griffin. A referendum on the terms of the merger was put before the citizens of Athens and Clarke County and approved on May 4, 1955. The districts had a little over one year to put everything in place so that by the beginning of the school term in 1956, the merger would be complete.

After the agreements were signed and the state had approved them, one of the first orders of business for the Athens city district was to sell off some properties that were no longer needed. The district hoped the sale of some surplus properties would provide funding for the final changes that would need to be made when the districts merged.

In June 1955 the Athens City School District listed the following properties for sale: the Newtown School Property, the old AHS football field (at Hancock and Finley), a portion of the old AHS property (on Prince at Finley), the AHIS school property, and the Reese Street Elementary property.

By July 14, 1955, the Board had accepted bids from various individuals and businesses to purchase these school properties. The only person who bid on all of the available properties was Mr. Malcolm A. Rowe, the owner of Rowe Warehouse and Fertilizer Company in Athens. The total value of the properties was deemed to be $165,050 but Mr. Rowe offered only $58,506, far less than half their value. Regardless, the Board voted to accept his offers, with one exception. The Coca-Cola Company had the highest bid of $31,150 for the portion of the old AHS property on Prince; the company did not bid on any other properties. The board approved this single bid. The Coca-Cola Bottling Company building, now known as the Bottleworks, still sits on the site of the old Athens High School on Prince Avenue.

When the merger was complete and the 1956-57 school year began in September, the school system was composed of fourteen schools for elementary children–ten for white children and four for Black children (East Athens, Lyons, North Athens, and West Broad)– and two high schools comprising grades eight through twelve: AHS for white students and AHIS for African American students. All students were assigned to a school based on attendance zones. Each elementary school had a kindergarten, though this program would be discontinued in 1958 due to budget constraints, as the state did not contribute any funds for kindergartens. The total enrollment in the school system in the fall of 1956 was 7,873, up from 5,334 the year before the merger. AHIS's student population increased from just under 500 to over 700 students.

College Bound

James knew very early on that he wanted to go away to college, preferably even farther than Atlanta, so in his junior year he set out to discover what options were available to him. Luckily, AHIS provided excellent guidance counseling to help students identify colleges for

AHIS Class of 1959

which they were competitive, aid them in completing the applications, and even help them find jobs to save money for college. The guidance office even advertised in the local newspaper that they had been "successful . . . locating part-time jobs for interested students." Potential employers were encouraged to contact the guidance department to post jobs for which students could apply.

The guidance department was diligent in informing students about all the possibilities for college and not just about universities that accepted African American students. James never had anyone tell him not to look at the schools that had not previously admitted Black students. However, he and his siblings wanted to go to historically Black universities. Some of his classmates, as well as prior and subsequent AHIS students did attend integrated schools, but these were all out of state and out of reach financially for many African American families in Athens at the time. James says he never really questioned the University of Georgia's motives for not admitting Black students. He recognized the irony of not being able to attend the university in his hometown, but since he wanted to go away to college, the University of Georgia was not a school he ever considered applying to.

It was through the AHIS guidance office that James learned about Tuskegee Institute. After some deliberation, he decided he wanted to attend this historic university. James' family was very supportive of this decision, but James knew he would have to work part time until graduation and full time for a while after graduation to help pay for it. In high school, James worked at a dress shop in downtown Athens, washing windows and performing other janitorial services. He also worked at the new Georgia Center for Continuing Education on the UGA campus, waiting tables in the restaurant.

By the time James graduated from AHIS in June 1959, he had been accepted at Tuskegee Institute, where he planned to matriculate

in January 1960. His father worked at the Alexander Wood Company at that time and recommended that James come work there, as he thought the money would be better than at the Georgia Center. The pay may have been greater, but the work was extremely difficult and dangerous. Nevertheless, James endured, keeping his eye on the prize. He was never happier than when he finally quit that job and prepared to leave home for college.

James graduates from AHIS, June 1959.

CHAPTER 7

Tuskegee Institute, Civil Rights, and Segregation: 1960-1965

In January 1960, James loaded a few essentials into the back of his father's Buick and set off with his parents on the long drive from Athens to Tuskegee, Alabama, where James would start college. Having never set foot on the Tuskegee campus, he was understandably nervous. This was all new territory for 18-year-old James. He wasn't sure what to expect, how he would be received, how to navigate the campus, or who to ask for help if he needed it.

As a high school student, James had read about George Washington Carver and Booker T. Washington, so he knew a little of the celebrated university's history. But he had no idea how the real-life experience would unfold. Nevertheless, he had waited for this moment for so long that excitement overshadowed his apprehension. Although James had lived in Virginia when he was very young and had been to Washington, D.C. with his high school safety patrol, this journey out of state was different. He recalls that he was probably the most anxious he had ever been as he watched the world rush by the car windows.

Tuskegee Institute

Founded in 1881 by former slave Lewis Adams, the Tuskegee State Normal School flourished under the inaugural leadership of Booker T. Washington. Its original mission was to educate freed African Americans in academic subjects as well as agricultural and industrial skills. As academic coursework and departments were added, it became known as Tuskegee Institute; in 1985 it obtained university status and was renamed Tuskegee University.

When James began his college years at Tuskegee, the institution had been rapidly expanding since World War II. New departments and fields of study included graduate programs in mechanical engineering, architecture, and veterinary medicine. In 1966 Congress declared Tuskegee a National Historic Landmark, recognizing "the significance of its academic programs, its role in higher education for African Americans, and its status in United States history." Tuskegee is the only Historically Black University to be named a National Historic Site by the National Park Service, a designation it received in 1974.

Life at Tuskegee

When James and his parents arrived at Tuskegee, James unloaded his belongings into a small room in one of "the Emeries," a group of four on-campus dormitories (named Emery I, II, III, and IV) that housed much of the freshman class. Two of the dorms were for men and two were for women. Three AHIS classmates and friends—Marvin Billups, Jr., Harry Tate, and Robert Thrasher—had entered Tuskegee the previous September. These friends helped James acclimate to life on campus, and it did not take long for James' apprehension to turn to joy. Tuskegee was his gateway to a wider world, new experiences, and the freedom to shape his own destiny. He reveled in making his own decisions and having responsibility only for himself. And while the dorms had resident counselors and strict curfews, and the demands of his schoolwork and extracurricular activities were at times overwhelming, James was thrilled to be there.

James jumped into college life with both feet. He signed up for the required freshman core classes and quickly realized he would have to "buckle down even more" than at AHIS. But his awe of and admiration for his professors fed his determination to excel in each class. James eventually decided to double major in political science and music.

James got involved in numerous extracurricular activities, including volunteering at the local VA Hospital near campus. He and other students would go there on Saturdays to "serve and encourage" the patients, sometimes sharing a meal, playing music and dancing, helping them with various tasks, or just sitting and talking. Many of the patients were World War I veterans.

This VA Hospital had a long and unique history. Authorized by Congress and established in 1923, the Tuskegee Veterans Administration Medical Center was built to serve the estimated 300,000 African American veterans of World War I. There were no other facilities in existence at the time to care for these veterans. Adjacent to the Tuskegee campus, the grounds of the hospital consisted of 27 buildings on 464 acres to accommodate the various wards and treatment facilities. The hospital attracted numerous African American doctors and eventually the facility gained accreditation to train African American physicians who were completing their medical residency programs at other universities around the country.

James does not remember having much time to explore the town of Tuskegee, but he says it was relatively small. In 1960, the population was just over 7,200 residents. He did visit with a family who had relatives in Athens, and he occasionally went to their house for a meal or just to chat.

As time allowed, James attended various campus events, including a graduation speech by Dr. Martin Luther King, Jr. and lectures by Muhammad Ali and Malcolm X. He enjoyed attending football and basketball games, especially the Southern Intercollegiate Athletic Conference (SIAC) basketball tournament held at Tuskegee every February. He would watch the band rehearse and play at games and attend social events sponsored by various fraternities or other campus organizations. He also made sure to explore the museums and historic monuments on campus. He describes these experiences as an opportunity "to do all the things I never could while in high school."

Air Force ROTC

At the time James attended Tuskegee, all young men were required to participate in either the Army or Air Force ROTC for two years. James chose the Air Force ROTC and says with a smile that

James as an ROTC cadet at Tuskegee.

there was a lot of friendly teasing between the two groups. "Of course, the Air Force ROTC was better! We dressed better, we were cleaner, our shoes were more highly polished, our precision drills were better, our cadence was better!" he says with pride, but also with a laugh.

James believes the purpose of this requirement was more than training young men for military service; it was to help prepare them for life after college. Military training taught them to be precise, pay attention to detail, follow orders, and complete a job well. James says that it was physically demanding, but also built a cohesive group. Some of the young men in his class joined the military as officers upon graduating from Tuskegee. This was not part of James' plan, but he says he learned a lot from this experience.

The Renowned Tuskegee Choir

When James arrived at Tuskegee, one of his first goals was to audition for the Tuskegee Concert Choir. His friends Harry and Marvin were already members and were eager to have James join them. Slightly nervous about his audition, but knowing it was one of the main reasons he came to Tuskegee, he gave it his all.

James had no formal training in reading music, but he had a good ear and learned new pieces quickly. To his delight, he was accepted into not only the Concert Choir, but the Touring Choir as well. The Touring Choir was a subset of the Concert Choir and consisted of approximately 40 singers out of the 70 or 80 in the larger choir. Harry and Marvin were also in the Touring Choir and all three young men sang bass. Here was one of James' dreams realized: He was going to sing with the famous Tuskegee Choir! The Music Department became his campus home and his abiding passion.

The Tuskegee Choir is nearly as old as the university itself. Book-

The Tuskegee Concert Choir, c. 1962. James is in the second row, fifth from right.

er T. Washington, the Institute's founder, encouraged and supported the choir's establishment in 1884. Mr. Washington believed the addition of a well-trained, professional choir would not only enhance the weekly chapel services that all students were required to attend, but also help preserve African American musical traditions. He felt it was an important part of the students' education to hear the music that helped sustain African Americans through hard times. He also recognized that a well-trained choir that could perform for a wider audience would be good ambassadors for the school, helping promote Tuskegee's mission. The choir quickly expanded beyond the original founding quartet and began performing at weekly chapel services and special campus events. It soon became a featured part of any cultural or religious activity on campus.

The choir has had a long list of directors over the years, but in 1931 its most renowned and decorated director took his place on the podium. William L. Dawson was not just a director, but also a composer and educator. He believed in furthering Tuskegee's reputation and respect through choral music. The Tuskegee Choir flourished under his leadership and by 1932 they were singing at events such as the opening of Radio City Music Hall in New York City, a performance at the Hoover White House, and President-elect Franklin D. Roosevelt's birthday party. The choir soon became a regular guest on a variety of radio programs.

When the choir was invited to perform on *The Charlie McCarthy Show* with Edgar Bergen in 1950, a national television audience saw the group for the first time. This appearance led to numerous other invitations to appear on television programs, including *The Ed Sullivan Show* in 1952. These appearances propelled the Tuskegee Choir to national prominence and requests for them to perform increased dramatically. Professor Dawson retired from directing the choir in 1955 after the choir recorded an album entitled *The Tuskegee Institute Choir Sings Spirituals.*

Mrs. Alberta Simms, a longtime and dedicated musician who had been at Tuskegee since 1913, stepped in to direct until a permanent director could be found. Tuskegee hired Dr. Relford Patterson as the new director in 1956.

Dr. Relford Patterson

Dr. Patterson was a North Carolina native who received his Bachelor of Music in Voice and Music Education from Howard University. He earned his Master of Arts degree in Composition and his Ph.D. in Composition and Musicology from Washington University. Before Tuskegee, he had taught at both Shaw and Wilberforce Universities. At Tuskegee, he became Head of the Department of Music and a Professor of Music while continuing to lead the Concert Choir to prominence. His promotion of the Touring Choir led to performances celebrating the 25th anniversary of Radio City Music Hall in 1958 and singing with the Atlanta Symphony Orchestra in 1959. While Professor Patterson was on leave from 1960-1962 to complete his doctoral degree, Mr. Odell Hobbs filled in. James remembers that Mr. Hobbs was like a big brother whom he idolized. James also proudly recalls that he was hired to wash and wax Mr. Hobbs' car on a regular basis.

Mr. Odell Hobbs

Ms. Ethel Smith

Numerous other members of the Music Department faculty also worked with the main Concert Choir. James remembers in particular Ms. Ethel Smith, who taught voice and worked with individuals and small groups of students to make sure every voice in the choir was singing their part correctly. James recalls that Ms. Smith was very stern and exacting, but he appreciated her approach and even her demanding nature. James remembered his mother's admonition that "if you are going to do something, do it well." Ms. Smith embodied that belief and James adhered to it when he became a director himself.

Choir rehearsals were held in the evenings after classes. This was a time James looked forward to even when his other class work was demanding his time and attention. He recalls that even when the choir was traveling, students still had to be sure to get their classwork completed. Professors were supportive of the choir and would give students their homework before they left for engagements. Sometimes the choir might be gone as long as a week, as the director might combine several performances in an area in which alumni would invite them to sing.

Mr. Patterson returned from his sabbatical in time to lead the choir at one of its most prominent performances. James recalls this event with great pride. "One of our greatest highlights singing with this group was in 1962, when we sang for the National Christmas Tree Lighting on the White House lawn and President John Kennedy was in office." President Kennedy attended this event and awarded the choir a special commendation. Mr. Patterson shook the President's hand and said it was one of the high points of his life.

James loved these tours and found his world expanding exponentially as a result. During his years at Tuskegee, the choir performed primarily in the Midwest and up the eastern seaboard, in cities includ-

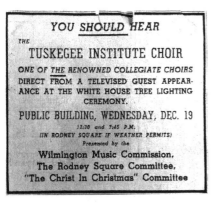

YOU *SHOULD* HEAR

THE

TUSKEGEE INSTITUTE CHOIR

ONE OF *THE* RENOWNED COLLEGIATE CHOIRS
DIRECT FROM A TELEVISED GUEST APPEAR-
ANCE AT THE WHITE HOUSE TREE LIGHTING
CEREMONY.

PUBLIC BUILDING, WEDNESDAY, DEC. 19

12:30 and 7:45 P.M.
(IN RODNEY SQUARE IF WEATHER PERMITS)
Presented by the

Wilmington Music Commission,
The Rodney Square Committee,
"The Christ In Christmas" Committee

ing Chicago; Gary, Indiana; Detroit; New York City; Washington, D.C.; Dover, Delaware; Columbia, South Carolina; and Chattanooga, Tennessee. These experiences continued to broaden James' world and expose him to people and places he might not have had a chance to see otherwise.

Another highlight for this group was the opportunity to meet the legendary Mrs. Mahalia Jackson, "The Queen of Gospel." When the choir traveled to Michigan for a performance, a reception was held for them at the home of a Tuskegee alumnus. Mrs. Jackson attended the concert and the reception. Choir members were thrilled to have a chance to meet this renowned singer and gathered around her for a photo.

The choir traveled to these engagements by chartered bus and stayed in hotels along the way. James doesn't remember much about

Tuskegee Touring Choir with Mrs. Mahalia Jackson, early 1960s. James is sitting on the floor in the middle, directly in front of Mrs. Jackson.

James and his good friend McArthur Fields in a hotel during one of the Touring Choir's trips.

their accommodations and assumes they had to stay in segregated hotels. They were all just excited to be traveling, and staying in hotels was a unique and exciting part of the trip. Of course, the director always exhorted them to be on their best behavior at all times. They were representing not just Tuskegee, but African Americans in general, and they were expected to be exemplary citizens. The choir was co-ed and the young men knew not to engage in improper behavior with the young women, and not to touch them or make any advances that could in any way be misconstrued.

Professor Patterson would remind the students before they left for any tour, "Here are the rules. If you don't follow them, you *will* be sent home." There were no second chances. As a result, James does not recall any incidents involving choir members. It was much too important to each of them to be able to continue singing in the choir and going on the tours. James admired and respected Mr. Patterson and says he learned about much more than music as a member of the choir. Mr. Patterson completed his tenure as director in 1967.

The Tuskegee Concert Choir and the Touring Choir were not the only musical groups James belonged to during his time at Tuskegee. He also sang with the Male Glee Club, The Cliques, and the Madrigal Singers.

The Concert Choir sang every Sunday morning at church services on the campus and was the only group that held consistent and regularly scheduled rehearsals. The other groups primarily sang for events on campus and performed a variety of styles. The Concert Choir sang sacred music; the Male Glee Club performed spirituals; the Madrigal Singers performed sacred and classical pieces; and The Cliques primarily performed popular music of the day and were a crowd favorite at fraternity events and other student-led programs.

The Cliques, early 1960s. James is fourth from left.

The Madrigal Singers, early 1960s. James is standing, fourth from left.

James recalls that there was a "Miss Tuskegee" competition every year and each young lady would ask various campus groups to support her campaign. James says that all the competitors wanted The Cliques to back them and perform at their events. This gave the group considerable power to choose who they would back, as they knew the young woman would receive a boost if The Cliques supported her campaign.

James and his friends Harry and Marvin sang in all of these groups. They also had the opportunity to perform for some theater productions at Tuskegee. James remembers singing in the chorus for *A Raisin in the Sun* one year.

Jobs at Tuskegee

While James was at Tuskegee, he continued to do various odd jobs to earn money for school. His parents helped with tuition and fees, but he still needed money for books, school supplies, and incidentals. Being an enterprising young man, he knew if he could find work that allowed him to be his own boss, he could work it into his busy schedule when and where possible. So he started his own business washing and waxing cars, and shining shoes for ROTC members. Tuskegee was a small town and many of the students were in financial situations similar to James', so his entrepreneurial spirit gave him an advantage when it came to finding work.

Social Life at Tuskegee

In addition to James' longtime friends from AHIS in Athens, he met several new like-minded students who would become lifelong friends: McArthur Fields and Abe Thomas from Savannah, Marvin Kelly and Nelia Coleman from South Carolina, and Marilyn Isabel from Memphis, Tennessee. These friendships lasted long past his college years. James had little time for socializing given the demands of his studies, the choirs, and working, but he does remember attending parties on campus hosted by the numerous fraternities and sororities. James did not join a fraternity while at Tuskegee, but he did join the local chapter of Kappa Alpha Psi when he returned to Athens.

Summer employment in the tobacco fields of Hazardville, Connecticut. James is in the front row, fifth from right.

Summer Months

During the school year, James would hop on a bus or hitch a ride with one of his friends from Athens to return home for the holidays or other longer breaks in the academic calendar. But during the summer months he wanted to find employment far from Athens or Tuskegee. The financial aid office at Tuskegee helped students locate summer employment all over the country. Businesses or individuals would send information to the office describing the work they had available and how many workers they needed. Students would fill out an application that would be sent to the employer, who would then notify Tuskegee who they would like to hire.

For the first two summers while a student at Tuskegee, James worked at L. B. Haas Tobacco Farm in Hazardville, Connecticut. James laughed at the irony of working in farming, as he had hoped to get as far away from farming and agricultural work as he could when he left Athens. But he knew he could do the work and it intrigued him to go somewhere new.

The four friends from Athens–Marvin, Harry, Robert, and James–were all hired for the job, along with several other Tuskegee students. They made the long journey to Connecticut by bus. Marvin recalls that the work "was the hardest, dirtiest, poorest conditions that we had encountered in our very young work history." At the Haas farm they met many other college students from all over the South who were hired each summer to work in the fields. They all lived in the rustic barracks of the farm called the "Haas Hotel," seen in the background of the picture on the previous page. The days were long and the work difficult, but James says they made new friends and enjoyed what free time they had. When the foreman asked James in his second year if he planned to return the next season, James' response was, "Hell no," noting that "he would eat rocks before coming back to Hazardville."

After two summers of farming the tobacco fields, James decided to seek out different summer employment. Through the financial aid office at Tuskegee he applied to work at a resort in the Catskill Mountains of upstate New York called the SalHara Hotel, located near the town of Woodbourne. The resort was named for Sally and Harry Friedman, the married couple who owned it.

Marvin remembers that not very long after James arrived at the hotel, he "called to tell me that he had talked to the owner and he had a job for me as well." So Marvin took the long bus ride up to New York to work at the SalHara Hotel with James. Working initially as dishwashers, the two young men quickly received promotions.

Marvin recalls,

> James advanced to the position of short order cook and I ended up assisting in the pantry and then assisting the baker. This was a real cultural experience. The chef was Hungarian, the baker was German, the owners were Jewish. Needless to say, all meals were kosher, prepared and served. During our downtime, James talked Harry into allowing us to borrow his car to shop for school clothes and catch shows at Grossinger's Hotel in nearby Monticello, New York.

Grossinger's was one of the largest "Borscht Belt" resorts in the

Catskills at the time. The young men met other university students from the South working summer jobs there as well.

The Civil Rights Movement

James attended Tuskegee in the early years of the Civil Rights Movement. He and his friends talked about what was happening in Selma, Birmingham, and other cities across the South where demonstrations were taking place. They knew that several Tuskegee students were involved in activities related to the movement. However, James and his friends were not active in most of the organizations or meetings.

This was not due to apathy or indifference. James always believed that it was long past time for society to acknowledge African Americans' rights to fair and equal treatment, that institutions should be open to all, and that no one should be judged by the color of their skin. But James felt like he had gone through so much in his upbringing that he just couldn't be a part of violence. And as much as he believed in and supported the nonviolent movement of Dr. Martin Luther King, Jr., he knew there was a good chance that by participating in a demonstration he might be beaten, and he was not sure that he would not strike back. James was not afraid, but he thought, "Why should I go put myself out there for someone to kick me, beat me, set dogs on me . . . I just couldn't do it." The unpredictability of what might happen was too unsettling.

James also felt that being raised in segregated schools did not hinder him. He treasured his education and his teachers, as well as the schools and community he belonged to while growing up in Athens. Many African Americans in Athens valued and appreciated what they had built *in spite of* segregation. Many were not eager to integrate the schools, as they valued the community, its shared culture and values, and the freedom having their own institutions provided.

Many also felt that while the schools were not at all equal in many ways, the African American community had thrived despite the limitations and lack of resources. Many of them also knew that when integration happened, the Black community had the most to lose and was likely to suffer the most. Integration did not mean equality. James knew that changing hearts and minds would not happen quickly, if at all. He also knew that the community in which he grew up was the reason he had gotten as far as he had.

While James was at Tuskegee, Athens was taking slow and incremental steps toward integrating the public schools. Although Charlayne Hunter and Hamilton Holmes had enrolled at the University of Georgia in 1961, most of the African American community in Athens was not as engaged in their matriculation as one might expect. It was dangerous for Black citizens to protest or voice their concerns, let alone demand action.

While James and his family were not directly involved in Hamilton's protection, he knew the family that housed Hamilton when it became obvious that living in the dorms was too dangerous. The Killian family (headed by Archibald Killian, one of the first Black police officers in Athens) took Hamilton in, and he stayed at Mr. Killian's mother's house off of Broad Street for some time while enrolled at the university. James knew that several community members carried guns to help protect Hamilton. Another activist in Athens at the time was Reverend William Hudson of Ebenezer Baptist Church. Hudson played a significant role in the Civil Rights Movement in Athens and was one of the more vocal African American pastors at the time.

While James was at Tuskegee, four Black girls in Athens were the first to enroll in one of the previously all-white elementary schools (James thinks it might have been Chase Street, although I was unable to verify this). In 1963, Wilucia Green, Margie Green, Agnes Green, and Bonnie Hampton bravely took the first steps toward integrating the public schools.

James also remembers the murder of Lt. Col. Lemuel Penn just north of Athens in 1964. Lt. Col. Penn was driving home from training at Fort Benning with two other World War II veterans in the summer of 1964. Spotted driving through Athens, they were pursued by members of the Ku Klux Klan to the Broad River and fired upon as they crossed the bridge on Highway 172. Lt. Col. Penn died at the scene. While a local jury acquitted the Klansmen, the federal government was "successful in prosecuting the men for violations under the new Civil Rights Act of 1964, passed just nine days before Penn's murder." An historic marker at Georgia Highway 172 and the Broad River Bridge at the Madison/Elbert County line commemorates this event.

African American Student Involvement in Civil Rights, 1960-1964

A generally acknowledged turning point for the Civil Rights Movement from isolated incidents of defiance to organized resistance was the 1960 student lunch counter protest in Greensboro, North Carolina. The burgeoning movement was significantly furthered by students at universities across the South and East. Prior to this moment several significant events, such as *Brown v. Board of Education* (1954), the desegregation of Central High School in Little Rock, Arkansas (1957), the passage of the Civil Rights Act of 1957, and Ruby Bridges' enrollment in a white school in New Orleans, Louisiana (1960) had awakened the country to the fact that the push for civil rights was not going away. After the lunch counter protest, demonstrations grew larger and increased in frequency. The Freedom Riders (1961) and Martin Luther King, Jr.'s "I Have a Dream" speech at the end of the March on Washington (1963) punctuated the various student movements around the country.

At Tuskegee, students formed a new civil rights organization, the Tuskegee Institute Advancement League, which was active in several protests and organized events in Alabama. However, many of the largely middle-class students at Tuskegee were wary of participating in a radical movement that might prove disadvantageous to their goals. Many, like James, hoped that change could come about without confrontation or violence.

The city of Tuskegee was involved in a civil rights case of its own during this time. In the wake of the Civil Rights Act of 1957, many African Americans living in Tuskegee had registered to vote for the first time. Since the Alabama constitution still had in place such discriminatory practices as poll taxes and literacy tests, the white residents grew fearful that African American voters would begin to prevail in local elections. So in 1957, the Alabama state legislature created new Tuskegee city boundaries that excluded nearly all Black voters and residents, but no white ones, creating a gerrymandered district that was certain to elect white candidates vying for office.

The city of Tuskegee was always predominantly African American (by a ratio of 4 to 1) and by 1960 registered Black voters almost equaled white ones. When most of the professional African Americans teaching and working at Tuskegee Institute and the Veteran's Hospital were disenfranchised by the redistricting, they organized a local economic boycott of white-owned businesses. This propelled the case to litigation. Unsurprisingly, the lower courts upheld the legislature's right to redistrict Tuskegee. However, when the case reached the Supreme Court in 1960 as *Gomillion v. Lightfoot*, the redistricting was deemed a violation of the Fifteenth Amendment. Immediately following this decision, the previous district boundaries were restored.

It must be remembered that George Wallace, a staunch segregationist, was serving as governor of Alabama beginning in 1962. He won the election due partly to his racist views, not in spite of them. When he tried to bar African Americans from enrolling at the University of Alabama, citizens throughout Alabama and across the nation were watching. The climate in the state was heating up and would soon explode.

One of the most devastating and violent moments in the Civil Rights Movement occurred in Alabama after James had returned to Athens from Tuskegee. March 7, 1965 became known as "Bloody Sunday" when more than 600 marchers gathered in Selma to march to Montgomery to call attention to the denial of their voting rights. Led by current Georgia congressman John Lewis and Rev. Hosea Williams, the marchers were forcibly stopped by a massive Alabama State trooper and police blockade as they tried to cross the Edmund Pettus Bridge. The brutality of the Alabama police force was televised nationally and seen around the world, sparking outrage, provoking fierce debate, and intensifying support for the Civil Rights Movement.

In Athens, a primarily student-led protest was inspired by the Greensboro, North Carolina lunch counter sit-in. The Varsity is a very popular fast-food restaurant in Athens that sells hot dogs, hamburgers, french fries, and milkshakes. It had been operating for many years at its downtown location at the corner of Broad Street and College Avenue, directly across from the University of Georgia. At this location, Black patrons were served, but only at a walk-up window; they were not allowed to sit inside. When the restaurant decided to expand in 1963, moving farther out Broad Street to the corner of Milledge Avenue, they hired African American teenagers to serve white patrons at their cars. White customers were still served inside the restaurant as well, but no African Americans were allowed inside the restaurant for any reason.

In 1964, several Civil Rights activists in Athens decided to protest this injustice. The protest initially involved marching in front of the restaurant and picketing. Local KKK members converged on the site to counter-protest and many Black Athenians were arrested. As these protests were not achieving the desired results, a large group of students, primarily from Ebenezer Baptist Church, decided to march from the church at Reese and Chase Streets to The Varsity, a couple of blocks away. They planned to sit at the counter just as the students had in Greensboro several years before.

The police department and the state patrol got wind of this plan and rounded up several buses to transport all the African Americans inside the restaurant to jail. However, Archibald Killian, the only Black officer on the police force at the time, refused to participate in the arrests, even offering the chief his badge in resignation. The police chief realized there was no good outcome to mass arrests. As Officer Killian recounts, the chief realized that "integration is here." He reversed his decision and dismissed the buses. While change was not immediate, The Varsity eventually allowed African American patrons to be served inside the restaurant.

When the Civil Rights Act of 1964 was signed into law by President Lyndon Johnson, it prohibited discrimination in public places, provided for the integration of schools and other public facilities, and made employment discrimination illegal. This document was the most sweeping civil rights legislation since Reconstruction. The Act was closely followed by the Voting Rights Act of 1965, signed into law on August 6, 1965, also by President Johnson. It outlawed the discriminatory voting practices adopted in many Southern states after the Civil War, including literacy tests as a prerequisite to voting.

However, when James returned to Athens in 1965, he did not see that much had really changed in his hometown. The schools were still predominantly segregated, most public places were still segregated, and African Americans still had limited access to facilities and jobs in the community. In some ways James saw Athens digging in rather than reaching out.

Segregation

James reflected on what it was like growing up in a segregated society.

> In the days while we were children, and growing up in Athens, most everything was segregated. I knew from the beginning that white folks were different. We knew where we stood as far as Black children are concerned. We went to segregated schools. When participating in any school activities or competing in any athletics or competitions, they were all done separately. Our sports teams used what we call "hand-me-downs." At our high school, the Coach, Mr. E. T. Holmes, would have to go to the white high school to get equipment that they didn't use anymore.

James remembers being aware at a very early age of the differences between his family and the white families for whom his mother did washing and ironing.

> We knew when we finished the work and we would take these clothes back to these folks, that we could go no

further than the front door. We never went inside their houses. We didn't feel any smaller than anyone else . . . but doing this for them . . . there was just something different about it. I realized that they were not doing any work for us. They were paying us and we would take the money back to our mother so we knew we were doing a service they valued, but I never saw any white people do something for a Black person. We didn't think about it as culture. We just knew they stay in their lane and we stay in our lane. We didn't always think everything was bad. No one had done anything bad directly to us.

James continued,

In Athens, during the fall, usually September or October, the fair would come to town and it was set up on Dunlap Road [in the far eastern part of Clarke County, off of Highway 78] for a week. There was a day for white children to attend the fair and there was a day designated for Black children to attend. As children we just thought that as long as we got to enjoy the fun, we didn't think about the fact that we had to do it separately.

In our home, segregation wasn't discussed that much. However, we knew who we were and our place in society. While walking to and from school, if you met someone white walking on the sidewalk, it was the correct thing to do to step aside to let them pass by. The eating places in Athens were also segregated and even if you were allowed to purchase food there, Blacks would be served in the back area or through a window outside. Water fountains were designated "colored" and "white" and it was imperative that you honored those signs. Of course, the bathrooms were segregated as well.

There has always been an interest in the University of Georgia football team among all the citizens of Athens.

There were many years that Black people had to watch the football games from the railroad trestle on the east side of the stadium. Once we got permission to go in the stadium, there was a segregated area where Black people were allowed to sit. I never thought about going to UGA for college because it was not integrated then. But then, I always wanted to go to Morehouse or Tuskegee anyway.

These negative aspects of life did not stop us or determine our outlook for a successful life. All of these negative things were teaching experiences to make our family work much harder to become strong men and women.

James' parents led by example and there were many discussions about appropriate behavior, especially how young men behave around young women. His parents talked about girls, and about not getting into trouble with them. The Smith children were always warned that if you do something against the law, a police officer *will* arrest you. They were also told not to call their parents if they did end up in jail, as their parents would leave them there. James doesn't recall whether his parents told him the police would treat him differently. He was simply raised to accept that "grown folks were always right."

When James looks back on some of the more radical actions of activists like Malcolm X and Angela Davis during the peak years of the Civil Rights Movement, he reflects that their approach might have had some merit. James "questioned their thinking at the time, but now [I] believe that maybe they were right about some things. I can no longer say that they were wrong." At the time, James thought MLK's nonviolent approach was the right way to go, but he also saw that it didn't stop white people from being violent. "Although we called it radical thinking then, the white man just dismissed the Black man's thinking. It didn't matter if you were radical or not, [white people] didn't think you were right anyway."

James felt he could not have put himself in physically dangerous situations. He was not only afraid of getting hurt but wary that if someone attacked him, he would attack them back. He just couldn't take that chance. When thinking about the possibility of being drafted and going to war, "It hit me real hard about serving my country. I love my country, but to give your life . . . is a lot. It's a lot."

James believes that at the root of prejudice is the fact that "people move away from what they are used to very, very slowly. We have lost a lot of opportunities because we just won't move." When I asked him about the fact that most churches in Athens are still segregated today, he says that they, too, move slowly. He also doesn't discount that some people and some churches are holding on to what they know and what they are comfortable with. James believes that "churches should come together as one, but they are each set in their ways and in their community." And James laments that "even if the doors are open, how do you get people to walk in?"

James shakes his head as he says that he does not see "that minds and hearts and souls have been changed much over the years." He sums up his view of prejudice and racism as "ignorance." He observes, "Some people won't let white people in their houses and some whites won't let Black folks in their houses. That's stupid. That's ignorance. That day has passed."

Deep in his heart, James knows

> that there is a man bigger than me. And He is not looking down on me because I am Black. He's the one that has kept me these 78 years. And if I am thinking, why is a white person going to a Black church or a Black person to a white one? . . . I have to think, You came to worship and it makes no difference to the Lord what color you are.
>
> I care about a whole lot, but it is a waste of time to worry about some things. But we can't get past it because we are not looking at it the right way. We are looking at it from the wrong perspective; we are not looking at each other and at our hearts the same. We have all lost a lot of opportunities because we all want to stay in our own little world. When it comes to the bigger things that would

help us all to improve and to grow, we got to move there. If I am a 78-year-old man, and I am still being held back because my people don't want to move, that's my fault. But then, too, we can't make anybody do that. Just like you can open the doors but can't make somebody walk through, it's the same with the brain. It's supposed to be open but most of the time it is closed.

I asked James when he became aware that there were very few representations of Black people in the media or in publications as he was growing up, and what he thought about that. He responded that Black folks knew that white America didn't want to see Black people as smart, competent, successful, or beautiful. He states,

> For some reason white folks thought Black folks didn't have any qualifications, or could do anything, or were smart enough. Although a lot has been done over the years, in their minds and hearts, they just want to keep it white. Some people don't want Black people to get credit for being able to think on or above the level that white people think. A lot of things have been squashed because of that thinking. We always could think, always been able to act. We are qualified to do anything. This is why others take such a hard stance, because they know they earned their place, that you had a mind and used it.

James recalls that when he and Marvin were at Tuskegee, they would joke with each other all the time "that if you don't think like me, you can't think at all or you are wrong." They each wanted to dictate their way or no way. James thinks that while they were joking around, on some level they meant it at the time. They would also comment on other people's thinking or decisions and judge them harshly. "We thought people were so stupid." And while some of this was just the hubris of youth, such attitudes also grew out of the frustration they faced throughout their lives because society didn't believe they were good enough, smart enough, or right about anything.

James recalls that as an adult, after he returned to Athens from Tuskegee and was teaching at Burney-Harris High School (the new name given to his alma mater, AHIS, in 1964), he became aware of another aspect of Athens' segregated and hierarchical society. He and other African Americans were aware that when white people in positions of power in Athens needed input about what the Black community might be thinking or wanted recommendations for who in the African American community they should nominate to appoint to (token) positions on boards or other civic organizations, there were two men in the Black community to whom they routinely went for this information. James speculates that the white community wanted to be sure they found the "right" African Americans for a post or to offer information on how the Black community might feel about or react to certain issues or decisions.

These two African American men were perceived as pillars of the Black community, but not everyone in that community believed it was right for these two to wield such power. It seemed that many opportunities for individuals in the African American community were in the hands of just these two men, who somehow spoke for the entire Black community. James doesn't remember when this "patronage system" changed or ended, but he knows that it rankled some at the time. If you were not part of the circle in which these men moved you might not be considered for positions or consulted about issues on which you might have made a difference.

Called Home to Athens

Toward the end of James' fall 1964 semester at Tuskegee, he received a call from Athens. His family was facing various challenges and he was needed at home. James remembers that many families were struggling at that time and he knew that he had to go home and help. He always intended to return to Tuskegee to finish his college education, but life and time moved on and he never got that chance.

While James regrets not completing his undergraduate degree at Tuskegee, he is not angry or disappointed. He knows he did what he needed to do at the time to support his family. Always the optimist, James even sees that some good came out of this time. His help at home made things a little easier for his younger siblings and he was able to help his parents build a better house. James says, "I have always taken the helping way."

When he returned to Athens, James knew he had accomplished a lot during those intervening years. He was grateful for the experiences and his expanded horizons. James remembers that he and Marvin talked endlessly during college about their plans for the future. They discussed what they were going to do, where they were going to work, and what lay ahead. Now James was embarking on this next chapter of his life.

in 1965 to more efficiently transport children to the school of their choice, but both the expense and the logistics were overwhelming. As a result, the district realized that it would need to create attendance zones for the 1967-68 school year.

However, by the spring of 1968 it was clear that even the attendance zone plan was not working as well as the district had hoped to balance enrollment at the various schools. So a committee of the Board of Education presented a districting plan for the 1968-69 school year that would "use a combination enrollment plan involving geographic attendance districts for some schools and freedom of choice for others." The proposal went on to note that "The plan is deemed desirable for the purpose of providing control of the distribution of pupils among the various schools and of continuing to meet legal requirements under the Civil Rights Act of 1964." Although the document reported that as of 1968, "more than 750 [African American students] are enrolled in formerly all-white schools," this number represented a mere 7.5% of the total number of students in a district in which African Americans represented approximately 30% of the school population.

The proposal went on to say,

> The plan for 1968-69 will require elementary children residing in "out-lying" areas to attend schools according to designated districts and those residing in an "inner area" of Athens will have freedom of choice among seven schools, in view of the fact that all of them reside within walking distance of a school. Freedom of choice will be continued . . . for junior and senior high schools. As the plan for 1968-69 is put into effect it is contemplated that there will be an increase in the desegregation of professional staff. For 1969-70 it is anticipated that completed districting will be put into place and no school will remain with an enrollment of one race. To go further will necessitate the entire elimination of freedom of choice.

By the fall of 1969, all of the Clarke County Schools were majority white except West Broad Elementary, which retained a majority of Black students, and Burney-Harris High School, which remained the only fully segregated school, both among its student population and its faculty. The district had 35 buses traveling over 2,000 miles per day to get children to school. To add to its woes, the HEW had rejected the district's plan to achieve desegregation by selective busing. As they wrestled with how to meet the demands of their district, the HEW, and the families of Athens, the school board actually considered whether they could just stop accepting federal funding and run the district as they saw fit. However, they quickly rejected this idea as unworkable and impractical.

In September 1969, several (mostly white) parents filed a lawsuit in the local courts disputing the legality of the elementary school desegregation plan, which "called for busing of some students and gerrymandering of school district lines to achieve racial balance in most of the schools." Judge James Barrow heard the case and effectively ruled that the desegregation plan was acceptable but that for the 1970-71 school year the district needed to come up with a better plan that was less disruptive to the community as a whole. He also noted that in the current plan, children who would be eligible for the free breakfast program were now attending schools that did not provide it.

As a somewhat odd addendum to his ruling, he ordered that the district either provide breakfast at all or none of the schools. By February 1970, the district decided to extend the breakfast program to all 13 elementary schools. However, it still struggled with the broader issue of desegregation. It was much easier to provide breakfast than true equality.

Some of the plaintiffs appealed Judge Barrow's decision to the Georgia Supreme Court. In June 1970, the state's high court reversed Judge Barrow's ruling, finding that the "school assignment plan" in place in Clarke County was illegal. The state supported a neighborhood school model, even though the HEW said this was unacceptable and would not approve it. Caught between these contradictory rulings and the HEW constraints, the Clarke County School District appealed to the Supreme Court of the U.S. for a final ruling on how they were to desegregate their system.

On September 1, 1970, an article in the *Athens Daily News* reported that the U.S. Supreme Court had "agreed to rule on the legality of the Clarke County school board's use of busing and gerrymandering of school district lines to achieve racial balance in county schools." The case from Clarke County was joined by five similar cases, including the Charlotte-Mecklenberg County, North Carolina school district. It was this county whose name became associated with the court's ruling on what was required of public school systems under the Fourteenth Amendment and the Civil Rights Act with regard to desegregation.

The court was scheduled to hear arguments on October 12, 1970. Athens Superintendent Charles McDaniel was quoted in the article as saying,

> I'm not nearly as concerned whether they uphold a position or rule one way or another as I am that not only this school system but all systems have some guidelines to go by. The main thing we want is to know exactly what is expected of us. We'll be better off and can carry out the mandate of the court.

On April 20, 1971, the Supreme Court published its ruling on the case. The following are direct quotes from the opinion but are by no means the opinion in its entirety.

> The objective today remains to eliminate from the public schools all vestiges of state-imposed segregation . . . to dismantle the dual school system.
>
> Our objective in dealing with the issues presented by these cases is to see that school authorities exclude no pupil of a racial minority from any school, directly or indirectly, on account of race.
>
> The constitutional command to desegregate schools

does not mean that every school in every community must always reflect the racial composition of the school system as a whole.

We hold that the pairing and grouping of noncontiguous school zones is a permissible tool and such action is to be considered in light of the objectives sought.

Bus transportation has been an integral part of the public education system for years and was perhaps the single most important factor in the transition from the one-room schoolhouse to the consolidated school.

In these circumstances, we find no basis for holding that the local school authorities may not be required to employ bus transportation as one tool of school desegregation. Desegregation plans cannot be limited to the walk-in school.

The District Court's conclusion that assignment of children to the school nearest their home serving their grade would not produce an effective dismantling of the dual system is supported by the record.

Neither school authorities nor district courts are constitutionally required to make year-by-year adjustments of the racial composition of student bodies once the affirmative duty to desegregate has been accomplished and racial discrimination through official action is eliminated from the system . . .

The high court affirmed that busing and less-than-contiguous school zones are adequate remedies for dismantling previously segregated school systems. As a result, Athens would continue what would become a long and complicated relationship with busing.

Merging Athens and Burney-Harris High Schools

While many white Athenians complained about their elementary age children being bused to previously all-Black schools, the African American community was struggling with what it would mean to lose their one Black high school. Many BHHS students and their families were not convinced they wanted to merge the two high schools. Moreover, while several African American students had already enrolled at Athens High School under the "Freedom of Choice" plan, BHHS' student body and faculty did not have any white members.

James reflected on what it was like at BHHS during that time. He recalls that many of his students didn't want their school to change, but most realized that they probably had no choice. He remembers the African American community wrestling with the inevitable integration of BHHS, uncertain that a complete merger with Athens High School would be in their best interest. James himself believed that because the student body and faculty were all Black it was easier for teachers to maintain discipline and connect with the students, parents, and administrators in a supportive environment.

James recalls the teachers' concern that after full integration they would not be able to maintain the atmosphere, discipline, and cultural cohesiveness that currently characterized their classrooms. At the same time, the students were certain they would not be treated fairly or have access to the same opportunities in an integrated school. James recounts, "Many people felt they were losing a lot by integrating the high school. They were losing their school and were afraid they would lose their culture."

A January 15, 1970 "Insight" column in the *Athens Banner-Herald*, written by staff writer Chuck Cooper, raised several questions regarding how to merge the two high schools in the most egalitarian and effective way. Cooper believed the students should be involved in the decisions and have a clear idea of what the merger of 1,500 white and 500 Black high school students would look like. In fact, the district had established a committee of a dozen students from each high school that had been meeting for the previous six weeks to discuss some of these issues.

While no substantive decisions had been made, the exchange of ideas was a start. The article listed some of the students' concerns regarding merging school colors, mascots, yearbooks and newspapers, athletic programs, student councils, clubs, faculties, and administrations. How would the leaders and students from these two separate schools and cultures find common ground? Many Black students feared their school and their culture would be subjugated or erased by the merger.

By April 1970, tensions were on the rise as decisions about the merger were imminent for the upcoming school year. The African American students asserted that they saw no advantage in losing their last remaining school. The climate became volatile enough that Judge Barrow issued a restraining order to curb protests at both high schools. An incident was reported in the newspaper in which a white parent brandished a gun at a Black student during one of the confrontations. The article noted that all the authorities asked of this white man was to put away the gun; they did not ask to see his registration nor was he issued a warrant.

The school board did meet with several Black student representatives from AHS who outlined the challenges they had faced as the first African American students at the previously all-white school. Shortly thereafter, a group of Black high school students from BHHS presented a "list of demands" to the school board. The students expressed concern about private clubs at AHS that would not admit Black students, a lack of understanding of Black culture, the loss of some African American teachers due to the merger, the lack of African Americans at the highest levels of the administration and as coaches, the desire for multiethnic textbooks and a Black studies program, and a need for full support for participation in extracurricular activities. After the board discussed the list in an executive session, Superintendent McDaniel read the board's prepared responses during a meeting of the full Board of Education at which the students were present. Most of the board's responses were along the lines of, "we will do our best to accommodate your concerns."

The students also referenced the incident in which the white parent pulled a gun on the Black student and the way that matter was handled. The students asked that AHS Principal Don Hight have a warrant issued for the parent's arrest. However, the school board's response was, "It is regrettable that rioting and disorder often precipitate illegal acts. Illegal acts of any sort by a person or persons will not be supported by the school district."

Not mollified by this response, the students insisted that the school board deal with this particular incident, but the board argued in response that "the student knew best what had happened and he could press charges." The students responded, "if the parent were Black and the student white, police would have charged the man." The students also accused Hight of demonstrating "racist attitudes."

These BHHS students were accompanied and supported at the school board meeting by Rev. W. G. Griffin of Ebenezer Baptist Church, Rev. Amos Jackson, Jr. of Hill First Baptist Church, and Rev. Clayton D. Wilkerson of First A.M.E. Church. At the end of the meeting, Rev. Griffin told the board that the ministers and students were "concerned about the communities' 'total good' and the improvement of race relations." The school board tried to reassure the students that they were taking all their concerns into consideration and were dedicated to finding ways to integrate the high schools "that would not be to the detriment of one race or the other." Among other promises, they committed to having the University of Georgia's Desegregation Center develop an in-depth in-service training program for teachers on Black culture. The students noted, however, that the Center did not have any African American staff at the time.

By May, some decisions had been made and the Superintendent proposed that AHS become an integrated 11th and 12th grade school and BHHS house an integrated 10th grade. (Ninth graders would be housed in the three junior high schools.) AHS would be renamed Clarke Central High School and BHHS would retain its name. Also announced among the decisions were that the AHS Trojans and the BHHS Yellow Jackets would merge and become the Gladiators. The new combined high school colors would be red and yellow, taking one color from each of the previous high schools (the AHS colors were red and white; the BHHS colors were blue and yellow). These mascots and school colors remain at CCHS to this day.

Over the summer, the newspapers reported several acts of van-dalism at some of the schools, including dozens of broken windows at East Athens Elementary and spray-painted walls inside Alps Road Elementary. Nevertheless, the headline for an article in the *Athens Daily News* on September 1, 1970 announced, "Clarke School Open-ings Go Smoothly." The 13 existing elementary schools (East Athens, North Athens, Alps, Barnett Shoals, Barrow, Chase, Fowler, Gaines, Oconee, Oglethorpe, West Broad, Whitehead, and Winterville); the three junior high schools (Clarke, Lyons, and Hilsman); and the newly combined high schools were beginning to settle into a new routine.

Of course, this "new normal" was by no means perfect and is-sues continued to crop up as the district struggled with ongoing ad-justments. The school board, for its part, felt it had done what it could for the time being. It turned its attention to other significant issues looming on the horizon, including the community's desire to elect school board members (in 1970 board members were still appointed by the city and county governments), a district budget crisis, disci-plinary issues, and a burgeoning drug problem in the schools.

James taught at BHHS until 1970, just before integration was complete. Some Black teachers from BHHS remained at the school, others moved to Clarke Central, while still others lost their jobs. For James, the decision to quit teaching involved a variety of factors: the final desegregation of his old high school, the fact that he could not advance without a teaching certificate, and, as James put it, "It could have just been that I was ready to move on." He was becoming more involved in various projects at First A.M.E. and had already been working some part-time jobs to supplement his income. As a lasting legacy of his teaching days, James' picture is in a collage of photos on the wall of the renovated BHHS (now the H. T. Edwards building) honoring the BHHS alumni who returned to teach there.

As a final note, many of the private schools in the Athens area were established during this challenging time. The oldest of these, St. Joseph Catholic School, opened in 1949, long before the issue of integration took hold, but Athens Academy opened in 1967, Athens Christian in 1970, Prince Avenue in 1978, and Athens Montessori in 1978. Given the events of the era it is difficult not to wonder to what extent, if any, their founding was related to the issues of desegregation in Athens' schools.

James Returns to First A.M.E. Church

When James returned to Athens in 1965, he returned to his home church as well. A new pastor, Rev. Clayton D. Wilkerson, had just been assigned to First A.M.E. that year. James and Rev. Wilkerson quickly bonded over mutual interests and goals. Thus began a long, close, and fruitful partnership at First A.M.E. that extended beyond merely that of a minister and a member of his flock. James became a valued and respected part of the administration and a lay leader at the church, especially among young people, a group he and Rev. Wilkerson shared a passion to serve.

History of First A.M.E.

First A.M.E. Church of Athens has a long and storied history. It begins in the 1820s when slaves were allowed to worship in the galleries of the (white) First United Methodist Church in Athens. In 1852 the white church built a new brick building and moved the old wooden structure to an empty lot on Foundry Street at the end of Hancock for use by African American worshippers. In 1866, the owner of the property where the wooden church was moved deeded it to the former slave congregation. At this time the church was known as Pierce Chapel. During the winter of 1866, the minister of the church, Rev. Henry McNeal Turner, obtained approval for the newly freed Pierce Chapel congregation to join the African Methodist Episcopal (A.M.E.) Church.

In 1874, the congregation, under the leadership of Rev. John M. Cargile, remodeled the sanctuary of the old wooden church. By 1876, the basement of the church housed one of Athens' first schools for African Americans. In June 1880, the congregation purchased the present church lot at the corner of Hull and Strong

Streets, just north of Dougherty Street, which included a house to be utilized as a parsonage.

When the old church on Foundry Street would no longer sustain the growing congregation, a new church was built on the Hull Street lot. The church hired Louis H. Persley, an African American native of Macon, as the architect. He and the builder, R. F. Walker, formulated the plans and completed construction of the church in 1917. In 1921 a new parsonage was built on Strong Street just behind the church for the new pastor, Rev. William A. Fountain, Jr. Unfortunately, this house would not survive the "urban renewal" of 1967, which destroyed many African American homes and businesses in the area.

In 1980, First A.M.E. Church was listed on the National Register of Historic Places. Additionally, an historic marker was placed on Dougherty Street in 2006 to recognize Louis Persley, the African American architect of the church.

The Rev. Clayton Duke Wilkerson

Rev Clayton D. Wilkerson

When Rev. Wilkerson came to Athens in 1965, he analyzed the needs, opportunities, and talent in the community. He had big plans for First A.M.E. and found the congregation supportive of his vision. James recalls Rev. Wilkerson and his mission:

He was a prepared and dedicated leader. In fact, he led by example. After being used to hard work in my life, it was refreshing to see a pastor who also believed in hard work. He was a communicator who encouraged his membership to do a greater work for the Lord. He became a great friend and an important helper in my personal life. He was a critical thinker and very observant. Very charismatic. A straight talker. Rev. Wilkerson's concern for the youth and children was a priority.

James as the Director of the Christian Education Department at First A.M.E.

When James returned from Tuskegee and rejoined his family in attending First A.M.E., he saw that Rev. Wilkerson, who had three daughters, had "adopted" his brother Leroy, Jr., treating him "like the son he never had." He readily took James under his wing as well and quickly recognized that James could be a valuable part of his mission to support, guide, and uplift young people. James jumped at the chance to help implement programs and initiatives to bring young people to the church. James soon became Rev. Wilkerson's sounding board for ideas regarding how to better serve the youth of Athens. James says they talked endlessly about the issues and problems facing young people and he saw how dedicated Rev. Wilkerson was to doing productive and meaningful work on their behalf.

James would become an integral part of the church's outreach to the youth of Athens and a trusted leader of several church programs. James recalls that a great deal of growth occurred in the church during Rev. Wilkerson's tenure and he was grateful to be a part of it. Under Rev. Wilkerson's leadership, the "Young People Department" became the "Christian Education Department," and James was appointed its Director.

The C. D. Wilkerson Choir

Another area Rev. Wilkerson wanted to revitalize was the church choir, and James was only too happy to help. Eventually James would conduct the newly named "C. D. Wilkerson Choir," which included a mix of young people and adults. With the assistance of Ms. Brenda Taylor (who was a music major at UGA at the time) as the pianist,

The C. D. Wilkerson Choir. Four of the Smith siblings sang in the choir. In the back row from the left are: James, Leroy, Jr., and Frank. Their sister Willie Mae is in the front row, first on the left.

Mr. Johnny Sims (who was also a music teacher in the Clarke County School District) as the assistant director and Leroy, Jr. as the assistant organist, the choir performed three Sundays a month at First A.M.E. church services and occasionally for other churches and local civic organization events.

In late 1971, just as the church was expanding and renovating (adding much-needed air conditioning in the sanctuary), a dispute arose between the Episcopal District and Rev. Wilkerson over an "unanticipated increase in the annual assessment." This dust-up with the bishop was sufficient for the church to wield its power in appointing pastors. Rev. Wilkerson was briefly moved to another church until the conflict could be resolved.

However, the congregation of First A.M.E. fought to get him back, and Rev. Wilkerson did return in February 1972. James recalls that Leroy, Jr. was very upset with how the church hierarchy treated Rev. Wilkerson during this time. But as James recalls,

> Rev. Wilkerson was solid in the faith. He would confront any lies or mess like is happening in the government now. He didn't care who you were. He had a doctorate and was a trained man. He was not afraid to speak the truth.

One of Rev. Wilkerson's primary goals was to build a community center on the church property where young people could participate in a variety of activities, including playing sports, doing schoolwork, meeting with mentors, and just having fun. Through Rev. Wilkerson's business acumen (he owned a tile business in Atlanta) the church was able to save a substantial sum toward the building of the community center. Additional seed money was raised within the church. As the project grew closer to becoming a reality, James was named Chairman of the Building Committee. He was flattered that he would be trusted with checking the plans, meeting with contractors, talking with the bank about financing, and making sure the project proceeded on time. Several trustees, including James, were signatories on a loan from Athens Federal Savings and Loan, Inc.

Groundbreaking for the new community center was held in October 1972. The center was completed by the summer of 1973 and dedicated as the C. D. Wilkerson Educational Center. Church records proudly report that the loan was repaid early due to sound fiscal management and to a bequest by Dr. Ellen F. Greene, a native Athenian and longtime member of First A.M.E. Church, who taught at Fisk University for almost 30 years.

After 13 years of pastoring First A.M.E. and achieving many of his goals for the church, Rev. Wilkerson left Athens in 1978. He subsequently pastored at a church in Atlanta for many years. The Rev. Dr. Clayton Duke Wilkerson passed away on November 20, 2006.

Youth Group at First A.M.E.

While James was teaching at BHHS, he encouraged many of his students and Leroy, Jr.'s friends to come to the church every Saturday for a youth group meeting. James felt there was a need and a desire on the part of these young people to gather outside of school. He thought this would be a good way to offer them an opportunity

> to learn lessons from the Bible, participate in health and physical education activities, learn proper etiquette, and have fun. Part of each Saturday meeting was also spent singing, dancing, and just communicating with one another.

Youth group leaders at First A.M.E. Church, c. 1967. From left to right: Eugene Terrell, James Smith, Rev. C. D. Wilkerson, Beatrice Goodrum, Willie Harris.

James and his sister Willie Mae were the primary leaders of this youth group, assisted by Beatrice Goodrum, Willie Harris, and James' friend and roommate, Eugene Terrell. Up to 50 young people would gather at the church every Saturday for a variety of activities.

Since the group included individuals from different churches, it also served as a social outlet for those whose home congregations might not be large enough to host a formal youth program. James recalls that they even put on performances such as the play *God's Trombones*, which was based on a 1927 book of seven sermon-poems by James Weldon Johnson. This book was one of the first written in the tradition of African American religious oratory as poetry and was frequently performed as a play. Rev. Wilkerson was very supportive of this endeavor. "Rev. Wilkerson was the kind of person that wanted young folk to do something. He would say, 'They are the church of tomorrow.'"

Both James and Willie Mae not only supported this new initiative financially, they also took it upon themselves to provide transportation for the many students who did not have a way to get to the church on Saturday. For many years James and Willie Mae would drive all over town picking up young people and bringing them to First A.M.E. One of the youth group members, (Dr.) Farris Johnson, Jr. recalls:

> Our earliest mode of transportation was James' 1960 silver grey Pontiac Catalina, "The Grey Ghost," which typically made at least five routes per Saturday transporting the youth group and one or two nights per week transporting the Ensemble to meetings, rehearsals, and performances. "The Ghost" ended up running a top speed of 20 mph with one forward gear in its automatic transmission. It was replaced by a blue-and-white Oldsmobile Cutlass, which James gave unselfishly to the cause.

The youth group members often placed bets as to how many people James could fit in his car.

The E. L. Terrell Ensemble

Since music and choral singing, as well as serving youth, were among James' passions, he knew he wanted to start a youth choir. Remembering how much he loved singing in the Men's Glee Club at Tuskegee, James decided to start this choir as an all-male group. Leroy, Jr. and Johnny Sims worked closely with James to identify members of the Saturday youth group who could sing and whom they thought would enjoy participating in a choir.

James says of the three organizers, "These three poor Black boys from Athens had a lot of musical ability. We all sang in our high school choirs, I sang at Tuskegee, Johnny was a music major, and then we all sang in the C. D. Wilkerson Choir." They were a talented group, looking for equally talented—and motivated—choir members. When they got the group organized, Ms. Brenda Taylor, the C. D. Wilkerson Choir pianist, accompanied them on the piano.

All of the original choir members were participants in the youth group, but not all of them were members of First A.M.E. Though the

The E. L. Terrell Ensemble, c. 1968. Back row (l to r): Bruce Holt, Johnny Sims, Farris Johnson, Jr., Harry Sims, Dewey Sheats, Ricky Hudson. Front row (l to r): Leroy Smith, Jr., Andy Hill, James Smith, Michael Hill, Reginald McBride. Not pictured: James Campbell and Michael Holmes.

choir rehearsed at First A.M.E., they performed primarily outside the church for various community events and civic groups. As a result, James' "Grey Ghost" was put into service as the group's "tour bus" as well.

Upon organizing, the choir members decided they needed a name for their group and agreed to honor their director. Thus, "The James Smith Singers" was born. However, this name did not sit well with James. In a lengthy newspaper article about the group in 1968, James is quoted as saying that he was embarrassed by the name choice. "All I wanted to do was to give the young men of our church something to do while providing a fresh and wholesome source of musical entertainment for the community."

The name was eventually changed, under very sad circumstances. James' roommate, high school friend, and fellow mentor for the youth group, Eugene L. Terrell, was killed in an automobile accident and James decided to honor him by renaming the choir "The E. L. Terrell Ensemble." James recalls, "Brother Terrell did not sing but was instrumental in helping to mentor and shape the lives of these young men."

Early in the ensemble's history, James decided the group needed a little outside inspiration and to "see folks in action other than the folks in Athens." So James asked his old Tuskegee group, The Cliques, if they would be willing to perform at First A.M.E. They agreed, on the condition that they could get transportation from Tuskegee to Athens and back. So Marvin Billups and James rented a van and went to pick them up in Alabama. The Cliques arrived in Athens, performed their concert, fellowshipped with the audience, and had supper. Then James and Marvin took them back to Tuskegee, all in the same day. James said it was very well worth it for him and his young choir.

When James reflects on this early experience as a director, he admits to being stern and wonders if perhaps he was too hard on the young men in the ensemble. But he wanted them to be the best they could be. He believed wholeheartedly the lesson his mother taught him that what you got out of something was equal in measure to what you put into it.

James wanted this group to shine, and eventually they began performing all over the area, and even outside of Athens. The demand for their appearances grew and they were invited to make a record on the Greenwood label. This 45 rpm had two songs per side: "King Jesus is a-Listening" and "My Lord, What a Morning" on one side and "All People That on Earth Do Dwell" and "An' I Cry" on the other. The record was played on local radio stations and continued to heighten the ensemble's popularity and increase their invitations to perform. Thus, while James may have been a bit strict with the choir, their hard work paid off. This experience set the tone for the kind of director James would be over the next 40-plus years.

The original nine members of the E. L. Terrell Ensemble were Johnny Sims, Samuel Johnson, Andrew Hill, Danny Favors, Michael

Holmes, Farris Johnson, Jr., James Campbell, Jr., Leroy Smith, Jr., and Prentice Jewell. Eventually the group added some female voices. Additional members over the years included John Hudson, Michael Hill, Dewey Sheats, Harry Sims, Bruce Holt, Reginald McBride, Josephine Morton, Debra Potts, Reba Haynes, and Agnes Johnson.

Here are some of James' recollections of the young men who made up the core of the E. L. Terrell Ensemble:

> All of these boys came from families that worked hard to care for their children. When I met them, they had all the values and qualities to be successful. They all came from different parts of Clarke County and became men with careers and different professions.
>
> Ricky Hudson played high school football and lived on Colima Street. Andrew Hill had a welcoming smile and lived on Magnolia Street. Reginald McBride lived on Plaza Street. His parents were educators. His father was a principal and his mother was an elementary school teacher. Reginald also had a long career in education and is now a retired principal. Michael Holmes was a musician. He lived on Plaza Street and his father was a biology teacher and high school coach. His mother was an elementary school teacher.
>
> Bruce Holt came from a large family and one brother, Tony, would attend our youth sessions, but only Bruce sang. They lived in North Athens on Athens Avenue. Bruce was an electrician for Georgia Power. Dewey Sheats was a little older than the other crew. He was always full of laughter. I remember him from years back. He lived off of Timothy Road, which is where we met while my family farmed in that area. He went on to become a professional barber and to own his own business.
>
> Harry Sims worked for many years as a teacher at Barrow Elementary School. He also served our community as a Clarke County Commissioner. Farris Johnson,

the story of the terrell ensemble

Not quite 'rags-to-riches'

By Chuck Cooper

The story of Athens' own E. L. Terrell Ensemble isn't exactly one of "rags to riches." In the first place, the 13 young men and women didn't start in rags, and they haven't yet caused internal Revenuers a great deal of concern.

But, they have been successful. Their success can be attributed to three things. They work hard, they love to sing and perform, and they are exceptionally talented.

Three years ago this month, what is now the Terrell Ensemble was organized by a young man named James R. Smith. Smith was, and still is, youth director at Athens' First A.M.E. Church.

In an effort to provide some worthwhile activity for teenaged young men and women Smith suggested to some in his youth group that they form a singing group. The more they stood around a piano vocalizing, the better they became. Soon, because any group wants to perform for an audience, they made a public appearance.

It just happened that they were a smashing success and got invitations to appear at other functions. It was at this point the group decided it would be better to choose a name than to continue being referred to as "that group from A.M.E. Church."

Because of their respect and appreciation for the efforts to organize that Smith had provided for them, the group unanimously selected "The James Smith Singers."

Smith recalls that he was embarrassed by the name choice. "All I wanted to do with the group," he says, "was to give the young men of our church something to do while providing a fresh and wholesome source of musical entertainment for the community."

But, young Smith accepted the name and began managing and administering their appearances which, as word of their talent spread, began to multiply.

Soon the Smith Singers began receiving more appearance requests than they could manage. They appeared at virtually all the Negro churches in the Athens area and requests soon came from places like Jefferson, Watkinsville, and other outlying communities, and finally from Atlanta.

Smith nurtured the group, and they spent untold hours improvising and practicing spiritual selections.

Finally, they were approached about making a recording on the Greenwood label and held a recording session here in Athens. Two of the local radio stations plugged their record extensively and they even appeared on a live radio show

several Sunday mornings.

The recording didn't exactly set the world on fire, but it did bring needed publicity. The single 45 rpm recording featured "King Jesus is A Listening" and "My Lord, What A Morning" on one side and "All People That on Earth Do Dwell" and "An' I Cry" on the flip side.

Now, they are preparing for another release sometime this summer, it too on the Greenwood label.

The original nine members of the group were Johnny Sims and Samuel Johnson, first tenor; Andrew Hill, Danny Favors, Michael Holmes and Farris Johnson, Jr. second tenor; James Campbell, Jr., LeRoy Smith, Jr. and Prentice Jewell, bass.

Over the years, only Danny Favors has left the group. But, the addition of John Hudson, Michael Hill and Dewey Sheats on first tenor; Harry Sims, Bruce Holt and Reginald McBride on second tenor; and Josephine Morton, Debra Potts, Reba Haynes, Agnes Johnson has improved their quality.

Fall, 1967, brought a change in names from the James Smith Singers to their present designation as the E. L. Terrell Ensemble. The group serves as a living memorial to the young man who had devoted his life to the betterment of youth.

Soloist Johny Sims, James Campbell, Leroy Smith and Reba Hayes

Back row (l-r) Reginald McBride, Leroy Smith, Johnny Sims, Harry Sims, Farris Johnson, Dewey Sheats, front row (l-r) Josephine Morton, Debra Potts, Reba Haynes, Agnes

Article in the Athens Banner-Herald *about the E. L. Terrell Ensemble.*

Jr., lived on Winterville Road in East Athens. His parents were friends of my family. My mother and Mr. Farris Johnson, Sr. were classmates and the family also attended First A.M.E. In the Ensemble, Farris would always find something to crack a joke about so he could keep the group laughing. But Farris was also very studious. He became a medical doctor and is still serving in Athens. Farris is my personal doctor and I'm very pleased to call him my doctor.

Johnny Sims lived on Nellie B Avenue in East Athens. Johnny not only sang with us, but after graduating from college he came back to Athens and served with me in the C. D. Wilkerson Choir. He was a choir director and band teacher. He and his family now live in Ohio.

Michael Hill lived on Magnolia Street. His father worked in the insurance business. His mother was an elementary school teacher. His mother is also a musician and played many years for Greater Bethel A.M.E. Church before her retirement. Michael lives in Albany, Georgia and has been a radio announcer for many years.

James Campbell was and still is one good and solid singer. His bass voice is one we all should hear. His voice range is very unique. He came to us from Magnolia Street and he served this community as a teacher.

Leroy Smith, Jr. is my brother and was responsible for most of these individuals. He had school connections with them. They had classes together and they were friends. He recruited most of them to come to our youth group on Saturdays. While in high school, Leroy began a job with the C&S Bank. He continued with C&S (which is now Bank of America) for many years, becoming a vice president.

It has been more than rewarding to have had the opportunity to know and work with these men.

Other Mentoring

Organizing the youth group at First A.M.E. marked the beginning of James' long dedication to mentoring young people in Athens. While teaching at BHHS, James worked with the youth group at his church, conducted both the C. D. Wilkerson Choir and the E. L.

While James Hurley and Kenneth Dious are often cited as the first African Americans to play football for UGA, Richard Appleby, Clarence Pope, and Horace King were the first to be offered scholarships to play for the Bulldogs. UGA offered Richard and Horace scholarships but said they would only offer Clarence a scholarship if the two of them both signed with UGA. Richard and Horace did sign, so all three of these young men received scholarships and played for the University of Georgia football team starting in the fall of 1971. Two other African American athletes joined them that fall–Chuck Kinnebrew from Rome, Georgia and Larry West from Albany, Georgia. As these young men were getting acclimated to UGA, they continued to reach out to James when they had questions or problems.

In 1972, Horace became the first African American player to score a touchdown for UGA's team. Of the three young men from Athens who played for UGA, Horace and Richard went on to play professionally. Horace was drafted by the NFL after graduation and spent nine years as a running back for the Detroit Lions. Richard was drafted a year later, and played one year with the Tampa Bay Buccaneers before moving to the Canadian Football League, where he played another three years. After his career in football, he became a businessman. Clarence went into the ministry and was also a firefighter.

During the high school merger and when the young men came to talk things over with James, Michael Thurmond was the de facto leader of this group. He later went on to become a leader in Athens and in the state. After graduating from Clarke Central High School, he earned his bachelor's degree from Paine College and his law degree from the University of South Carolina. Early in his career, Mr. Thurmond became the first African American elected to the Georgia state legislature from Clarke County. He also led the state Division of Family and Children Services.

In 1998, Mr. Thurmond was elected Georgia's Labor Commissioner, a post he held for three terms. One of his signature programs was "Georgia Works," which earned him national recognition. He practiced law in Atlanta with a major civil trial firm, Butler Wooten Cheeley & Peak LLP. Mr. Thurmond also served as interim Superintendent of schools in DeKalb County, Georgia, one of the largest school districts in the state.

Mr. Thurmond ran for U.S. Senate in 2010 as the Democratic party nominee. Although he did not win the election, in 2016 he ran for the post of DeKalb County C.E.O. and won overwhelmingly. Mr. Thurmond is also the author of the newly re-released book, *A Story Untold: Black Men and Women in Athens History*, a source I have drawn upon heavily for this story.

James says he hesitates to claim that he "mentored" these young men. Nevertheless, they clearly sought out and trusted his insights when they were getting acclimated to life in the "desegregated" communities of their high school and the University. James was always ready to lend an ear and provide a place to gather and talk.

"Urban Renewal" and the Model Cities Program

In the mid- to late-1960s, Athens undertook several major federally funded projects directed at removing "blighted" areas of the city and improving housing, infrastructure, and social services. The first phase of this set of initiatives was a massive "urban renewal" program designed to "clean up" two areas of the city that were deemed "unsightly" and in rapid decline. One area, near the University of Georgia, would be sold to the University for expansion of the campus as soon as the residents were relocated and their homes razed. The second area was located just north of downtown Athens. A good portion of this area was known as "Lickskillet"; the area close to the Oconee River was known as "The Bottoms." Both of the targeted areas were predominantly African American and poor. All of the funds made available for these projects were a direct result of decades of social programs and Presidential initiatives, beginning with the Roosevelt Administration's "New Deal" and continuing under President Truman's "Fair Deal" and President Johnson's "War on Poverty" and his "Great Society."

(Author's Note: I put "urban renewal" in quotation marks as it was really a slum clearance program and not, for all practical purposes, "renewing" anything.)

History of "Urban Renewal"

The concept of "urban renewal" had its seeds in the "New Deal" of President Roosevelt. When the Great Depression hit, Roosevelt realized that many communities would not survive without federal help, in the form of an infusion of jobs and money to stimulate the economy. His "New Deal" included many programs that were created by Congress as well as by executive order, including the Social Security Administration, the Farm Security Administration, and the Civilian Conservation Corps. In 1941, when the U.S. entered World War II, war production further stimulated growth. Thus while citizens were encouraged to sacrifice, save, recycle, and ration, jobs were plentiful.

With the war's end in 1945, President Harry Truman turned his focus to the needs of America's urban areas and the returning troops. New housing, health care, and social programs were needed to re-stimulate a peacetime economy. Truman's "Fair Deal" program put forth a set of proposals primarily targeting education, health care, and fair employment practices. Truman faced an uphill battle in getting these programs funded, as Congress was controlled by conservatives. But he did accomplish one piece of landmark legislation: The Federal Housing Act of 1949.

The Federal Housing Act represented a complete overhaul of the federal government's role in mortgage insurance and funding for public housing. It included funding for "slum clearance" as part of the "urban renewal" projects deemed necessary for many American cities, primarily those with a population of over 500,000 citizens. The Act stimulated some of the largest and most sweeping responses to perceived "urban decay" in history. It provided cities with the means to purchase privately owned land, demolish areas of their cities deemed to be in decline, and sell the property to private investors or use it as city property "for the good of the community." Initially projects related to "urban renewal" were sent to HEW for review.

Lyndon Johnson's 1964 "War on Poverty" included some of Truman's proposals and a few from President Kennedy's abbreviated attempts to attack the problem of poverty. The national poverty rate was rising and that year had reached around 19 percent. Johnson felt this was unconscionable for a country as prosperous and innovative as the U.S. His proposals resulted in legislation that established the Office of Economic Opportunity, which would administer applications from municipalities requesting funding for local anti-poverty initiatives. Lyndon Johnson's master plan, "The Great Society," was grounded in his belief that the federal government had a major role to play—especially in education, health care, urban issues, and transportation—to combat poverty and racial injustice.

Johnson's success in passing many of his programs was due in large part to the election in 1964 of many new liberals to Congress who supported his initiatives. It was during this time that Medicare and Medicaid were established. By 1965, as the number of projects submitted to HEW became overwhelming, Congress approved the establishment of the Department of Housing and Urban Development (HUD) to administer programs specifically related to "urban renewal" and public housing.

"Urban Renewal" in Athens

In 1963, Athens applied for HEW funding for two "urban renewal" projects, Project GA-R 50 and Project GA-R 51. (See maps for the targeted areas.) Project 50 was an area near the University

"Urban Renewal" area, Project GA-R 50. (Map courtesy of Hargrett Rare Book & Manuscript Library/University of Georgia Libraries.)

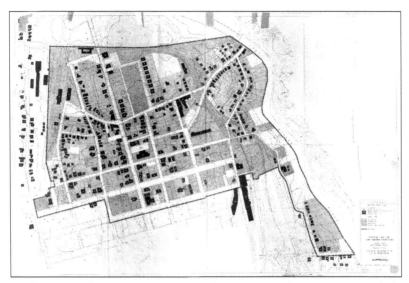

"Urban Renewal" area, Project GA-R 51. (Map courtesy of Hargrett Rare Book & Manuscript Library/University of Georgia Libraries.)

of Georgia that was considered a "slum in the middle of Athens." Eighty families lived there and by 1967 they were all relocated and the area razed. As agreed, the city then sold this land to UGA for roughly $200,000. The University quickly built high-rise dormitories on much of the site.

Project 51 involved a much larger area north of downtown. It consisted of 128 acres and involved 310 parcels of land and 350 structures. More importantly, the destruction of this area caused the dislocation of 233 families (nearly 850 people), the majority of whom were "non-white" according to the statistics gathered at the time.

All of this area was cleared by wholesale demolition. Some of the properties were burned on site as training for the city fire department, but most were bulldozed and the refuse burned or hauled away. Even some of the oldest houses in Athens and its only synagogue were not spared. However, one house was saved and relocated. The Church-Waddel-Brumby House is considered to be the oldest existing house in Athens, built around 1820. It was moved to its current location at the corner of Dougherty and Thomas Streets and serves as the Athens Welcome Center. The Athens-Clarke Heritage Foundation was founded as a result of the efforts of citizens who joined together to save the house in 1967.

When these projects began, Capt. R. M. Bowstrom was the Director of Urban Renewal in Athens. He was succeeded by Mr. Paul Hodgson, who served for most of the time this project was implemented. The final report for the two major "urban renewal" projects indicates that both were finished in 1967. The GA R-50 project near UGA cost the federal government $987,143. The GA R-51 College Avenue project cost $4,469,549.

Controversy over "Urban Renewal" in Athens

In the wake of a desire to "beautify" and "renew" areas that were considered "blighted" parts of Athens, many African Americans lost their homes, their businesses, and their neighborhoods. It was as if they were told that their way of life was substandard and unacceptable. While it may be true that the properties to which these residents were relocated were in better physical condition than the ones they lost, the lack of self-determination for many Black residents created renewed frustration and reinforced their sense that they were not a valued part of life in Athens.

Most of the African American community was not aware of the "urban renewal" project until after the city had purchased the land upon which they lived. By that time, the residents had no choice but to be moved. If they owned the property, they were compensated so that they might have seed money to buy another home, but for many residents, Athens did not offer enough decent affordable housing options to make this financially feasible.

There are numerous letters in the archives written by the Urban Renewal staff to local real estate companies and developers asking if they had, or would have in the near future, additional housing stock, especially for African Americans. Many of these businesses responded that they were adding housing, but it might not be enough to meet the needs of all the people being displaced. The Jack R. Wells Housing

Project (known as Pauldoe) would open in March 1967, but residents of "Lickskillet" needed to be out long before then.

To be fair, there did exist newly created federally backed mortgage loans for low-income citizens, and the city assisted homeowners with the application process. However, this did not solve the problem of a lack of sufficient affordable housing for those who were displaced. If a family did not own the land on which they lived, the displacement often meant being moved to government subsidized housing, if there were any units available. Many evicted residents were given temporary help, but no long-term solution to their housing problem. In any case, residents did not have much choice about where they might live or whether they were close to their work, family, or previous neighbors. Once again, in the name of "improvement," African Americans were excluded from the discussion and the decisions.

In an article by Matthew Pulver, a UGA librarian, published in the February 25, 2015 issue of *Flagpole*, Pulver lays bare the real motivation for the "urban renewal" of the 1960s. "Black Athenians were a problem to the white power structure. Black poverty was in the way, never mind that white power and affluence were absolutely predicated on that subjugated underclass."

By the time cotton was no longer "king" and rural African Americans were heading to urban centers for employment, the majority-white cities were not prepared for the influx of the remaining agrarian citizens of their counties. Athens was no different. Most of the land in Athens settled by African Americans was either in flood plains, originally occupied by the Black "help" for white families, or was land that the city deemed unsuitable for other purposes. As these communities grew on what little they were able to earn in the city, the white power structure became uncomfortable with the obvious lack of resources the African American community had to build homes and businesses that were sustainable. Pulver writes, "whites in Athens wanted the advantage of cheap, subsistence-wage Black help, but not the effects of keeping half the city unconscionably poor." To make matters worse, "Lickskillet" was too close to downtown and such obvious poverty was not good for Athens' image or prospects for attracting investment.

As these "urban renewal" programs gained traction as a way to deal with the "blight" of urban areas, their methods went unquestioned. Many of the "solutions" they provided disregarded or dismissed the value of the communities African Americans had built within a segregated society. In the words of Eldridge Cleaver, Pulver writes, the idea that there was a problem in urban areas was synonymous with the question, "What do we do about the Blacks?"

Pulver continues,

> Athens' answer was no different than that of many Southern cities: Remove them en masse from wherever they interfere with white wishes. Push them out of areas close to the downtown commercial center. Federal "urban renewal" legislation gave Southern cities like Athens eminent domain power and control of the purse strings of federal cash.

Rather than involving and including the residents of areas like "Lickskillet," the city decided unilaterally to raze their homes and displace the residents.

In the words of James Baldwin, "urban renewal" was really "Negro Removal." Most attempts by the white power structure to deal with poverty involved eradicating the symptoms while failing to acknowledge root causes. Athens, like many other urban areas in the South, was reluctant to acknowledge that decades of Jim Crow laws, racism, and society's determination to keep an entire segment of citizens in an "underclass" were responsible for the "slums" in the first place.

James remembers the demolition of "Lickskillet." He knew several people, including some of his students, who lived in that area. He also knew Rev. Frank Maddox, of Greater Bethel A.M.E. Church on Rose Street, who purchased some of the land cleared by the project to build Bethel Church Homes, a low-income housing development that still exists today.

While Bethel Homes was a private enterprise, the Athens Housing Authority also used part of the cleared land to build the Jessie B. Denney Tower on Dougherty Street for low-income senior citizens. Much of the remaining area was purchased by private enterprises or became city property. Notably, two of the old passenger train stations survived, and long after the last passenger train ran through Athens, the station on Hoyt Street became the headquarters for the Athens Community Council on Aging.

Model Cities Program

On the heels of these "urban renewal" programs, Athens decided to apply to become a "Model City." The Model Cities Program, begun in 1966, was part of President Lyndon Johnson's "Great Society" and "War on Poverty." According to the legislative wording, the purpose of this program was to rebuild or revitalize slum and blighted areas; to expand housing, job, and income opportunities; to reduce dependence on welfare payments; to improve educational facilities and programs; to combat disease and ill health; to reduce the incidence of crime and delinquency; to enhance recreational and cultural opportunities; and to establish better access between homes and jobs.

This constituted an extremely ambitious list of goals for any city, let alone one of Athens' size and demographics. The program, funded and overseen by HUD, would identify 150 municipalities that proposed the most comprehensive five-year anti-poverty initiatives.

Some of the push for the Model Cities Program was born out of the urban riots and unrest of the 1960s. Poverty, the build-up of the Vietnam War, continued racial discrimination, inflation, white flight to the suburbs, and the assassinations of several prominent civil rights leaders and politicians had shaken the nation and lawmakers in Washington, which led them to be more proactive. The "scorched earth" results of "urban renewal" demolitions, which were just wholesale slum clearance projects, may have destroyed substandard housing but did not offer a vision of what should replace it so that it would not return to the same conditions. Destroying the physical signs of poverty did nothing to ameliorate its causes.

What made the Model Cities Program different from previous attempts to combat poverty in inner cities was the insistence that local citizens, local government, and local agencies work together at all levels as partners to formulate solutions. This was not to be another top-down model of problem solving. Instead, it was a multifaceted and multi-pronged approach to combating poverty and its attendant ills that would need new ideas for interventions, new community-wide initiatives, and money . . . lots of money.

Model Cities were selected based on an application completed by the municipality in cooperation with all the various departments, businesses, nonprofits, government entities, and—most important-ly—the people who would ultimately benefit from this program. The plan had to identify every possible problem and remedy for poverty and blight in the city. All ideas for new initiatives were welcome and vetted.

Black leaders in many communities were very supportive of the Model Cities Program, especially as one of its prominent features was a prohibition on housing discrimination. They saw the previous de-cades of "redlining" (the practice of refusing a loan or insurance to someone because they live in an area deemed to be a poor financial risk) as a major roadblock to minority wealth building. Under the program, fair housing laws were to be enforced or funding would be revoked.

To be competitive for a Model Cities grant, the proposal had to be very comprehensive, beginning with an in-depth analysis of ex-isting conditions and the underlying causes of poverty. The city then had to provide a detailed list of goals and strategies for achieving those goals. The proposal had to cover the required areas of improvements in housing, income opportunities, education, health, criminal justice, transportation, and living conditions. This was the first time federal and local governments acknowledged that just providing better hous-ing and some job training was not the way out of poverty, especially in the South. Moreover, as an economic development engine, the resulting programs and initiatives were expected to include some economic development authority that would see these programs through to completion and accomplish the identified goals.

When Athens submitted its proposal to HUD on August 19, 1968, the city described its purpose as:

> To locally develop a carefully coordinated comprehensive system of inter-related programs which will have substantial impact on physical, social, and economic problems to arrest blight and decay in the model neighborhood area; and demonstrate to other cities the manner in which problems can be successfully attacked to improve the quality of urban life for all persons in the community.

The program was extremely ambitious and the initial component committees represented the areas of housing, employment, transportation, recreation and cultural activities, health, education, social services, law enforcement, legal aid, physical environment, and citizen participation.

Athens was awarded a Model Cities grant in the amount of $2.6 million per year for the first three years of the program. UGA's Institute of Community and Area Development had agreed to work with the city on this project, providing much-needed resources such as research facilities and expertise, as well as administration of some of the components. Gordon Dixon was named the Director of the Model Cities Program for Athens. Some of the early African American activists during this time included Evelyn Neely, Miriam Moore, Jessie Barnett, and Virginia Walker. They were all involved in the program from the beginning and were determined to have a seat at the table and provide voices that would be heard throughout the process.

The program began by conducting house-by-house surveys to gather the essential demographic and economic data needed to write an action plan. It was this part of the project that James worked on. This survey of households in the targeted area was conducted in 1968

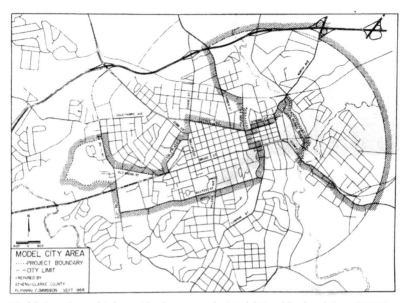

Model City Area of Athens. Also known as the Model Neighborhood Area (MNA). (Map courtesy of Hargrett Rare Book & Manuscript Library/University of Georgia Libraries.)

and asked a variety of questions including who was the head of the household; the number of household members and their ages, employment status, and job location; ideas and attitudes regarding problems facing the city and particular neighborhoods; ideas for changes to the city; where residents go for any and all types of assistance, public or private; quality and priorities of neighborhood schools; opinions about the performance of city council and school board members; views on integration; leisure activities; programs available for children outside of school; availability and affordability of daycare; availability and affordability of housing; access to loans; police protection and interactions; medical access; illness; prenatal care; income; and race.

In addition to these individual surveys of households, the program had to document current businesses in the target area and their economic impact on the city, existing programs to help the poor, goods and services available in the target area, existing employment and economic opportunities, and access to social services and programs that were already in place. This required taking a hard look at the roadblocks to economic development for citizens in the target area.

The target area of the project, known as the "Model Neighborhood Area (MNA)," included 13,500 residents and was considered to contain "the highest concentration of the city's social, physical and economic problems." It overlapped with the "urban renewal" area that had just been cleared, but included a much larger area of Athens, both east of the Oconee River and west of the downtown business district.

The goal of these federal grants was to help Model Cities establish new programs, but not for the cities to become dependent on federal funds to maintain them. Part of the agreement was that after the initial five years, the city would identify outside or local funding to continue all the component projects that were established and proved successful under the Model Cities Program. In its fourth year of funding Athens was granted $1,078,000—less than half the amount it had received in each of the previous three years—to help wean the city off of the federal infusion of money.

In a letter to the mayor and City Council dated August 28, 1972, Walter A. Denero, the Director of the Athens Model Cities Program at that time, emphasized the progress that had been made but also stated:

> The time has come to begin thinking even more seriously about what will happen to the jobs and services now being provided with Model Cities funds once the Model Cities Program terminates. A realistic analysis and evaluation must be made to avoid a drastic and abrupt elimination of jobs and services two years from now. If it is determined that it will be impossible to maintain certain projects, it is felt that serious consideration must be given to planning for that eventuality now.

This was a critical reminder that without the generous grants from HUD, many of the established programs would flounder.

Athens' participation in the Model Cities Program yielded some very positive and long-lasting results. Athens Transit was born out of the program, as was the Athens Neighborhood Health Center. Programs for senior citizens, many of which were housed in the newly built Denney Tower, were established, as was the Athens Community Council on Aging. Infrastructure in the Model Neighborhood Area was improved as streets were paved, sidewalks installed, water and sewer lines added, and bridges built.

There were also improvements to recreation programs and parks facilities. The Thomas N. Lay Community Center and Park next to the Lyndon House was created as a result of Model Cities planning. Youth counseling services and police-community relations programs were also established. The Athens Downtown Development Authority was created shortly after the Model Cities Program ended to continue the work the program had begun.

However, a very long list of programs were discontinued or funding was drastically reduced when new funding sources were not identified or secured by the end of the fourth year. In addition, many of the initiatives have fallen by the wayside since the program ended, due either to lack of leadership, political will, or financial backing (see Appendix 8). The Model Cities Program ended in 1975 and was replaced at the federal level with the Community Development Block Grant (CDBG) initiative.

Moving On

By the end of 1971, James was focusing most of his time on his programs with youth at First A.M.E. He had been working part-time at Penn-Lo liquor store on Washington Street in downtown Athens, waiting for the next employment opportunity to come along. The next phase of James' life would bring new jobs, community recognition, and the realization of some long-held dreams. It would also involve meeting his future wife, getting married, and starting a family of his own.

Chapter 9

Marriage, Children, and Career: 1971–1980s

One Sunday in 1971 at First A.M.E. Church services, James noticed a young woman he had not met before. Since James knew most everyone in the church community, he made a point of introducing himself and asking how she came to attend services there. She responded that she was a teacher in Oglethorpe County and had heard about First A.M.E. from friends. She had met Rev. Wilkerson, who invited her to worship at the church. She was impressed with his vision and enthusiasm. As James walked her to her car after that first meeting, he asked for her name and, boldly, her phone number. "Rosa Burgess," she replied, giving him her number. James was already smitten.

What James didn't know then, but learned shortly thereafter, was that Rosa already knew of him through his younger sister Christine. Christine and Rosa met while they were both attending Morris Brown and had even worked together at the college. Christine thought highly of Rosa and was glad to hear that she and James had met. Rosa had also crossed paths with James at some of the local dance spots in town, but she had never introduced herself. James says that in spite of all this, "She still wanted to go out with me!" Thus began the courtship of James Smith and Rosa Burgess.

Rosa L. Burgess

Rosa was born near Ashburn, Georgia, a very small town in Turner County about 160 miles south of Atlanta. She is the youngest of four girls born to Shelton and Tilda Black Burgess. Shelton Burgess

Rosa L. Burgess

was a sharecropper who was compensated very meagerly at the end of the harvest season, and he struggled to take care of his family. Nevertheless, says James, "they continued to have faith and they survived."

At the age of five Rosa began attending a one-room church school in Rebecca, Georgia, at the church her family attended. The girls walked to school until they entered fifth grade, then rode the bus to Eureka Elementary School in Ashburn. They later attended high school in Ashburn as well. Rosa was in the sixth grade for only three weeks when she was skipped ahead to the seventh grade because she was bright and the school was short of teachers. A gifted student, Rosa graduated in 1964 at the age of 16 as valedictorian of her high school class.

In late August of that year, Rosa left home to attend Morris Brown College in Atlanta. She recounts what happened upon her arrival that Sunday. "When I arrived at the college in a cab, they didn't have a room for me. I told the room mother that I could not go back home and they finally did find me a room." Rosa says there were others who also arrived to find they had no room, but eventually everyone was settled. Rosa continued,

> I began working in the dining hall the following day, which was on a Monday. I worked the entire four years and one summer while in college. My college days were very busy studying and working. I graduated in June of 1968 with a B.S. in elementary education. I was the only one in my family to attend and graduate from college.

Upon graduation, Rosa moved to Lexington, Georgia in Oglethorpe County to begin her teaching career. She taught at Oglethorpe County Elementary School under principal Mrs. Mamie Sapp Dye and lived in a boarding house with other African American teachers. Her first three years were spent teaching first grade and the next three teaching second grade. At some point during this time, Rosa moved to Athens and shared an apartment with a friend. She describes the rest of her teaching career,

> In September of 1974, I began teaching at Hilsman Middle School in Athens as a math teacher. My main subject was math even though I taught science, reading, and language arts to sixth and seventh graders during the course of my career. I retired in June of 2001 after 33 years of teaching. However, after two years I returned to teaching for three more years and finally retired for good in 2006.

When I asked Rosa to describe her first impression of James, she said that she did not like him. She initially thought he was very mean, but after getting to know him better she says she fell in love with him. During their courtship, James and Rosa attended concerts and parties in Athens and went out to eat when both their schedules allowed. He would also visit her at her apartment after she moved to Athens. James says he doesn't remember if they ever went to the movies but asserts that he has never been particularly fond of going to see movies. Rosa, in contrast, "likes to go and see movies, especially about integration issues, but they just make me mad," says James.

The couple talked on the phone frequently and their connection grew deeper. As James got to know Rosa he learned that she, too, had grown up poor and in a large family, and had worked her way through school. James was charmed by her and impressed with her steady and serious demeanor. He felt they shared a philosophy and an approach to life that was a result of their early life situations. James says, "I was concerned about her background and the type of environment she had to endure in growing up. It was so similar to mine." His "concern" was really sadness that she had endured a hardscrabble childhood, but he admired that she had thrived in challenging circumstances. He says that their experiences taught them both to "be content with what they had and to look forward to a better day and a brighter future."

James says that before meeting Rosa, he noticed that a lot of the young women he had dated were interested in a lot of "things." They wanted a world of material goods that did not particularly interest James. But Rosa was raised just as poor as he was and things were not that important to her.

Rosa was also a Christian woman and that mattered greatly to James, although he recalls that he was not always doing Christian things himself at that time: he was still happy to go clubbing, he drank alcohol, and he ran a liquor store. None of these activities were particularly virtuous, but James was able to compartmentalize his secular life from that of his church community. Upon reflection he says he was looking for someone who did not do any of the things he was doing. Perhaps he hoped that if Rosa saw him as worthy, he would not feel quite as conflicted himself. But James stresses that he asked Rosa from the beginning not to try to change him. He was who he was and it was important that she understand that.

Rosa herself had been independent for a while and knew who she was and where she was going. Thus she did not feel a need to change or "rescue" James. She appreciated his forthrightness, his energy, his commitment to what he believed in, and his good sense of humor. James was impressed that Rosa was thinking about her future: "Not what had been done or was in the past or where she had been but moving forward." He respected that she had worked while in college at Morris Brown, as he had to do at Tuskegee. And, like James, she had a lot of responsibility for helping her family. James says with love and respect, "She was just about something," and it was obvious that he meant she had substance, determination, and grit.

James and Rosa dated for two years and James recalls the day he asked her to marry him. "During the school holidays, Rosa would go to Atlanta to be with her sisters. I bought a ring and decided to take it to her while she was visiting them. I don't remember if she was surprised or not, but she said yes!"

James and Rosa's wedding. From l to r: Rosa's older sister Annie, Rosa's father Shelton Burgess, Rosa, James, Vallie and Leroy Smith, Sr.

Wedding and Early Married Life

Rosa and James were married on Sunday, December 30, 1973 at First A.M.E. Church with Rev. Wilkerson officiating. When I asked James to tell me about his wedding day, he shook his head and said, "It rained from morning through midnight. Rained like nobody's business!" When I said I thought that was supposed to be a good sign, he countered, "No! It's a bad sign. Black folk say it's bad. But the wedding was nice." Since they are still married, it couldn't have been a predictor of anything too terrible to come.

Their wedding reception was the very first one ever held at the C. D. Wilkerson Center. This was particularly wonderful for James given his involvement in getting it built. James' mother and father were in attendance, as was Rosa's father. Her mother had passed away several years before. All of Rosa's and James' siblings and numerous friends and colleagues were also there to help them celebrate.

James and Rosa cut their wedding cake.

James' best man was Anthony White, who worked for the Dean of Students at UGA. He had been one of Willie Mae's high school classmates who James grew close to after his return to Athens from Tuskegee. James remembers that they enjoyed attending football games together. Rosa's maid of honor was Joyce Harrison, a close friend who lived in the same apartment complex during Rosa's early years of teaching. James says they couldn't afford a honeymoon, but later that evening after the reception they went to a party at the Alpha fraternity, celebrating with friends there. The newlyweds returned to work immediately after the New Year's holiday.

James and Rosa purchased a house on Lyndon Avenue in Athens. Married life required some adjustments, but James says he had been single for so long that he was glad to be getting married and felt he could deal with whatever changes his new status brought. He says adapting to being part of a couple wasn't hard, but it did involve new responsibilities, both large and small. One thing he remembers learning was "knowing when to speak and when not to." Rosa observes:

> Married life has many challenges: working, being a wife, and keeping up with the daily chores at home. I worked hard at trying to balance life's demands. The finances of most married couples can be a problem. Being married can have its ups and downs.

Rosa and James didn't really divide up the household chores, since both were used to living on their own and taking responsibility for their own needs and upkeep. They both worked full-time and knew that sharing the chores would come naturally. However, James said early on that he would do his own laundry. He had a very definite idea of how he liked his clothing cared for and Rosa was happy to let him continue with that routine.

Rosa has always done the cooking but James is quick to say that he told her, "You can cook if you want to, but you don't have to." He says he didn't want to be a burden or demand anything of her; he wanted her to continue to make decisions for herself about how she spent her time. He was determined to treat his wife with respect and to remember that she was capable of making up her own mind about things. He says he can get upset sometimes and has always had a stubborn streak, but "you have to be careful. Little things can become big things if you let them" and he didn't want to let that happen.

James says of his wife of 46 years,

> Rosa is a special woman and a special wife. She's a great mother, a gifted and talented lady. As a homemaker she is a good cook and great baker. She is also a seamstress! She is a Deaconess and the head cook for the Ebenezer Baptist Church Food Ministry. The Food Ministry serves the homeless each week and students who attend Bible Study each Wednesday evening.

He is unabashedly proud of his wife and her commitment to faith and family.

In retirement, Rosa enjoys being a "couponer" and James is impressed with how much she saves the family by being so diligent in using coupons when shopping. Rosa enjoys shopping as well as cooking and watching TV. She also says that "reading the blogs on the Internet is a relaxing pastime."

Working at Penn-Lo

While James was still teaching, he was offered a part-time job at a liquor store at 224 Washington Street, in the heart of "Hot Corner."

He doesn't remember how he found out about the job at Penn-Lo, but many employment opportunities in the African American community were conveyed by word-of-mouth. An older African American man owned the business and was eager to have some help. The store, located next to the barber shop on the corner of Washington and Hull Streets, was relatively small. Penn-Lo had been a fixture for some time and James was happy to supplement his income through his work there.

Not long after James left teaching, the owner of Penn-Lo was ready to retire and asked James if he wanted to take over the business. James considered the offer and decided this was a business opportunity he did not want to pass up. James had to pay for the inventory, but no other money changed hands. James was now a business owner in Hot Corner.

Hot Corner

The area around the intersection of Washington and Hull Streets in Athens is known as "Hot Corner." This area of downtown Athens has historically been the hub of many Black-owned businesses in the city. African Americans were not always welcome in the white-owned businesses of Athens, and in response a rich tradition of Black entrepreneurship emerged in the late 19th century. This area of Athens flourished with a theater, dentists' and doctors' offices, barbershops, restaurants, a funeral parlor, and dry goods stores. Hot Corner was also a place for African Americans to gather, socialize, share stories, and find out about jobs, entertainment, and other opportunities in a segregated society. It was also just two blocks from First A.M.E. Church.

Much has been written about Monroe B. "Pink" Morton, who built the theater and office complex on the southeast corner of Washington and Hull, but he was not the only contributor to this thriving district. Dozens of Black-owned businesses came and went over the years. Ironically, it was integration that caused many African American-owned businesses to close. Once African Americans could shop anywhere, it was not as essential to have businesses that catered just to

Blacks. Moreover, most white people did not shop in the Black-owned stores. So over the years the number and variety of Black-owned businesses in Hot Corner waned.

In 1999, Mr. Homer Wilson, owner of Wilson's Styling Shop, formed the Hot Corner Association. The group revitalized the area as a cultural hub in Athens, highlighting its African American heritage and its prominence in the development of Black-owned businesses. Every year the Hot Corner Festival draws thousands of participants to share in and celebrate the area's history and its contributions to life in Athens.

Reflections on Penn-Lo

When I asked James to tell me more about working at and subsequently owning the liquor store, he replied, "Penn-Lo! Oh Lord, the bad old days!" He confessed that while he himself never did anything illegal while he was the owner of the store, he did allow many of his patrons to drink and play cards on the premises, which was technically illegal. He now believes that "God protected us. We did some crazy things." He recounts that men would get off work and come to Penn-Lo to relax and unwind in a little room off the main part of the store. He shakes his head as if he still can't believe they did it and got away with it—and that he let them.

James is quick to reiterate that he didn't do any of these illegal things, but he knew he would have been in big trouble if anyone found out. He says he was lucky that in all the years he owned the store, he never had trouble with the law while running it, "not one day." No one ever tried to rob him at the store either. James acknowledges that he did have a pistol, sold to him by a sheriff's deputy who also showed him how to shoot it.

James recalls of his patrons,

> All of the people who came by the store were not only people who bought or drank alcohol. Of course, there were many who did buy or drink. That was what the business was for. But both friends and other patrons gathered

after their work day or work week to chat and fellowship with African brothers. From time to time ministers, deacons, stewards, coaches, postmen, teachers, UGA professors, funeral directors, Board of Education officials, civic persons, retired persons, men with nothing to do, and just the everyday citizen would come around to interact with one another at Penn-Lo.

To say that James felt conflicted about running the liquor store is an immense understatement. When he got married, he knew Rosa did not necessarily like what he was doing, "but she didn't say much." James reflects now, with great self-awareness, that he was "the kind of person who let you know that whatever I'm going to do, I'm going to do. No woman can change me. She understood that." Rosa knew that she could not "program or predict" James. He says with some chagrin, "I was crazy 40 years ago."

James' mother was also not happy with his choice of occupation. She would ask him how he could serve two masters—the Lord and the Devil. She would remind him that mixing the work of the two was wrong. She also worried about his safety and feared he was placing himself in a dangerous situation. James says, "I never stopped working for the Lord during this time, but I did take heed to her concern. My main reason for this job was a paycheck. But this was one thing that troubled my mind daily."

Rev. Richard B. Haynes

James' days as a liquor store owner came to an end in the late 1970s. He was beginning to formulate a plan to start a community choir and was searching for just the right people to help get it off the ground. It was at this point that James met Richard B. Haynes, who would become one of James' best friends, colleagues, and confidants. Richard would also be another voice that helped convince James that running a liquor store was not consistent with his faith or life goals.

Richard had just recently moved to Athens and tells the story of how he and James met and what transpired after that fateful meeting:

One day I asked a young man about a church and he pointed me to the Hill First Baptist Church, which was in sight of where we were standing. I left him and drove over there and the pastor, Rev. Ben K. Willis, just happened to be coming out of the building. I met him and started attending there whenever I was off work.

One particular Sunday that April, they were celebrating Men's Day. They had a special men's choir but no music. I felt totally guilty sitting there knowing that maybe I could be of service, so I got up and moved to the organ just to help out if I could.

It was that Sunday that a visitor, there for the program, introduced himself to me after the service was over as James Russell Smith.

He was somewhat overbearing and straightforward, to the extent that he made me a little uncomfortable. "Who are you? Where did you come from? What are you doing here?" I answered very little and kept walking. I had started to sort of enjoy being an unknown and staying to myself. He asked me if he could have a contact number so that he could follow up with me concerning a vision he had for the community. I did give him a contact number and kept moving.

He called me that night and the moment I heard his voice on the phone I knew that I had made a mistake by giving him my number. It was the end of my solitude. He began to share with me his vision of organizing a community choir. I heard him out and then told him that I wasn't interested. I really was not that great of a musician and that when he saw me, I was just filling in because I saw a need. He said, "I heard you play and you have the gift I so need, so just think about it. I'll call you in a day or so."

A few days later, my phone rang. I knew it had to be him. I didn't know anybody else. Again, he began to tell me about this great plan that he had for this choir and how I was going to help him. I honestly thought that I had gotten myself hooked up with a crazy man.

After a few conversations he began to talk in a way that sort of caught my attention. "Whoever you are, I don't believe that God sent you here for nothing, and you can't take a God-given gift and just hide it away. At the very least you are going to have to use that gift somewhere."

I finally said, "OK, I'll try," and that was the beginning of a lifelong friendship.

As I got to know him better and as we worked on his vision to put together a community choir, he carried me by his job at a liquor store. He got out of the car and went in. I stayed in the car. He came out and told me that I didn't have to sit in the car, I could come in. I said, "No thank you, I'm fine." When he came out and we were leaving, I asked him, point blank, "What kind of choir is this we are organizing?" He told me a choir that could do all kinds of sacred music. I challenged him on the spot. The conversation went sort of like this:

"Before I can go any further with you in this endeavor, you have some decisions to make. If we are going to do this, we've got to do our best to represent God well. While I am far from perfect and have more flaws than I care to talk about, I'm serious when it comes to my service to God." We talked about my concerns that we had to try to be the best examples that we could be.

The next time I saw him he told me he had given notice that he was leaving that job. It was then that I realized that this brother is serious about this choir.

As we continued to get to know each other I began

to assure him that I, just like everybody else, had more shortcomings than I even wanted to talk about, and never ever wanted him to think that I was some "holier than thou" character. But I was at a point in my life where I had been given an opportunity for a new start and I refused to blow it. With me it's all about where God has brought me from and where he's trying to get me to. At that point I had no idea where that was.

So James gave up the liquor business. He just closed the door and walked away. He did not want to sell it and have someone else bear the burden of what it might do to the community, what he saw it do to too many men. He says now that the liquor store was a foolish mistake. But he was young and just didn't think at the time that the decisions he made might have an impact on other people. By the time he left the business, he was married and his first child had been born. While his baby was still very young, he realized that his actions would speak louder than words. He thought about how he wanted to raise his children and was determined they would not make the same foolish mistakes.

James was also very serious about starting the community choir and realized that Richard was right. Others might judge him harshly if he were to start a choir that specialized in sacred music while he also ran a liquor store. That was not the impression he wanted to make and he certainly did not want people to question his motives or commitment. Before then, James says, it really didn't cross his mind that continuing to work at Penn-Lo could compromise his dreams and goals. He told himself that "you could do one thing over here and another over there and justify both fine."

However, James realized that once they started the choir, others might think like Richard. And starting the choir was critically important to him; he wanted nothing more than for it to succeed. James has always been a man who makes up his own mind about things, but he also listens to those he respects. The combined voices of his mother, Rosa, and Richard made him take a harder look at what he was doing and convinced him to move in another direction.

James says,

> I never left the church since I was a little kid. But Richard was on point. He had been through some problems and knew what he was talking about. Just this morning I was doing my meditation and this one was about, "Thank God for your problems." Sometimes they help you move to another place in life. Richard kept his head even when things were tough. He wasn't judging me; he just had a way of looking at it and shared it with me.

James laughs and says, "Richard is different. He was put here for some reason." And James is tremendously glad he was.

Subsequent Employment and Recognitions

In 1972, James became the first African American to be named "Outstanding Young Layman of the Year" by the Athens Jaycees. He had been nominated by First A.M.E. and an article in the *Athens Banner-Herald* listed his many activities at the church and beyond. This recognition came at a time when Athens was making significant attempts to reach across cultural and racial divides, and working on many initiatives as part of the Model City Program.

The article also mentioned James' involvement with another civic organization he had helped launch. The One Hundred Percenters was begun by a group of African Americans in Athens who

Jaycees Name Smith Young Layman of Year

James R. Smith was selected Outstanding Young Layman of 1972 at the Mayor's Prayer Breakfast this morning.

Smith, a member of the First AME Church, was chosen from candidates nominated by area churches. The Athens Jaycees, which hosted the breakfast, made the final selection.

Smith was cited for his church activities which include: Sunday School teacher, president of the Youth Choir, president of the Young Ushers Board, member of the Trustee Board, member of the Steward Board, chairman of the Project Committee, director of the Building Committee, and director of Christian Education.

He is director of the Eugene Terrell Ensemble, a singing group of young people from different churches in the community.

Smith is also president of One Hundred

Per Center Inc., an organization which provides students with scholarships for further education and also helps needy families in the community.

Smith said of his selection, "I appreciate the Jaycees awarding me this plaque. I really don't feel I'm worthy. What I did, I did for the young people. When I see their progress I feel that is the answer for the work I've put in."

Athens Mayor Julius Bishop presented the plaque to Smith.

The 5-year-old Mayor's Prayer Breakfast was established at a time when business and the church communities came together for spiritual uplift. It also honors a young layman, between the ages of 18 and 36, who exhibits Christian character and principles. Last year's winner was David Clements, a member of Young Harris Memorial Methodist Church.

JAMES R. SMITH (R) SELECTED OUTSTANDING YOUNG LAYMAN OF 1972
Mayor Julius Bishop Presents Award on Behalf of Athens Jaycees

wanted to provide college scholarships for young people. Interested students from the Athens area could submit an application describing their goals and plans for college. The Athens Area Human Relations Council (AAHRC) reviewed the applications and selected the award recipients, whose names were announced at the annual AAHRC breakfast each year. James is proud that both of his children received scholarships from this organization.

Wear-Ever and Cutco

For a short time James was employed as a salesman with a company that sold the Wear-Ever and Cutco brands of cookware. In this position, he sold the products and was tasked with recruiting and interviewing other prospective salesmen. The highlight of this job for James was receiving the "Quota-Buster Award" for being the top salesman. He won two trips for Rosa and himself as a result of his salesmanship: one to Tampa, Florida and one to Hawaii.

However, James didn't stay with this job very long. He didn't feel that sales was his calling even though he was clearly quite good at it. He says he had to sell to friends, neighbors, and acquaintances, but he knew "you can't make nobody buy nothing." Working on commission was also challenging. Nevertheless, like everything else in his life, whenever James set out to do something he did it well.

Dairy Pak

James had a friend who knew of jobs available at Dairy Pak, off Newton Bridge Road in north Athens. This Cleveland, Ohio-based company manufactured milk and juice cartons and had opened a branch in Athens in 1951. James started work there in 1979 and worked for five years in the Case Loading Department and the Shipping Department.

Seeking to advance at the company, James asked for an interview to move up to an office job. At the time only two African Americans were working in the office: the receptionist and a computer operator, both women. There were no African American men in any supervisory position. James recalls that his persistence paid off, as he was granted a formal interview and was subsequently offered the position of Assistant Scheduler for the company.

James had worked at Dairy Pak for almost 21 years when suddenly the company was sold and the new owners downsized the staff. James was offered an early retirement. He was uncertain at first what he would do next, as he was not in any way ready to stop working. The first thing he thought to do was return to substitute teaching in the Clarke County schools. But a lot had changed since he had been in the schools, and after a few assignments he realized that substituting would not be a long-term replacement job.

In 2000, after contemplating in which direction to head next, the 59-year-old James bought a lawnmower and started a business cutting grass. James says proudly, "It has been 19 years and I'm still in the same business, as my own boss." When asked when he might consider retiring for good, he replied, "probably at age 80. Yes, that would be a good time. As soon as I pay off my truck, I'll be ready. But I won't just be sitting around. I always gotta be busy!" James says he will take a little time to do things he hasn't had a chance to do in many years. He looks around the room in which we are sitting at his house and says he might begin with cleaning out his rec room, which is full of the history of the past 40 years. He also says he might join me in running and even teased me that maybe we could run a marathon. I don't think I can, but I don't doubt that he could!

James and Rosa's Children

"It has been a joy to parent two children, Tiara Latrice Smith and James Ricardo Smith. Both children are very keen, alert, and active in the Athens community," James says with much pride. Having children was always on James' list of priorities and he was thrilled the day his eldest child, a daughter, was born.

Tiara Latrice Smith

James relates:

On April 10, 1976, we became the proud parents of a

baby girl. Like most parents just beginning a new road with raising a child, I'm sure we made some left turns when we should have been making right turns. I'm sure we didn't make all the right decisions, but the good Lord brought us through it.

Tiara and Rick, c. 1984.

The new parents took this new responsibility in stride. Tiara, by all accounts, was an easy baby. After a brief maternity leave, Rosa returned to work and Tiara was cared for by Mrs. Bernice Hancock in her home. She later attended Magic Years of Learning daycare until she started elementary school.

James Ricardo Smith

James and Rosa welcomed a baby boy on May 24, 1983. After being blessed with a healthy daughter, James was thrilled to have a son. Having one child of each gender completed their family. All of James' single life he had wanted to raise a son, and here he was! Named after both his father and his father's close friend, Richard Haynes, he has always been called Rick.

Parenting

As James and Rosa settled into life as parents, they were dedicated to providing all they could for their children. James says their primary focus was to "expose the children to everything that is possible." This included teaching them the importance of an education, what it meant to be a Christian, and to appreciate what they had in life. James also wanted them "to be exposed to some of the better things . . . things I wasn't exposed to because my parents weren't able to or didn't have the opportunity to show their children."

James says the adjustment to being parents for the first time was not as difficult as one might expect for him and Rosa. Both had waited quite a while to marry and then to begin a family. They both loved and worked with children so they already had a glimpse into all that parenting involved. James also helped with his younger siblings for many years, an experience that was invaluable when he became a new father. Rosa says,

> Raising a family can be a hard job and needs the cooperation of both parents. Most of the responsibilities fell on me. We did not have a lot of money, but we made sure that the children had what they needed to succeed in life. I sacrificed a lot for my family. It wasn't easy being a working mother but through the grace of God, I made it!

As a student at Timothy Elementary, James says, Tiara was "progressive, smart, talented, never gave me any trouble." Tiara was a model student and quickly moved into the gifted program. She loved to read and always got her work done on time. When Rick started school, he too was an eager student and was also identified as gifted. Both children were involved in numerous extracurricular activities and were active in their church youth group at Ebenezer Baptist Church. Rick also played football and basketball in community leagues. James recalls telling both of his children as they moved into middle and high school, "it doesn't matter the color of your skin. Just do your work. Do what you are supposed to do. You can compete."

James is proud that from his children's kindergarten days to their high school graduations, he attended all of their parent-teacher conferences, concerts, performances, sporting events, and family nights. He never missed an opportunity to engage with their schools and be an advocate for his children. He recalls that he enjoyed these experiences "because my children were well-behaved and their grades were good. I always left the schools with an upbeat spirit."

James describes Rick as a very active little boy who did all the boy things. He had a lot of energy and natural ability but also a lot of empathy. James could tell he had a keen interest in learning. But one thing especially stood out about Rick as he was growing up: he practiced preaching. Often. James says,

> His calling was to preach. He practiced what he saw Dr. Hope [Rev. Dr. Winfred Hope, pastor of Ebenezer Baptist West Church] do. Richard [Haynes, who had become a pastor] lived nearby then and Rick would go visit him and try out his preaching. He spent a lot of time there.

Rick is now the pastor of Browns Chapel Baptist Church in Bishop, Georgia.

James believed it was important to expose his children to all kinds of music from a very early age. Not knowing if they would pick it up, he nevertheless gave them every opportunity to sing and try various musical instruments. As a result, they both played several. Tiara learned to play flute, oboe, violin, piccolo, and piano. Rick played trombone, baritone horn, cello, drums, tuba, and piano. James paid for the children to take piano lessons from Ira Cobb, who had been trained at Julliard. James says he couldn't really afford it but he wanted them to have the best. The exposure to music clearly paid off.

I asked James if he ever had to discipline his children. He said it was very rare. He attributes this to the way he and Rosa raised them and how they set expectations and were consistent in enforcing them. Rosa adds that James was a very strict parent. He also says that he raised his children on Proverbs. I asked him to explain what he meant and he responded, "Proverbs brings discipline." James was raised with the Bible by his mother but had his own ideas about how he wanted to raise his children. Proverbs provided the tools and lessons he felt were most important for them to learn. He also says he emphasized that they must "Have the sense to recognize that you are not the only one on this earth. You have to listen to another person as well. No one is always right or wrong."

Because he and Rosa so rarely had to discipline their children, James could remember two very specific incidents when he did have to discipline each child.

One time when Tiara was six, she and Richard's daughter, Sheena, went to my sister Willie Mae's to get their hair done. Some kind of confusion went on over there. Tiara may have been disrespectful to my mother or something like that. I am not sure what it was about, but I was told about it when I went to pick them up. When I got Tiara home, she got a whupping.

As for Rick, James recalled that once as a teenager Rick had "borrowed" one of James' jackets without asking, then lied about it. James says he had to teach him the lesson that you have to ask, even at home. He told Rick, "If you do that some other place, you would get in trouble. And I won't be there to bail you out. I am just letting you know the consequences."

James also recalls that at one point in middle school when James would ask if Rick had any homework, Rick would say "no." James would ask again, "They didn't give you anything to work on?" Rick would again say no. While James knew that Rick was a good student and always got his work done, he didn't believe in being idle. So he would say, "Okay, come sit over here, I got something. Tell me everything you learned at school today." Sometimes James would even have Rick write out what the teacher taught and what he had learned. He believed that even if the teacher had not given specific homework, as a student, "you always got some kind of assignment." He would even suggest to Rick that he should do more than what was required to get ahead of the game. James knew he was tough, but he also knew "how easy it was to slip, or get behind and make it seem like you don't have anything to do."

James says that it was somewhat different raising the two children. He describes Tiara as more like him: "outspoken, firm, believes in getting things done, on time, professional." He laughs and adds that Tiara is "much more [professional] than me!" He goes on to say, "Rick is more like his mother. Soft-spoken, observant, and eager to please. At least growing up. But since he has been a pastor he is beginning to be more like me." From all accounts, the siblings were and

Tiara, Rosa and Rick, c. 2001.

continue to be very close, despite their seven-year age difference. They look out for each other and share a deep bond.

James was very aware that he did not want to be like his father when he parented his own children. He realized that while he might get angry with his children, he did not want to react the way his father had. James was determined not to be as harsh as Leroy, Sr. had been. He stresses that his children "didn't know it, but I was aware of it." He says that when he felt like he was overreacting he told himself not to go there. He recognized that "Leroy might have done so-and-so in this situation, but I won't do that."

Tiara and Rick did get to know their father's parents. The children would visit them often and James' mother took care of Rick when he was little. Leroy, Sr. was attentive and showed more love to his grandchildren than James felt Leroy, Sr. was able to give to his own children, "even though he didn't know he was giving it." James knew that his parents were proud of his children, although they were not overly demonstrative. They did insist on the children remembering their manners and treating their elders with respect.

James recalls that his father would always give Rick something—

candy or a dollar—and on one occasion Rick didn't say thank you. James says that his "dad didn't get on him, but my mother did. They believed that children were to be taught the right way to act. They wanted to instill in them that you were polite everywhere." When I asked James if his relationship with his father had changed as a result of having children, he looked at me and said, "No. I was still not inclined to spend a lot of time with him or communicate with

Tiara and Rick, c. 2005.

him." But James did want his children to know their grandparents, regardless of the past.

When I asked James if he has learned anything from his children, he replied, "Yes, I learned a lot from them. Their actions and the lives that they are living speak volumes." James acknowledges that "There are a lot of things that I might have wanted to say that I didn't have to say when they were growing up. They were always striving to do good and please their parents." Seeing them achieve success in school, church, and the community makes him very proud. Sometimes, however, he sees them "doing just what I did and I want to tell them that's not the way to go." He doesn't say it to them, but he believes they need to be "more selfish." By that James says he means they need to take better care of themselves, be more protective of their family time, and limit how much they are always doing for others. James knows how short life is and he doesn't want his children to struggle as much as he did. But above all, he is enormously proud of the adults they have become.

Tiara's Reflections

Music has always been a part of our family. When I started kindergarten, my grandmother felt I should learn piano as well. I began lessons on Fridays at age 5 and continued to age 15 (no, I don't play now). I went on to also learn how to play the violin, flute, oboe, and piccolo. I don't remember the actual forming of the Athens Voices of Truth, but I am told I sang, "Yes Jesus Loves Me" at their first concert. As a toddler my brother directed "All These Blessings are Mine" after being caught mocking my dad during rehearsal (that was when the choir rehearsed in our den).

My first memory is one of being disciplined. I don't remember if it was accidentally or on purpose, but a box of crackers ended up on the floor; I was made to clean it up. I did so reluctantly.

I also remember my dad playing the devil in a play I think was called Heaven Bound. I'm sure it was explained to me that he would be playing this part, but when I saw him in full costume, carrying out his role, I cried tears of GREAT FEAR.

I'm not sure how old I was, but my brother was school-age which means I was in middle school, our family went to Walt Disney World.

Parents' child-rearing style

I would say my parents strived to raise us based on the following Bible verses:

Proverbs 13:24 NIV - "Whoever spares the rod hates their children, but the one who loves their children is careful to discipline them."

Proverbs 22:6 NIV - "Start children off on the way they should go, and even when they are old they will not turn from it."

As children, especially teenagers, we did not always like the decisions they made. (I'm certain I thought they were mean, but knew better than to say that to them out loud.) However, we were better equipped to deal with life's challenges because of it.

Valuable lessons

- Developing a personal relationship with God—this began with family devotions each Sunday morning before going to Sunday School
- Having a song in your heart
- Loyalty to those you love

College/Education

Tiara attended Spelman College and received her Bachelor of Arts in Political Science. She subsequently attended the University of Georgia and received her Master of Education in Health Promotion and Behavior, focusing on violence prevention. Her studies at the University of Phoenix culminated in her earning a Doctorate in Education in Curriculum and Instruction. She is now the Clinical Supervisor at Brightpaths (formerly Prevent Child Abuse Athens). She also serves as the Children's Ministry Leader at Ebenezer Baptist Church, West and is a published author.

Rick's Reflections

I struggle to remember the earliest memories of my father. There are two that seem to stick out and are wrestling for first in my mind, so I'll share both. These memories also taught me two important principles in life.

The first I'll give attention to is when a childhood friend twice my size hit me. I ran away, scared to respond. My dad came and got me, told me to stand up for myself, and wouldn't let the other child hit me again. While some might have seen that as him teaching me to retaliate, I now understand he was teaching me about manhood.

Secondly, every Sunday I would come downstairs from my Sunday School class, he would be at the bottom of the steps waiting to take me to the restroom. Even if I didn't feel the urge to go, he would tell me "Well, you need to try." He wasn't going to tolerate me getting up in the middle of church to do something I could have done before. That was teaching me discipline.

Parents' child-rearing style

Stern would be the word choice for me! All my friends, both growing up and even now, think my dad is the funniest guy in the world. That wasn't my testimony. He was firm but fair. My mother actually was the stronger disciplinarian, but my father definitely was not a walk in the park. What's amazing to see is the people who raised me as their child are noticeably different with their grandchild. Similarly, I find myself doing much of what my dad did and I know that his philosophy works!

Valuable lessons

The lessons learned are too innumerable to name. In summary, I've been tremendously blessed to be born to my wonderful parents. As I reflect on the life of my dad with the Voices of Truth, I'm reminded of him going to work, church, and still having time to work with the choir. That left an indelible mark on me. I had to learn that him staying busy was to provide and to fulfill his God-given purpose. That requires a great deal of sacrifice and becomes a family affair. There are members of the Voices that will tell you I grew up in their laps. While the group has been in existence longer than I've been alive, the impact of my father and many others will forever be etched in the Athens religious music fabric. For that, I'm grateful.

I've learned to give God my best, love my family hard, stand up for what's right, and enjoy life because it's fleeting fast.

I've also learned to do what the commandment on Moses' tablet in Exodus 20 that Paul borrowed in Ephesians 6 tells us to do: Honor thy father and mother that thy days may be long on the Earth.

College/Education

Rick attended Morehouse College and received a Bachelor of Arts in Philosophy and Religion. He is now the pastor at Browns Chapel Baptist Church in Bishop, Georgia. He has also served as a conference host at the Classic City Conference in Athens and is the author of *Managing Ministry Misfits: Helping Members Find Their Place.*

Grandchild

In 2009 Rick married Ms. Rhondolyn Jones and they now have a son, Jameson Isiah Smith, born July 24, 2017. This is Rosa and James' first grandchild and he is the light of their lives.

Rick and Rhondolyn's wedding, 2009.

Transition from First A.M.E. to Ebenezer Baptist Church, West

Before Rick was born, James and Rosa had long talks about moving to a new church. James explains:

> After being reared in the A.M.E. church, it was more than a blessing to know who Jesus is. I had great teachers and great preachers. I had the opportunity to be involved in so much during the years we spent in First A.M.E. Rosa joined First A.M.E. Church after she moved to Athens, but she grew up in the Baptist Church.

After moving to their house on Rhodes Drive in 1981 and enrolling Tiara at Timothy Elementary School, James and Rosa decided to change churches. They began attending services at Ebenezer Baptist Church, West on Chase Street. James stresses that they didn't leave First A.M.E. because they were unhappy. They just felt like they needed a change and a different environment in which to raise their children. James says, "I believe if you are a Christian, we all serve the same God; denomination doesn't matter."

The Smith family has deep roots now at Ebenezer. James watched both his children grow up in the church and become leaders there. Tiara still serves as the Youth Director and Rick received the call to preach at Ebenezer. As the Rev. Dr. Winfred Hope retires in 2019 after 40 years as senior pastor, the family is still deeply engaged in the church, with James serving as a Deacon and Rose as a Deaconess.

CHAPTER 10

Music Ministry and the Athens Voices of Truth

James has been worshiping through music for as long as he can remember. From the time he was very young, listening to the choir at church he felt empowered by the music, the message, and the energy emanating from the voices. Performing sacred music became a calling and a passion. Singing in and directing choirs over the years also became his way to honor and uplift his community.

By 1979, James felt the need to further expand his musical horizons and to expose others to the full range of sacred music. He had observed that many church choirs had a particular style or a set repertoire and he wanted to build on the diversity of musical approaches taken by these various choirs. He sought to create a community choir that was well versed in all types of sacred and classical music, comprised of dedicated members who were willing to try new choral renditions. He also set out to bring together individuals from various faith communities who could bring different styles of music to the group. And he wanted to do all of this with great integrity.

James tells the story:

> In 1979, one of the most depressing times of my entire life (brought on by myself), I needed God to deliver me out of this depression. Thanks to Him, and to Johnny Sims, an adopted son, a musician, and most of all a friend, the darkness began to lift. Johnny had been a student of mine in school and in church. He participat-

ed in the youth group and sang in the E. L. Terrell ensemble. He left Athens to attend Shaw University, where he received his B.S. degree in music. When he returned to Athens, we worked together as director and assistant director of the C. D. Wilkerson church choir at First A.M.E. Church.

When I resigned as director of the church choir, Johnny became the full-time director. One evening during my down time, Johnny came to my home for a visit. Not only did he come to visit, but he came with a message: "I've just attended a male choir rehearsal at Hill First Baptist Church. They are preparing for their Men's Day program on Sunday. You should come and join us and sing on this occasion. By the way, there's a man there playing the organ that I've never seen or heard before." I responded to his request, but it has always been a point of mine to practice what you preach, and that is: if you haven't rehearsed, don't sing. So I said I would go, but as part of the congregation.

On that fourth Sunday morning, Johnny came to my house to pick me up. We proceeded for worship at Hill First Baptist. As I sat and meditated, the time came for prayer. During prayer time, this young man that Johnny had spoken about on the Wednesday night earlier began to play "Sweet Hour of Prayer" on the Hammond organ.

Sweet hour of prayer
Sweet hour of prayer
That calls me from a world of care
And bids me at my Father's throne
Make all my wants and wishes known
In seasons of distress and grief
My soul has often found relief
And oft escaped the tempter's snare
By Thy return, sweet hour of prayer.

-Alan Jackson

Through the powerful message of Almighty God, through the encouragement of Johnny Sims, and because of the touching of the keys of a Sunday morning worship experience, it was a blessed joy to meet Richard B. Haynes.

After worship we met and I shared with Richard what the playing of the message through music—"Sweet Hour of Prayer"—meant to me. Johnny and I were amazed at the touch he had on the organ and the inspiration he brought musically. This meeting led to many calls and a discussion about church choirs and music in the Athens community. In one of our many discussions, I expressed to Brother Haynes my desire to organize a community choir, a choir that would glorify God through all types of sacred music.

Since he didn't know me, he was reluctant to jump on board immediately and I didn't blame him. After many conversations, I found Brother Haynes to be sincere and dedicated to the work of the Lord. Our families met and we became brothers.

This chance meeting led to the beginning of the Athens Voices of Truth choir. For a couple of months, the three men talked and shared ideas about how to get this community choir off the ground. They wanted a group that would perform sacred music but would be more than a regular church choir. James explains,

In church choirs you are limited to whatever style that church is doing. But in a community choir you can be more versatile. There is a lot of talent in the Athens community and we felt that people shouldn't limit their talent. As we continued to share and work together, we all understood what God had done in all of our lives, and the touch and talent he had given to us individually.

The choir's name came after hours of brainstorming; when Richard suggested "Voices of Truth" it struck all three men as the perfect name. James says, "The name had to reflect what we were doing, why we were creating this group. We hoped that this name would be true to what we intended and that folks who joined knew what we were about from the start." Soon after, they added "Athens" to the name to identify where the choir originated and where most of the members called home, but the choir has continued to be known as simply the "Voices of Truth."

James could read music, but he knew additional musical training would benefit him and the choir. And while he had been singing and directing for many years, he had not tried to play an instrument since his abbreviated attempt at the trombone back in high school. James recalls,

> In order to hone my musical skills and to teach and train a choir, it was important for me to get training and to take piano lessons. My first piano teacher was Ms. Willie G. Owens, who taught lessons in her home. She also played for many churches in the Athens area. My second piano teacher was Mr. Ira Cobb, a very detailed man and a graduate of the Julliard School of Music, who also taught my children. I was blessed also to study under Ms. Cindy Tandy and Mr. Bruce Ware. Mr. Ware is the Minister of Music for Timothy Baptist Church.

James laughs as he reflects that he was never going to become a concert pianist, but the lessons did help make him a better director.

The Early Years

The Athens Voices of Truth began in 1979 with eight members who rehearsed at the Central Athens Community Center. The original eight are still singing with the choir today: Brenda Bellinger, Gloria Bizzle, Shirley Butler, Joelene Cherry, Larry Johnson, Shelia Neely-Norman, Sylvanus Turner, and Connie Woodall. During

Athens Voices of Truth, c.1980.

its 40 years of existence the choir has had several "homes" in which to rehearse, including First A.M.E. Church, Greater Bethel A.M.E. Church, Hill First Baptist Church, Timothy Baptist Church, East Friendship Baptist Church, and even James' home. James is grateful that the churches have allowed them to rehearse in their sanctuaries, but the choir never really had a permanent home. They wandered from place to place relying on the kindness of the religious community to provide them with a choir stand, a piano, and ideally, an organ, all necessary to hone their craft.

When the choir was formed James insisted that they specialize in sacred music— hymns, spirituals, anthems, and traditional gospel—as well as some classical pieces, such as Handel's "Messiah" and Mozart's "Lacrymosa." James has always dug deep in the canon to find music that may not be as well known, so audiences would learn to appreciate the full body of work in the genre. Working with the true foundations of sacred music, especially as they relate to African American history, and keeping the traditional forms alive was essential to James. As a result, the choir has performed spirituals by Black composers and arrangers like William L. Dawson and Hall Johnson; hymns by Robert Fryson; gospel songs by Margaret Douroux, Richard Smallwood, and Walter Hopkins; and anthems by Glenn E. Burleigh, among many others.

This variety of music gives the Voices of Truth a chance to show their expertise in four-part harmony, with and without musical accompaniment. Some of the most challenging scores are a cappella renditions of old anthems and spirituals. Each piece of music represents a unique contribution to the hundreds of years of expressions of faith, hope, hardship, love, anguish, and praise in the Black community. James reflects,

> A lot of times when we focus our attention on what is popular, it doesn't last. Hymns will always be there. Spirituals will always be there. We don't want to forget our heritage and the music that brought us through slavery. We cannot forget that this generation of children does not know much about what has happened in the past.

James has welcomed people from all faith traditions, all walks of life, and all races to perform with the choir. Choir members come from many different denominations, including Baptist, Methodist, Catholic, A.M.E., Presbyterian, Holiness, Unitarian, and Seventh-day Adventist. James believes the diversity of the group has helped the choir to grow. And while it has remained predominantly an African American choir, it was never his intention that the Voices of Truth be an all-Black group.

Nor was it his intention for the group to be solely a gospel choir. While the choir has performed contemporary gospel, it is not his personal preference. James doesn't mind that some choir members and many audiences love the upbeat, "foot-stomping, hand-clapping" modern gospel music. However, he was careful to communicate to the choir members that their commitment was "to be a part of learning something new and doing something different." James did not want the Voices of Truth to be known as a gospel choir, as there was so much more to their repertoire than just one type of sacred music.

James has always been very clear about the choir's purpose. "Our first priority is to know the Lord," James affirms. "If you know something about Him, you know what you're singing about. We want the audiences to ascertain a message. Singing is as much ministry as preaching."

The Voices Musicians

James recalls:

> When we began the community choir, we decided that Richard would play the organ and Johnny and I would teach and direct. We just needed someone to play the piano. In the end, there were several young musicians who shared this responsibility, but Joelene Cherry was a godsend and agreed to handle this task from the beginning. Joelene had been playing the piano for quite some time and was the musician at St. James and Timothy Baptist churches.

Tom Broadnax and Joelene Cherry.

In addition to Joelene, Richard, and Johnny, other musicians have dedicated themselves to the choir over the years. Dr. Ron Campbell, Rev. Lonnie Johnson, Dr. Carl Walton, David Bolton, Judy Sikes, Cindy Tandy, and Bruce Ware have played for the Voices of Truth. Eric Johnson is a current musician and continues to accompany the choir.

Joelene describes her longtime involvement with the choir: "The Voices is a choir that is different than the normal church choir. They are a dedicated, well-trained, Christian organization. They are also like a family." Joelene is a very talented musician who loves playing the piano, directing, and teaching. A longtime employee of the University of Georgia, Joelene continues to work with other church choirs in Athens as well.

James also expresses gratitude to Tom Broadnax, another talented musician who has been with the Voices of Truth for almost 30 years. James says, "I could not do what I do without Tom." Tom recalls how he learned about the choir:

> While in college at UGA in 1992, I became friends with Bruce Ware. One Saturday we had plans to "hang out," but Bruce had to go to a rehearsal first. Since we were both church musicians, I offered to tag along to his rehearsal "just to listen" and then move on with our plans for the day. That rehearsal at Timothy Baptist Church was my first experience with the Athens Voices of Truth, and also with James Russell Smith, who I would soon know more affectionately as "Smitty." During the rehearsal, the choir sang "One More Day," "I Have a God," and "Just a Little Talk with Jesus," among others. Bruce usually played the organ, but he was playing piano at this rehearsal and accidentally on purpose told Mr. Smith that I could play the organ. As a result, I am still accompanying the Voices of Truth 27 years later!

Tom described what being a part of the Voices has meant to him over the years:

> Through the years, the Voices of Truth has been a great strength to me both musically and spiritually, because of the many opportunities to sing and play a variety of musical styles and worship through music and song. Gospel music is uplifting, no matter the condition of one's emotional and/or mental state. Gospel music is comforting and encouraging when one is despondent. The Voices of Truth has been a family of sorts to me for many years, and my time spent with them will be cherished always.

James preparing for a concert.

James as Director

James is as serious about directing as he is about everything else he has done in his life. He acknowledges that when it comes to music and singing, he is a perfectionist. He has been accused of being too tough, but he asserts that he is only tough when choir members don't give their best.

James knows that people have called him mean, and that some don't like him. But he believes that when you commit to doing something, you must do it to the very best of your ability, regardless of how you might feel about a particular person. He thinks that many people don't really know what they are capable of until they are pushed. He would prefer not to have to push quite so hard, but he believes there is always something more one can achieve.

Part of James' intention in creating a community choir was to teach choir members a broader repertoire and a wider variety of techniques so they could go back and help their home church choirs do more. James' goal was for the Voices of Truth "to be so good that we can sing all over the world." He always encouraged the choir to take on new challenges and expand their horizons, both musically and spiritually.

James never set out to make a name for himself and always kept his focus on the message of the music. In a 2009 *Athens Banner-Herald* article about the Voices of Truth's 30th anniversary, James is quoted as saying, "I believe in quality; the notes, articulation, phrasing, and lyrics, they are to be clear. And I believe in doing professional work."

What James does not believe in is giving anyone special treatment. The rules for participating in the choir are clearly stated and James believes that the music can't be spiritually meaningful to the audience or the choir member if you are not fully committed. He shakes his head and says, "People get away with things they have no

Carl Walton, musician; Johnny Sims, First A.M.E. choir director; James Smith; and Ron Lowe, a former musician at Ebenezer Baptist Church and current musical consultant for the Athens Voices of Truth.

business doing. Shocking how people get away with things. What do people think these words mean–dependability, punctuality, responsibility, discipline, commitment?" He tells choir members that if they do not attend rehearsals regularly, they should not expect to perform at their next concert or scheduled event. He reiterates that he is not trying to disrespect anyone, but he must respect the people who attend every rehearsal.

Rehearsals

James has always been a taskmaster when it comes to rehearsals. He encouraged anyone and everyone who wanted to sing sacred music to join the choir, but choir members also had to commit to regular attendance at rehearsals, to working hard during rehearsals, and to practicing diligently. "One of the most important aspects of the Voices is its rehearsals. In rehearsals is where the work begins and ends. This is where the foundation of this choir was laid. Nothing can stand without a sound foundation."

James explains:

Athens Voices of Truth, c. 1995.

In order to receive everything that is offered in each one of the rehearsals, I stressed first and foremost to arrive on time. Rehearsal began at 7:30 p.m. and ended at 9:00 p.m. sharp each Tuesday evening. This has been the case for 40 years. We never changed it because no matter what day we might choose to rehearse, there will be conflicts with other things going on. But if choir members know this is when we rehearse and what the expectations are, then they know they must be available every Tuesday.

Some people think they can make excuses for not coming to rehearsal; I don't. Some people will ignore what you are trying to do and go on their way to do other things on Tuesday night when rehearsal is in session. We try very, very hard to remind people that excuses are not accepted. Of course, if you are ill or there is a death in the family, we know these things will happen. But when members join the group, they know they must commit to our schedule. Whether you joined in '79, '89, or '99, rehearsal was on Tuesday and we expect you to honor Tuesday nights for rehearsal. How are you going to learn new music if you aren't in rehearsals? How are you going to keep up, if you aren't in rehearsals?

Each rehearsal begins with a devotion, especially prayer. We must invite God in and thank God each and every rehearsal for everything. Without Him there is no spiritual rehearsal. Then the choir must do warm-up exercises. In order for the individual voices to blend in with their section and to sing the correct part and pitch, the voices must be conditioned, trained, and in tune with the other three sections and the instruments.

Choir members are encouraged to pray all the time, whether in rehearsal, riding along the highways, at home, at work, in church . . . just everywhere. They are asked to study the scriptures as well. We have several scriptures that are important to the Voices, but Colossians 3:12-17 deals with us directly:

[12] Therefore, as God's chosen people, holy and dearly loved, clothe yourselves with compassion, kindness, humility, gentleness and patience. [13] Bear with each other and forgive one another if any of you has a grievance against someone. Forgive as the Lord forgave you. [14] And over all these virtues put on love, which binds them all together in perfect unity. [15] Let the peace of Christ rule in your hearts, since as members of one body you were called to peace. And be thankful. [16] Let the message of Christ dwell among you richly as you teach and admonish one another with all wisdom through psalms, hymns, and songs from the Spirit, singing to God with gratitude in your hearts. [17] And whatever you do, whether in word or deed, do it all in the name of the Lord Jesus, giving thanks to God the Father through him.

James reflects:

Choir members preparing for their 20th Anniversary concert, 1999. Front row (l to r): James Smith, Brenda Bellinger, Shelia Neely-Norman, Gloria Bizzle, Derrick Ellis, Reginald Willis. Back row (l to r): Sylvanus Turner, Eric Johnson, Willimenia Haynes, Erwin Greene, Homer Thurman.

While working with choirs and different singing groups, it was never my intention to just have a group of people singing. You can do that anywhere and in any place. In music ministry, organization, understanding four-part harmony, what it means to blend, and rehearsing regularly is mandatory. When the message of the music is conveyed it must be simple and clean. If we are not sincere, and do not have time to put into an organization or choir to make it the best, we need to check ourselves. In any undertaking, there must be a vision; to develop the vision there comes direction, dedication, and structure.

Performances, Awards, and Recognitions

The choir's first concert was held at Hill First Baptist Church on October 7, 1979 to great acclaim. The program for what was, at the time, called The Athens Community Choir listed James as director; Larry Blount as assistant director; Johnny Sims as assistant director and arranger; and Joelene Cherry, Richard Haynes, and Anthony Rucker as musicians. Since that first performance, the Athens Voices of Truth have performed in hundreds of venues, garnered numerous awards, and earned recognition as a pillar of the community. The choir has performed in Georgia, Florida, South Carolina, Alabama, and Utah. The group has both organized and participated in a variety of spiritual and professional programs, conferences, and workshops.

One of the Voices of Truth's earliest performances, in response to a personal invitation from Coach Vince Dooley, was for a Georgia Bulldogs football team pre-season worship service in the 1980s. In 1987, the Voices of Truth won the Athens Cultural Award from the Clarke County Community Relations Division. The Voices sang both at the dedication ceremony for the Athens Tutorial Program in 1988 and again for their Gospel Fundraising Program in 1998. The group sang for the Georgia Legislative Black Caucus annual prayer breakfast in Atlanta in 1992. They also sang for a CBS telecast and performed for the official opening of Athens' new civic center in 1995. In the same year, the choir performed at the Athens Public Library at a day-long symposium sponsored by the Georgia Humanities Council that featured noted African American authors.

The Voices of Truth appeared in several programs during the 1996 Olympic Games, hosted by the state of Georgia, including performing during the opening ceremony that welcomed the Olympic torch to Athens and for the Australian Olympic team. At the end of 1996, the choir performed at the Georgia Museum of Art's annual Kwanzaa celebration. In 1997 the choir participated in a two-night pre-Christmas concert tour with award-winning country singer Kenny Rogers.

One of the pinnacles for the choir occurred in 1999, when they performed at Tuskegee University for the Eighth Annual William Levi Dawson Institute for Classical and Folk Music. The choir was also featured at a "Celebrate 2000" concert at the Athens Classic Center, which included gospel singer Teresa Haynes. In 2002 the choir sang for the 17th Annual MLK Day Celebration at the State Capitol in Atlanta. Also that year, the choir participated in a choir festival in Salt Lake City, Utah.

The Voices also performed for a 2015 event sponsored by the Willson Center for Humanities & Arts at UGA, that featured a lecture by celebrated poet, writer, and activist Alice Walker. The choir has also received numerous accolades and letters of appreciation from elected officials, colleges, civic groups, non-profits, communities, and congregations. Numerous feature stories have been written about the choir and their concerts in local newspapers and magazines.

Early on, James decided that the choir would always perform for free, and as a result the Voices of Truth has never charged for its concerts. The group has done some fundraising events, including fish fry dinners and an "International Tea," and sells its CDs to help pay for travel, purchase music, and make recordings. They have performed at events where admission is charged, but the choir never charges for its participation. The group accepts donations and over the years many generous benefactors, hearing that the choir needs funds for a trip or to make a recording, have helped the Voices reach their goals. But James believes everyone should be able to listen to, participate in, enjoy, and be uplifted by their performances. The message of the music and the choir's delivery of that message thus remains free for everyone.

Tuskegee University and Mormon Tabernacle Concerts

The Voices of Truth have performed at many venues in the Southeast, but two highlights for James and the choir were the invitations to sing at Tuskegee University in 1999 and at the Mormon Tabernacle in Salt Lake City in 2002. These opportunities were special for everyone in the choir and are a testament to the quality, reputation, and dedication of the director and the members.

James, of course, was thrilled and proud that the Voices were invited to perform at the Eighth Annual William Levi Dawson Institute for Classical and Folk Music at his alma mater. William Levi Dawson was an African American composer, choir director, and musician who taught at Tuskegee from 1931 to 1956. He was born in Alabama but went to Chicago for his musical education. He began writing music at a very young age and was a prolific composer of spirituals.

Athens Voices of Truth at Tuskegee University in front of the famous statue of Booker T. Washington, "Lifting the Veil of Ignorance," 1999.

The performance at Tuskegee was in honor of Dawson. Each choir that was invited was to sing at least one piece composed by Dawson, and the Voices performed his, "Soon Ah Will Be Done." It was an amazing and uplifting experience for the choir. Before and after the performance the choir was able to tour the campus and marvel at the award-winning chapel and various monuments to the achievements of the University's founders, alumni, and faculty.

Another highlight of the Voices' career was singing at the Mormon Tabernacle in Salt Lake City in the spring of 2002. James learned about the opportunity from his longtime friend Ron Lowe, a former musician at Ebenezer Baptist Church, West who lives in California. Ron told James there was to be a gathering of church and community choirs from all over the country who would perform in a concert at the Tabernacle. Ron's church choir was participating in the event and he invited the Voices of Truth to come as well. James presented the idea to the choir and they were very excited about the prospect.

Choir members in Salt Lake City, Utah.

The music that was to be performed at the festival was sent to all the participants so they could learn it ahead of time. James was especially pleased to see that some of the spirituals were by Moses Hogan. James asked his longtime friend and choir supporter Greg Broughton, a professor of music at the University of Georgia, to work with the choir because some of the music was difficult. James was determined that the Voices would be prepared and know their parts. The trip was relatively expensive so as they had in times past, the choir held fundraisers to help pay for their airfare and hotel costs. James made sure each person knew exactly how much money they needed to make the trip.

Flying to Salt Lake City was a new experience for several choir members. James recalls the excitement and anticipation of taking such a momentous trip. Some choir members had never been that far from home and he was glad they were exposed to something completely new and different. The rehearsals were held in the Tabernacle and James says the acoustics were amazing. On Sunday, they worshiped with the Mormons and heard the Mormon Tabernacle Choir sing.

James recalls that it had snowed just before they arrived, but the city was full of flowers blooming everywhere. He and the choir marveled at how beautiful and clean Salt Lake City was. When it was time to perform with the other choirs in the Tabernacle, it was an awe-inspiring moment. As the group sat in the huge choir loft and prepared to sing, James thought, "We have been blessed."

Outreach Ministry

Since the very beginning, the Voices of Truth have performed regularly at community events, festivals, church revivals, and nursing homes as part of their outreach ministry. Over the years, the group has also sponsored a variety of music workshops for their members and other local choirs. They have often retained the services of renowned artists and songwriters in the gospel music industry, including Mr. V. Michael McKay, Dr. Margaret Pleasant Douroux, and Mr. Samuel Sander, to facilitate these workshops. The choir holds an annual concert each fall, typically at Ebenezer Baptist Church, West for the whole community.

The choir is often asked to sing at funerals. Although this might seem a sorrowful duty, the choir sees it as a blessing, as James explains:

> Through the years, it has been rewarding to know that the Voices have been able to lift people. Our mission is to carry our singing ministry to as many people as possible, whether in Athens or outside of the city. During the years that we have been singing, several of our members have "gone home." We worked with the families to plan the homegoing music for the services. Several community members have also asked the Voices to provide music for the homegoing of their relatives as well. We want to serve as a source of encouragement to all who will hear our message in song.

Recordings

In 2000, the Voices received a grant from R.E.M. to help them record a CD. This would be their first professionally produced album, and would become a source of great pride and a way for the choir to raise funds for their various out-of-town performances. Over the years, the choir has recorded seven CDs. The first was completed in 2004, followed by recordings in 2006, 2011, 2013, 2014, 2017, and 2018.

Reflections from Current Voices of Truth Members

At various points in its history the choir has had as few as eight members and as many as thirty-eight. When current members were asked what the choir has meant to them, they almost unanimously

Athens Voices of Truth at a performance in Elberton, Georgia, 2000.

spoke of fellowship, spiritual growth, and witnessing through music. They all describe the choir as a family who not only sing together but also uplift and support one another. They recall how they helped raise each other's children and took care of one another in times of struggle.

The fact that many of the members have been singing in the choir for over thirty years is a testament to the camaraderie and cohesiveness created through their regular rehearsals and performances. Many current members talk about feeling blessed to have had the opportunity to be part of the choir and emphasize how meaningful it is to them to share the Word of God through sacred music. They view it as their mission to bring a message of hope and love to the community through song. They emphasize the joy of sharing sacred music with members of other church families, making new friends, and learning to accept others as they are. Some report that crossing some of those boundaries has broadened their lives.

Seeing the joy their singing brings to audiences is gratifying for the choir members and reinforces their commitment to providing this music for Athens. One current member is the daughter of former members. She says that as a young girl she would travel with her parents when the choir performed at various events. She notes that hearing the songs that were sung by the choir then—some of which the choir still performs—brings joyful memories of growing up in the choir community. The fact that the choir has such a lasting effect on its members is a testimony to its mission.

Some members noted that this choir is stricter than church choirs, and I know they really mean that James is stricter! But this has not dissuaded them. They know James is sincere in praising God, and they describe their Tuesday evening rehearsals as food for the soul. They also note that after performances they are amazed at the effect their performance had on the audience. Audiences always have prolific praise and gratitude for the choir. Choir members say they have seen spirits lifted, broken hearts healed, and lives changed after hearing the message of the music. For all members, it has been an extreme joy to belong to this musical family and the experience will always be dear to their hearts.

James' daughter Tiara writes of her life with the choir,

> Since my Daddy is the founder of the choir, I honestly don't know life without the Voices of Truth. My mother says that I sang at the very first concert, so I guess that makes me an original member. I was three years old at the time. I have a unique point of view of the ins and outs of the group. I applaud those who have remained dedicated to exalting the name of the Lord through song.

Athens Voices of Truth c. 2004.

Choir members Alfreda Ballard, Aurelia Scott, Brenda Bellinger, Eric Johnson, Joelene Cherry.

The End of an Era

James has decided that after the Voices of Truth celebrate their fortieth anniversary in 2019, they will still perform when asked, but regular Tuesday evening rehearsals will cease. He is pleased with what the Voices of Truth have accomplished and grateful for the blessing of belonging to this community of musicians, singers, and audiences. He says although the choir has had its ups and downs, the group never lost sight of its purpose. He hopes the choir has touched lives, uplifted those who needed it, brought hope to the dispirited and joy to the weary, and given people a reason to keep going. James says he will accept requests for the choir to sing at special events or invitations from family and friends of choir members to perform for their churches or special occasions. But the group will no longer meet regularly to rehearse. James says, "Forty years is enough. But I have been richly blessed."

CHAPTER 11

Work, Family, and Church: 1990s to Present

As James' dream of creating a community choir was finally achieved and the Voices of Truth became well established, his life seemed to hit an even stride. With work at Dairy Pak, two children to raise, responsibilities at church, choir rehearsals every week, and various commitments in the community, life was full and James felt blessed. There was a consistency and calm to this phase of his life as he and Rosa continued to work, raise their children, and support one another.

However, as the truism goes, the only certainty in life is change. The next disruption in their lives came in 1999, when Dairy Pak was sold and its employees were told the company was downsizing. Unfortunately, James was one of the employees they let go. However, always being able to see the glass half full, he says he was actually among the "lucky" ones. Since he had worked there for over twenty years and had been a valuable and steadfast employee, they gave him an early retirement package. This softened the blow of losing his job, but at fifty-eight years old, James was far from through working and pondered what he would do next.

James the Business Man

James' first thought was to go back to teaching, so he signed up to substitute in the Clarke County Schools. He realized fairly quickly this was not a good fit for him after so many years out of the classroom. As he contemplated how he might be gainfully employed he wondered if he could do something that would allow him to be his own boss. After many years of working for others, James relished the idea of a job that would provide him independence and flexibility.

So one day he decided he would try cutting lawns for a living. He was not sure this was his ultimate calling, but he was going to give it his all. He bought a lawn mower and started at his mother's house. He had business cards and flyers printed up and passed them out wherever he went. His brother, Leroy, Jr., was only too happy to help get this fledgling business off the ground, and James says that through Leroy's generosity he was able to buy his first U-turn mower and an eight-foot trailer. James says he had to ask various people how to use his new equipment as he acquired it, since he had never worked with this type of machinery before.

His business grew by word of mouth and his ability to self-promote was a huge asset. It also helped that James is a perfectionist and the jobs were always immaculately completed. Clients began calling and he soon had a list of regular accounts. Before long, he purchased an Exmark turnaround and a walk-behind mower, which necessitated the purchase of a sixteen-foot trailer and a larger pick-up truck. He learned quickly that this type of work is more than just cutting grass, and he soon added hedge cutting, leaf collection, gutter cleaning, flower planting, mulching, and pine straw spreading to his list of services.

Once he had twenty regular clients, James realized he would need help to keep up with the schedule. He knew that men looking for manual labor jobs would gather by Home Depot. So James joined the legions of employers who picked up workers from the store parking lot. James says there is a unique culture to this method of getting day-laborers and he had to learn the process. He would pull up to the end of the road by Home Depot in his truck and trailer and immediately men would ask him how much he was paying. James would respond with an amount that he thought was a fair hourly wage, but many of the men would just say "No" and begin to walk away. He would then offer a bit more and some would still say "No." This could go on back and forth for a while before he hit on an amount that someone was willing to take.

For James, the employees negotiating their wage was new and surprising. He also said that no one really wanted to work for less than a full eight- or ten-hour day. If he said he just needed help for a couple of hours, it was harder to get someone to come with him. He knew, however, that he would never commit to anyone for more than that day of work, so he could see how it went and if it would work out with any particular person. As many of the men were not native English speakers, James was worried that the language barrier would prevent him from being able to communicate what he needed them to do. But he also says that the men didn't ask what the work was; they just wanted to settle on the hourly wage before they agreed to hop in the truck.

After many years of having a revolving roster of helpers, James finally found one man who was a perfect fit for him and the work. This man stayed with James for over six years, only moving on when he was offered a regular construction job that paid a higher wage. No matter who was working for James, however, he always required thorough, meticulous, high-quality work from them. If they were not serious about quality, they didn't last long. As James said, "I was not mean to my helpers, but I was mean about the work."

Because many of the men James hired over the years were immigrants and his best and longest-term worker was from Mexico, James reflected on the realities of the changing nature of the U.S. workforce. He observed:

> We are going to have to learn it from the White House to my house that the culture of the United States has changed. We may not all agree with this but you have to give these people the opportunity. If a man wants to work and he is here, let him work. You can't run these people out of the country. What would happen if we round all these people up and throw them out, who is going to do the work? Of course, I am not for letting criminals or drug dealers in, but the men I have worked with . . . they are not those folks. They talk to me about their family,

the bills they have to pay, the things their kids need, just like anyone. Everybody's got issues, debts, worries. Trouble goes everywhere. But they are just trying to make a life and do right.

Just recently, after James lost his best employee, he began to partner with some other independent small businessmen to collaborate on some of their bigger jobs, helping each other out while continuing to serve their regular customers. Some of these other businessmen have equipment or skills that James does not and vice versa, so the collaboration benefits all of them. He hopes this can continue for the remainder of his working days. Still, when he needs extra hands for a large job, he makes the drive to Home Depot to pick up a willing worker.

Since becoming his own boss, James never complains about the work, the heat, or the long hours of his employment. He is meticulous and determined that all his customers be satisfied with the results. His philosophy is, "If you commit to doing something, you do the absolute best job you can do, and you can feel pride in it no matter the work."

James says he will continue doing yard care as long as he can, perhaps stopping when he turns 80 years old. He still has the strength, drive, work ethic, and desire to stay physically active. On one particularly hot day, I asked him how he does it, especially in the summer. He responded, "I just get up, do the job, and come home and take a shower. There's not a lot else to it. You just do what you have to do." It is this spirit that has propelled James, day after day, throughout his life.

Family

Over the last twenty-five years, as the Smith children grew up and began careers of their own, James and Rosa settled into a new routine while remaining active and engaged in their family, church, and community. Tiara graduated from Clarke Central High School in 1994 and matriculated at Spelman College. After earning her degree in political science, Tiara returned to Athens to work and attend graduate school at the University of Georgia, earning a Master's degree in

Tiara, Rosa, James,
and Rick Smith, c. 2000.

education. At about this time, Rick graduated from Clarke Central and entered Morehouse College. Yet while James and Rosa were intermittent empty nesters during this time, the Smith home remained a nexus of activity, due to the frequent comings and goings of their children, friends, family members, choir members, and members of their church community.

Rosa retired from teaching in 2006 and was happy to have more time for her hobbies and her duties at church. She continues to work with the Food Ministry, cooking for the homeless and for evening worshippers every Wednesday at Ebenezer. She is also a deaconess and coordinates activities for families, especially around the holidays. She is a loving and dedicated grandmother who frequently cares for Rick and his wife Rhondolyn's son Jameson.

James is always grateful when his siblings are able to gather. They enjoy coming together as often as possible and have had some wonderful reunions. During these gatherings they always made sure to take a family photo. When their mother Vallie died in 2003 and

The Smith family, l to r: Leroy, Jr., Willie Mae, James, Vallie, Joseph, Christine, and Frank, c. 2000.

they gathered for her funeral at First A.M.E. Church, they realized that the time when they could all be together was growing shorter. But they continue to stay close and keep each other appraised of what is happening in their lives. James notes that although they have each walked a different path in life, he cherishes the love and support he has received from each of them through the years.

In 2009, James attended his 50th high school class reunion. He was happy to see that so many of his classmates were still around and he enjoyed catching up with everyone. As one of the last classes to attend the old Athens High and Industrial School at Reese and Pope, they had cherished memories of the old school while also reaping the benefits of attending a brand-new school when they were soph-omores. And while the old school had been torn down, some AHIS alumni created a website to memorialize their time there (www.theye-llowjacket.com), which features some photos, a brief history, and a few reminiscences.

Church Involvement at Ebenezer Baptist Church, West

When James and Rosa decided to move to Ebenezer Baptist Church, West in the early 1980s, they were eager to volunteer for various committees and responsibilities at their new church home. The pastor of Ebenezer, Rev. Dr. Winfred M. Hope, asked James to serve in several different capacities from the very beginning. One was to be the director of the Baptist Training Union, which met every Wednesday evening at the church. The BTU is a longstanding part of the African American Baptist Church and a foundation of its adult Christian education curriculum. It was designed to instruct church members in the basic beliefs of the faith, church doctrine and history, their responsibilities as members, and church policies and procedures. James' job was to make sure the teachers got the training they needed and were assigned to the various sections they were to teach.

One year, Rev. Hope also asked James to head up the Men's Day Program. Some older members were skeptical that this newcomer could do the job and do it well. Little did they know James Smith. James says that it often takes some time to be accepted and welcomed when people are used to doing the same thing year after year. Change is hard, but James never took it personally when someone criticized the way he did things. He just kept doing the best he knew how.

Due to his experience with the construction of the C. D. Wilkerson Education Center, James was also asked to work on tasks related to rebuilding the Ebenezer sanctuary. The main portion of the church was razed in 2009 and reconstructed on the same footprint as the old one. James thinks there were a variety of reasons they had to tear down the old sanctuary, including the presence of asbestos. James was in charge of organizing crews of volunteers to take on tasks that would help the church save money on the reconstruction. James recalls that one especially arduous task was removing every pew and either selling them or finding out where they could be donated. The pews had been in the sanctuary since it was built in 1938 and James says it was no easy task to wrench them up from the floor.

Ebenezer Choir

Dr. Anthony Rucker has been the choir director at Ebenezer Baptist Church, West for over 30 years. James sang with the choir for several years after joining the church in the early 1980s, but once the

Voices of Truth became his focus, he knew it was best if he stepped down from his church choir. He knew if he could not devote all his attention to the choir, he would feel he was shortchanging the group and himself. However, he was asked if he would still serve as the hymn director each Sunday morning at Ebenezer. James has been performing this function at his church for nearly 30 years now and considers it an honor. Dr. Rucker leads the choir in other types of music, but James has been grateful for the opportunity to lead them in the hymns. The Ebenezer choir is accompanied by musicians Ms. Dierdra Stroud and Ms. Monique Darrison.

James as Deacon

James has been a deacon at Ebenezer for many years. The qualifications, duties, and responsibilities of a deacon in the Baptist Church are spelled out in 1 Timothy.

> [1] Here is a trustworthy saying: Whoever aspires to be an overseer desires a noble task. [2] Now the overseer is to be above reproach, faithful to his wife, temperate, self-controlled, respectable, hospitable, able to teach, [3] not given to drunkenness, not violent but gentle, not quarrelsome, not a lover of money. [4] He must manage his own family well and see that his children obey him, and he must do so in a manner worthy of full respect. [5] (If anyone does not know how to manage his own family, how can he take care of God's church?) [6] He must not be a recent convert, or he may become conceited and fall under the same judgment as the devil. [7] He must also have a good reputation with outsiders, so that he will not fall into disgrace and into the devil's trap. [8] In the same way, deacons are to be worthy of respect, sincere, not indulging in much wine, and not pursuing dishonest gain. [9] They must keep hold of the deep truths of the faith with a clear conscience. [10] They must first be tested; and then if there is nothing against them, let them serve as deacons. [11] In

the same way, the women are to be worthy of respect, not malicious talkers but temperate and trustworthy in everything. [12] A deacon must be faithful to his wife and must manage his children and his household well. [13] Those who have served well gain an excellent standing and great assurance in their faith in Christ Jesus.

1 Timothy: 1-13

In describing his duties as a deacon at Ebenezer, James noted that caring for families is a priority.

> Supporting families is the biggest part. You help directly sometimes and indirectly sometimes. Each family in the church is assigned to a deacon. That deacon is responsible for making sure the family is okay. A deacon may not necessarily do something for them personally, but you need to care for the well-being of the family. You can let the pastor know if they have needs that are not being met, whatever they are. Deacons are not to get in the families' business but to support their needs. I have ten families that I care for. This responsibility is an awesome way to encourage and keep in touch with members of the congregation.

James explained the full embrace of democracy at Ebenezer. All of the church's major decisions are voted on by the entire membership. The congregation votes on everything from the budget to hiring a new pastor. Decisions are made during called business meetings held in the evening at the church. There must be a quorum present and the congregation votes in person.

James explains that the trustees of Ebenezer are responsible for the financial health of the church. They make all the suggestions for the budget and take care of all aspects of the buildings and grounds. At one time you could be both a deacon and a trustee at Ebenezer, but it has since been decided to prohibit members from serving in both capacities so they can dedicate themselves fully to one position. James

Ebenezer Baptist Church, West wished Rev. Dr. Hope well upon his retirement, August 2019.

says this ensures that no one person is taking on too much responsibility and that everyone can concentrate on doing one job well.

Rev. Dr. Hope retired in 2019 after serving as head pastor at Ebenezer for 40 years. The church is seeking a new pastor and the congregation is confident it will find someone who can both carry on its rich traditions and also inject new energy and ideas. James has never been afraid of change and looks forward to seeing what lies ahead for his church family.

James and Retirement

James remains fully engaged in his work, his family, and his church. And while he says he will consider retiring from work in a couple of years, this does not mean he will be sitting still. It is simply not in his nature to be idle. However, at the very least, Tuesday evenings will become his own after the Voices of Truth 40th anniversary concert in November 2019, when the choir ceases regular rehearsals. James will undoubtedly find many ways to stay busy, although he has certainly earned some time to rest.

CHAPTER 12

Character, Values, and Beliefs

"Not everybody can be famous but everybody can be great
because greatness is determined by service. You only need
a heart full of grace and a soul generated by love."
– Dr. Martin Luther King, Jr.

For as long as humans have contemplated their reason for being and the nature of existence, there has been debate about how to assess a person's character. Who decides whether a person has been virtuous? What constitutes a "life well lived"? How do you assess the value of an individual's accomplishments? How does society determine what is worthy of recognition, praise, or veneration?

From the ancient philosophers to the many authors, educators, and leaders who have contemplated these questions through the ages, much has been written about how to appraise someone's worth. In attempting to answer these questions, probably the most widely read and frequently quoted text in our culture is the Bible, whose Old and New Testaments contain numerous verses devoted to the expectations of a good, just, and righteous person. And yet, it remains for each individual to choose for themselves what kind of mark, impression, or legacy their life will leave. While fame or fortune are two of the ways our society measures a person's worth, for most people it is the manner in which they have journeyed through good times and bad, their strength in enduring challenges and achieving triumphs, their experiences of pain and of joy, and the manner in which they treated their fellow human beings that will provide the ultimate evidence of their character.

Most of us lead lives out of the spotlight and far from the effects of fame. We struggle with everyday circumstances and strive to live our lives as best we can, working hard at our jobs; trying to raise our children to be good people and good citizens; being grateful for our health, friends and family, and a roof over our heads; and hoping that no great tragedy will befall us or those we love. And yet, these lives are no less worthy of remembrance and appreciation than are those marked by fame or fortune.

Thus while James is not "famous" in the traditional sense, neither did he strive for that type of recognition. His life, however, stands as an example for others precisely because of the long and winding road he has traveled through this earthly existence. He has weathered many storms, found reasons to rejoice, taken occasionally questionable turns, and always lived each day to its fullest. Ultimately, he has found his way, and with it a measure of peace along the path he has trod.

James is a complicated man with many facets, but in many ways he is also an open book. He is firm but never cruel, demanding yet loving, serious but with a keen sense of humor. He embodies both confidence and humility in an exquisite balance. Gregarious and thoughtful by turns, he has strong convictions and is comfortable speaking his mind, but he also knows how to listen. He grew up in some of the most challenging times for African Americans, especially in the South, but despite facing his own hardships he never lost his compassion for others. He never dwells on the past, nor does he live for the future; instead, he is grounded in today. He strives to make each day the best possible, regardless of what is happening in the world. His focus is on how he can do right and be a good person with the time he has been given.

James is not without flaws and he readily acknowledges his own shortcomings. He can be harsh, and at times his bluntness rubs people the wrong way. He is sometimes impatient and can be critical. He will tell you exactly what he thinks, leaving no uncertainty about where he stands.

James is a man who grew up in a difficult time, with limited resources, who fought every step of the way to make something of himself. Perhaps for this reason, he is not tolerant of "half-stepping," nor will he allow others to make excuses for not giving their best. He may become frustrated with people's actions or attitudes, but he never takes that frustration out on anyone. He does not believe it is helpful to let people get away with just going through the motions in life and will demand excellence.

James has never blamed anyone else for his limitations or expected anyone to forgive his trespasses without his true contrition. Despite his humble beginnings, he has never depended on others for his own sense of well-being. Though he can become angry at the way certain people behave, his anger never leads to harm, nor does he hold grudges.

James is not judgmental, but can be piercing in his assessment of others' actions. He believes that prejudice is born of ignorance and that ignorance must be addressed through education and an open mind. He has friends from all walks of life and of all races, all professions, and all faiths. He assiduously treats everyone the same. He is proud of his ability to get along with anyone and says with a sly smile:

> I can mingle with anyone. I can mingle with Obama or with the homeless. I can deal with the alcoholic or the minister. That doesn't mean I am going to stay with any one of them, but I know something of what they are going through, where they came from, and what is important to them. And if I don't know, I can listen and learn.

Reflecting on how he was raised, James says, "My upbringing taught me not to forget where I came from. But what is most important about knowing where you came from is knowing where you are going." He says he learned early that "no one owes you anything. You have to work hard for what you want in life and you have to do it the right way."

James has never let anything from the past hinder his ambition or purpose. Part of that purpose was to raise his children to believe they could do and be anything in life. However, he also emphasized that success would not just be handed to them; they had to work hard and persevere in difficult times. James recognized the importance of talking with his children about everything: the good and the bad, the joys and the challenges. He emphasized that they always had choices about which direction they went. He understood the importance of being honest with them, of loving and nurturing them, while also reminding them that they are not the center of the universe and that nothing worth having is achieved without hard work.

Growing up in the Jim Crow South in a family that faced a variety of struggles, James recognized that he had the ability to choose how he responded to challenges. He knows he could have taken a different path, and he is thankful to have drawn strength from small successes along the way, the support of his teachers, a loving mother, and an innate drive to achieve. He is always grateful and punctuates his conversations with many exclamations of, "I have been blessed."

James loves to talk. Oh my, how James loves to talk, but he is also an amazing listener. He is sometimes surprised by the things I remember from our conversations. He is humble in that he often doesn't expect people to pay much attention to what he says. When he would expound on one topic or another, often getting off track from our original conversation, I loved just listening to the cadence and depth of his voice. He can convey so much with just a few words, condensing complicated and nuanced points into clear and succinct ideas. James does not just speak, but often declares with vehemence. He can become very animated when talking of things about which he cares deeply. His intensity, however, is frequently punctuated by self-deprecating jokes. He can be as insightful about his own character as any critic.

James' faith is his rock, his family is his solace, and his friends are his ballast. James' life has not been easy, but he believes that life's struggles are a test of one's faith and commitment to doing the right thing. James believes in the importance of prayer, meditation, and Bible reading every morning because "the Devil can sneak up and ruin your life." But he also believes in people and that only good can come from joining together to do something worthwhile.

James believes it was part of his destiny to cross paths with all the people he has met in his life. He is especially grateful for all the young people he has met and mentored, and hopes his support and encouragement has had some small part in helping them find their way. He knows that his life has been deeply enriched by the people he has mentored, befriended, and led.

> I think about all the people I have met and worked with and I don't know if I did anything for them, but if I hadn't gone toward them, to tell them about what they could be doing, they might not have heard the message. Only the Lord saves, but someone has to lead you there.

James firmly believes that one must always be ready for change . . . in life, work, family, and community. He reflects on years of seeing "that often people will say they want something new, but then when it happens, they just cling to the old." He doesn't believe in throwing out the old, but he does understand the importance of accepting change. People have to be prepared to change their thinking, how they look at things, and what they're doing. "If the old works, keep it. But if it doesn't, be ready to move on." However, he knows how hard it is to bring about change.

> People are set in their ways and if you move too fast, you are going to upset people. You have to look at the total picture and say, "Let's sit down and figure out why we are doing what we are doing," especially if you aren't getting the results you want.

James is wary of people who are arrogant or think they know everything. He doesn't believe that anyone knows everything, even those with advanced degrees or years of experience. He does believe that life experience in addition to a formal education can give you a seat at the table, but also that you must be humble in how you present what you know.

In many churches, civic groups, and other organizations, James has seen how having a closed mind toward someone or something new prevents people from moving forward. He asks, "If a group decides one thing but you supported another, why not accept it, jump on board, and make the new direction even better?" He also believes that strong leaders are needed, but have to earn their following. "You can't just tell people what to do. They have to see a reason to follow your lead. The way you can tell if someone is sincere is to look at whether they do what they say. Or are they just talk?"

James feels we are in a new day in this country. He believes that some institutions and some organizations aren't willing to change with the times and as a result leave lots of people, especially young people, behind. He gives the example of a church not reaching out to youth and meeting them at least partway on their terms. James doesn't really like rap music, but he realizes that it is a language that young people speak and if you want them to hear a message, maybe you need to speak to them in their vernacular. If they tune you out because you aren't willing to walk across the bridge to meet them, there is no conversation to be had and consequently there is no coming together. He says this is true in politics as well. As long as people are shouting at one another and not even trying to listen, we won't move forward. He says, "Things have got to change. You have to meet people where they are in order to get to some agreement."

At seventy-eight years young, James says he is still working on being a better person. He describes his younger self as wild and impulsive, someone who would say whatever came to mind without caring what people thought of him. But he soon realized that this kind of bluster was not the best way to approach situations or people. He says he keeps more things to himself now and listens more. Whereas he used to want everything to be done to his high standards, he realizes now that not everyone believes his ideas are always right or good. However, he remains committed to never doing anything halfway. If he is in charge of something or is even just a participant, he is "going to do the best I can. I know I can count on me."

James recognizes that life is short and no one knows how many years the Lord will give them. But he says if you examine your own shortcomings and do all you can to be the best you can be, it won't matter when your life ends. James knows that he, like everyone, is flawed, and believes the best thing you can do is examine your intentions, monitor your actions, and lead with your heart. He understands there is only so much one person can do in their life but he is proud of his accomplishments, his family, and his dedication to his church and his community. He has brought joy and inspiration through directing the Voices of Truth and has helped many young people grow into the responsible citizens they are today.

Community Engagement and Hope for the Future

When James and I talk about the high poverty level in Athens, the children we know who are struggling, and the challenges facing families and schools in our community, we realize that these circumstances can't easily be changed. There is a great deal of hopelessness that goes hand in hand with poverty and James believes that people have to want change in order for things to get better. He thinks that too many families have lost hope, and are so disheartened and discouraged that they struggle to keep putting one foot in front of the other. For those who have unstable housing, are under- or unemployed, have insufficient education, lack medical care, and possess few job skills, it is difficult to see a way up and out.

James' view is that many issues begin in the home and that things won't get better unless the needs of the whole family are addressed. He believes that if more churches and other organizations or individuals who have resources work with families, they are more likely to feel supported and uplifted during difficult times. He believes that churches have an important role to play in providing a support system for people in need. James knows that many of the churches and other non-profits in Athens are doing good work in the community, but he would like to see more churches reach out to people in need on a daily basis.

James worries about young people, especially young Black men. He wants to find ways to inspire them to do as much as they can with their lives. He bemoans the violence he sees every day on the news, and says he can't understand this level of brutality. He says that even if you are desperate, poor, and feeling hopeless, you don't have to take someone else's life. It just doesn't make sense to him.

James says he wants to ask everyone, "What is your ministry and what have YOU done?" He acknowledges, "Every last one of the men in the E. L. Terrell Ensemble could have gone on and become what they wanted to be without me. But at least I told them I was concerned. I told them, I am here for you. I care about you." He wishes more individuals would hold themselves accountable for what they can do in the community.

James also acknowledges how challenging it is to raise children today. He says, "Thank goodness I had a good mate to help me raise our children." He talks with his family members, many of whom work with children, about their shared and ongoing concerns. And while James is not sure how to resolve the problems he sees, he knows the community will have to work together to find solutions.

A Conversation with James about His Faith and Core Beliefs

James' faith is a huge part of who he is, and forms the bedrock of his life. I wanted to dig deeper into what it means to him, its evolution, how it sustains him, how it influenced the way he raised his children, and what he hopes others can take from his faith.

How did your faith evolve? When did you feel your faith meant more than just going to church every Sunday?

Well, really it started when I was a boy, and I was putting [my faith] into action but not knowing it. When I was helping my great aunt and her blind son, I was doing work that Christians ought to be doing but were not always doing, even though I was very young at that time. Also, everything that we had learned as children, at home and going to church before we knew what church really meant, something was still being built on the inside. There is more to be done than just going to church, singing in the choir, fellowshipping with brothers and sisters. Because I saw the needs not only in my family, but also needs in other folks. And as I learned more about the Bible and what Jesus really did, in my heart was a feeling that I needed to do something more. And I guess that was when something in me started telling me to work with young people. You need to sacrifice more for others or think about others, and sacrifice sometimes to help others move to the next level.

My faith has always been strong, from the time I went off to school. I knew it was the Lord who really took care of me. I was young and dumb but I can always remember that I thought of my faith when I wanted to do some things that I knew I shouldn't be doing. As I grew older, from decade to decade, my faith just got stronger and stronger.

Now, a lot of times when you meet different folks it changes you. My faith really got stronger when I met Rev. Haynes. He is so different than I am but he is strictly about what you ought to be doing for the Lord and for others. And in each situation, I saw him in action. He was not necessarily the first person I saw walking the walk, because I have met several folks, like Rev. Wilkerson at First A.M.E and different other folk there and at Ebenezer, who did as well.

But Rev. Haynes was special, and some things I saw him do were special. He took me to a job he had at a nursing home in Gainesville where he played the piano for those folks. And they loved him to death. Then when he became pastor of Springfield Baptist Church in Comer, those members who were in a nursing home and didn't have a way to come to church, I saw him pick these people up and bring them from the nursing home and carry them back home after the service. I saw the Lord moving in the life of this man. He did several things, but especially to see him go and pick these people up before he would preach on Sunday morning and then when he was finished preaching, he would take them back home, was really something.

So my faith has always been strong; I believe in helping others. I believe in giving back, not necessarily being on the receiving end, because when you give you are blessed. And with Richard it got stronger and stronger because of the things I saw him do and the way I saw him live.

Were there other people who influenced your understanding of your faith?

I have always tried to be open and expose myself to other people's thinking. So many different folks—parents, school teachers, preachers, Sunday school teachers—helped me understand. During the time I was in public schools, the laws were not as strict about people talking about religion. So my teachers were important to my education in more ways than just the basics. Even in these latter years of my life I have been involved in and attended lots of seminars (some at the state meetings of the General Missionary Baptist Convention of Georgia) and different sessions and workshops on music and so forth, where I learned more about what my faith was telling me.

Was there a difference in your faith or your thinking once your children were born and you had a child to raise up?

Not necessarily changed, just now I had two! The Bible says, "Raise up a child in the ways they should go and when he is old he will not depart from it." Always when you have your children you have to think about sacrificing. And I have never given my life like Jesus, but I know there are some things you have to sacrifice to raise a child.

What helped hold your family together?

Teaching. I always taught my children. I didn't wait until I got them to Sunday school or to school. I have teaching materials at home. Bibles at home. Things that I have experienced and learned at home. I shared the things that I had learned, daily. Especially on weekends. We had to sit and study the Sunday school lesson before Sunday school. I was stricter about studying Proverbs because it is the discipline chapter. My son says he doesn't preach from Proverbs now! He had enough of Proverbs growing up.

I am proud that my children haven't strayed from our faith. They didn't waver. In wavering (you learn this as you get older), sometimes you don't get back. And sometimes you do. But it is easier to just stay on course. Just keep following the teachings. Sometimes it might be hard and difficult, but once you've been taught, if you read it for yourself, exercise it, and practice it, then it is easier for you to stay on course.

There are some things we are told to do but our minds are like a seesaw. We know we ought to do it but we don't do it. Then we stray and get too far out there. You can get back, but it can be hard. It depends on the person and their mind. God gave everybody a mind. But you have to use your own mind; nobody can use it for you. I think my children are kind of independent in their thinking and they use their mind.

What would you like people to take from your steadfast, long-term commitment to your faith?

When you are born, when everybody, each person is born into this world, God has anointed them to do something. You just got to find out what it is. Maybe you find out in your younger days or you might be old like me before you find out what it really is. There is a calling on everybody's life.

Some folks think that there is a calling only on the life of a preacher. But each individual was born into the world just like the preacher; although he may have a calling to preach on his life, there is a calling for you to do something. You got to find out what your calling is. And instead of an individual worrying about someone else's calling, they need to talk to the higher power to find out what their purpose is in life. But bear in mind that whatever it is, it's not going to be easy.

Also, you need to find out or establish some goals. You may not meet them all or may not meet any of them, but you need to establish some and work on trying to meet them. I was reading in my meditation this morning that a man had 127 goals and at the age of 47 he had completed 103. And so I believe that you establish goals and stick with them. And don't just establish them and don't work on them. But complete at least one and then two and then when the hard times come you just have to pray. You have to believe in prayer. You have to trust God, you have to trust Him.

You also got to establish friends but you got to establish some positive friends. In my lifetime I had a whole lot of friends, some of them were negative and some were positive, but you got to think about the positive people to help you reach your goals. Not necessarily that they are there intertwined in what you are trying to do, but at least they won't be negative and always keep you down. Sometimes negative folks can cause you to stray. You can't listen to the negative folks. You can't listen to the folks about what you should be doing. You got to know for yourself.

Know who your God is and who you are going to serve and which direction you are going in regardless of what others say. I listen to a lot of folks going through difficult times, but I make my own decisions and I trust in God to see me through those decisions and I depend on Him to hold me up. He has held me up through some rough times or I could have gone down the wrong road.

What do you say to people about prayer? What do you say to people who feel that God doesn't answer their prayers?

You have to establish a relationship with Him and in doing that you must read the Word of God. He speaks to us through the Word. And if you don't pick up the Bible and read it, and pray to Him, you won't be able to recognize what he is saying.

I have learned through church, reading the Word, listening to preachers preach the Word, the Lord hears your prayer but that doesn't mean he answers every prayer. If you really go to the Lord humbly, pray to Him, not always asking but being thankful, have a thankful heart, call on Him yes, but really thank Him even that you breathe, even that you have achieved what you have achieved. You can thank Him for so many things, that you get up every day, you still can think, that you aren't sick, or if you are sick, he can heal you, all these kinds of things.

Be more grateful and then when you feel like maybe he didn't hear your prayer, I would ask, "Well, why do you think that?" You have to ask, Why do you think he didn't hear you? Not all prayers are answered immediately, but he will come on time. Trust in God and believe that he WILL do it. The answer will come. Waiting is hard. My patience has always been short on waiting on the Lord. I don't just want all my prayers answered, I want the situation fixed! My patience has been short but I learned to wait.

How important is forgiveness?

Forgiveness is also huge. It might be one of my weaknesses. I don't ever try to get even or get revenge, but I have always kept things in my mind. I remember things that people have done, not just to me but to others. But I had to learn to just let some things alone. Sometimes things are put on us for us to learn to wait but not to get back at someone. What we do, including me, we try to take matters in our hands that we should carry to Him and just leave them. And then our burdens will be lighter. Because the person who did something to us, they are all right cause they did it! But [their satisfaction in upsetting you] can keep you always in an [agitated] state of mind that you shouldn't be in and that can make them happy. But if you handle it the Lord's way, that can make you happy.

What do you think kept you on the right path in life?

My mother. In spite of the challenges, she was always encouraging. She always said, "You can do it" and "You can do better." And the things you do have, be grateful. From the big things to the little things. My mother taught me years ago, even in the little things, like you take what you have and make it look nice and it's enough. But my point is, she taught us and encouraged us to do these different things. And to stay on the straight path. We wavered, all of us, but we tried to stay on the path, and listen to her teaching.

And as I said earlier, all those kinds of things like not having things growing up, and being poor, and white people not being responsive to integration, and all that we lived through, I guess we just felt like we had to tough it out. We didn't worry about that. We just toughed it out. Also, as one [sibling] would see the older one move on, there was encouragement and help. Help from each other to move on.

That doesn't mean we didn't get discouraged. And many, many, many times we did. But we saw the need to just move forward. We had plenty of kinfolk who were poor. All our cousins, and other families that had more children than were in my family. But we saw the need to keep pushing. Some people thought my mother wanted her children to be better than others because she was doing things to help us to move forward, but she just wanted us to see the world and succeed and have better things. She sent us to school and she worked to do that. They don't know how hard she had to work at the poultry plant. So it wasn't easy but she wanted her children to do better. Not necessarily better than anybody else's children, just better in life. That was a good lesson.

In some ways, the little things kept me going. When you have little, you can have less if you don't do nothing to get more. Instead of going backwards, my thing was always to go forward. And from a young age, although we didn't know it then, by working hard we would move forward and do better. Because we were young and didn't know better, when we had to work hard, we just keep working. I know some people don't have the inner being to keep moving. They don't have the inner faith that things will get better for them.

What would you tell your younger self knowing what you know now?

Everything I just told you. [We laughed.] I would tell my younger self don't go down some of the paths that I took, that I walked. I should have walked a straighter path. All young people wander, but some are more focused. It's in them to be more focused.

I know my children have not been perfect, but their actions showed me that there was something in them that caused them to try to stay focused and on the right path. They made mistakes. But when I see the sickness [acts of senseless violence] in others, I just wonder, What are they thinking? We don't have the answer, but my thing is regardless of what your religion is, what you believe in, we better turn back to God. Cause that is the only thing that will save us. We tried everything else. We got to turn back. Regardless of what we believe in, you better turn back to something. When I hear about all these shootings, I would guess that there is no God in their lives.

Would you forgive your younger self some transgressions?

There are some things I wouldn't do over. I would go a different way. It has been difficult for me to forgive myself for the foolishness I have done in my younger days. But as I have learned more about my faith and what the Lord would have me do, I can more easily now forgive myself for everything I have done. Because the Lord will forgive you. And not only forgive myself but to forgive others, because even if they did me wrong, I have to forgive them because Jesus forgave them. And I got to love my enemies. It's not that I know I have enemies, but if you live in this world, you do have them. I had to learn to forgive.

Do you think people are basically good?

Everybody is born a sinner but saved by grace. And so I am saved. I am going to heaven regardless. Not that I can do whatever I want, but the Lord will forgive you. Once you are old enough to know your sins are wrong, you can't just do whatever you want. You have to know the difference. But once you acknowledge the Lord and Savior Jesus Christ, you are saved. And you must be baptized.

What about people who call themselves religious but do wrong?

I don't know about those people. I don't have the answer. But, they can't just "call themselves religious." You got to know. You got to know that you are saved. I know in Romans where in order to be saved you must acknowledge the Lord and Savior Jesus Christ and be baptized in his name. You got to know what you are and who you are. The things I have learned have caused me to know who I am and what I believe in and who I believe in and what direction I am going in.

What would you want to say to young people, especially young Black men, when they feel discouraged or angry or like there is no hope?

That's the thing that the Black boy must get in his mind and get in his soul, is that there is hope. And that sometimes while they are looking for other things, they need to be looking for the hope. And hope is their future. A Black kid, any kid, can be whatever they want; they have the opportunity. Things are better than when I was coming up. The world is better, although we have our problems. The United States is better. But you got to find out what your calling is and pursue it.

You can't just sit around and cry about what the government is doing or not doing or that you are poor. I was poor! I'm still poor! There's no making excuses for being poor. Excuses are not important. Anybody can make excuses, but you got to do something. I don't believe in using the word *can't* when you're supposed to be using the word *can*. I *can*, instead of I *can't*. Or saying, so-and-so is keeping me from doing something. So you find out what your purpose is, pursue it, set goals, and do it. Sometimes your goals are going to fall short. Your ambitions are going to be short. All those things may keep you from reaching some of your goals, but you can reach goals if you pursue them.

Another thing Black boys need to do is get their minds straight. Regardless of what they think of us who go to church, they need to go to church. Young people got to get into an environment and be a part of something where you can share your ups and your downs. You might have a vision and somebody might be a part of that team or group or church that you are a part of who can help you pursue that vision.

We just had Rev. Hope's fortieth anniversary celebration luncheon. And he's retiring so we were honoring him. There were over five hundred people at the house. The most meaningful thing that was said to everyone there was one of his daughters said, "Y'all helped us [Rev Hope's children] to be what we are. And just like you all helped us when we came [to Ebenezer] and we were young, this new preacher who is coming in has three small children; do the same for them."

So many people talked about all that Dr. Hope has done and that's fine. He did. But his daughters were grateful for what the congregation had done for them. Her statement was fitting for just this. For what young boys need today. She told us to help this man [the new pastor] to raise his children. We all got to help raise all our children.

Hope is the answer. Belief that you can be something. Ask yourself, Is it that I want to stay in poverty? That isn't going to solve the problems. You'll still be waiting. It's been going on for so long. If you're going to wait that's just like saying I'm going to wait to go worship. I am going to wait till everything gets right. I'm not going to school this year. I'm just going to wait until it gets right. Unh uh! You can't wait. You can wait but don't expect that this thing is going to get cleared up before you do anything. So get up off of your behind, go to church, go to school, and do right.

I taught my children to go to school and do right there. Don't go disrupting, cussing, fighting. I didn't even expect them to do those things anyway; I didn't have to tell mine, but I mentioned these things because I knew they might see that, be in a classroom with that. But I told them you don't have to do that. Get your work done. That's your only job.

There are a lot of children who need tutoring and there are people and places who do tutor. I would say to that child, "Don't just sit there and not understand. You got to go find help. Go to somebody and tell them, I need help. They aren't coming to you. You got to find that help to get out of that situation." That's what I would tell them. But you gotta make a move. And I would say, Your parents might not go to worship. It might not be one of those things that they do. May not be in your family. But you can make that decision if you want to do better and get out of poverty. Athens has one of the highest poverty rates in the country. It's shameful. But there is hope.

What are your greatest hopes for your grandson Jameson?

That he continues to grow, to be a solid child, a thinking child, like he is now. That he will listen to his parents. Honor his mother and his father that his days might be long. That he will stay focused. That he will watch and see what others are doing and the things that are wrong, don't do them. Find out what the right things are. I want him to grow up to be a responsible teen. Learn to work. Regardless of what anybody says, you got to work. And grow up to be able to succeed in high school. Go on to college and do as well and choose a profession and come out and be the man he ought to be in his life.

What do you think keeps you going? What keeps you getting up every day?

First thing is I have to pay for my truck. Then I quit. I gotta do that regardless. [We laughed.]

But really, as long as I am healthy and the Lord has given me strength and I am in my good mind I want to keep going. I don't want to sit around and lie around here. I still see some things I want to help my children to do, although they are not asking me for anything. I want my grandson to have a bright and somewhat easier future than his dad. So my grandson, my children, my wife keep me going. They aren't pushing me to do anything. But the Lord gives me strength to do things. I am happy about doing. I don't want to be a person who is remembered by, "he just sat down." I would love for them to say, "he is one who really got up."

You see, the teachings over the years that I have heard and seen, and I still hear folks preaching and talking about them, and I hear at conferences, folks say they want to be more like Jesus. But a lot of them [are] lazy. A lot of these things wouldn't have happened in the world if Jesus hadn't come. And if he wasn't involved with the people.

And so I see myself . . . I'm not like Jesus, I know that, I know

I'm still growing . . . but I don't want to say I didn't do nothing. And especially to help somebody when I had the opportunity to. Or I could have and I did not do. So those kinds of things keep me going. I just believe that from my childhood and what I was taught and how we worked, you have to keep getting up. What also keeps me going is I like to be happy in doing what I am doing. Whether it is working or working with the choir or worshiping, to see somebody else be successful, all these things make me happy.

Political Thoughts

I told James I wasn't sure I wanted to include anything in this book about politics, because I wanted to stay away from any topic that would detract from his life story or be polarizing. But as we talked over the months, I realized there was no separating him from his beliefs, convictions, and opinions. James has some unique perspectives on what is happening in our country and I think it is valuable to include a few of his thoughts on where we've come from, where we are, and where we are headed.

James thinks a lot about the state of the world and is fully engaged in keeping up with the latest news, but spends little energy worrying. He watches the news consistently and listens to all voices but draws his own conclusions. He is not really surprised at what is currently going on in our country, but rather than judging people, he tries to understand where they're coming from and why they're doing what they're doing.

James is not at all gullible and is not easily convinced by others' arguments or positions until he has reflected on all perspectives on his own. He is uncannily aware of who is sincere, who is manipulative, who is honest, who is lying, and who is on the right or the wrong side of history. He can become very animated when discussing the state of our country, but he also seems curiously open to just seeing where we are headed. He is not particularly judgmental and is calmly certain that "this too shall pass."

This is not to say James does not have very strong opinions

about many things; he absolutely does. But he seems able to compartmentalize what is happening, staying on top of what is going on while not giving in to despair. He may express dismay, but he knows there is only so much one can do to counter the larger forces shaping the direction in which our country is headed.

What do you see as the biggest challenges going forward for our country?

The first thing I would tell the people of the United States is you have to listen to your heart. You can't listen to nobody else's heart unless you're a doctor. Listen to your own heart. Read your Bible and ask the Lord, What should I do to make things better? No matter what anybody else is doing, what anybody else is saying. Cause we all are talking, but very few of us are listening. And the first person to listen to is yourself and your heart. What am I doing to make America, or my environment or my place, city, or state or whatever, where I live, to make it better?

Once I listen to myself, and hear from what the Lord has said to me in my heart, then I can express that to other people. We can't get nobody's heart right as individuals. We can't even get our own right. It takes the Lord's intervention to get us right if we really believe and read.

How did you feel when President Obama was elected?

James is especially animated when talking about the effect of having a Black President on where we are now. He believes it was a complete shock to many people when Obama was elected and many people were not happy about it. He recalls,

When Obama was elected, I think I cried. We watched it at church. It was something else. The U.S. was doing okay [moving forward] and then a Black President was elected. But there were folks who didn't want a Black man to be President, who didn't think it would ever happen. But he was elected to be President of these United States of America. That's a powerful goal. There were enough people in the U.S. to say that we want this man to lead us as President. Not as king, not as dictator or nothing else. Just as President of the United States.

Although his color is Black, he still achieved that goal. A lot of America didn't think that a Black man would achieve this milestone. But he did. With the help of others, not only Black, but it was all different races and nationalities that live here who are now citizens of the United States.

And even though [some people] tried everything in the world [to get rid of him] it didn't work, and some people are still angry. Some people wanted to find things to really to ruin him because he is Black. Only because he is Black. [People] thought, "We are going to *ruin* this Black man." But they couldn't find nothing. Don't think they weren't looking. But they couldn't find anything. People want the worst of what they can find on you.

[It seems like] there are so many people that still want America to be like it was in Jim Crow time and slavery time. All that was not discussed during the Obama years like it is now. But those folks were always out there. And that's why there is so much division now.

Nobody I know wants to go back to slavery. Nobody I know wants to go back to George Wallace. I was coming up during that time. Like I said, I was always taught to move forward like my family. Why do we want to go back to those days? And why would anyone support someone who wants that? I would be ashamed to support somebody with no morals. None. That's terrible. I just don't get it.

What we need to do is go back to what I said earlier and search your heart. Obama didn't do anything to [white people] directly. His policies and some of the laws that were made might have affected you, but he didn't bother you personally or directly. He was the President of all the people. He tried to work in that capacity. And some people are still mad.

But you know what, the country is moving on while you mad. But in order for us to move, we got to forgive. And we are not willing to do that. There is no way in the world that we can be sitting in our home watching TV and this madness is going on. This is bad for young people, Black and white. This is bad, y'all!

So let's get it together. And in order to get it together the Senate got to get right, the Republicans got to get right, the Democrats got to get right, the Independents, all of us. We got issues. We got attitudes. We got problems. But we got to sit down and listen to our own hearts and get ourselves right and then contribute something positive to this ongoing mess. That's what I would say.

What would you say to young Black men and women, considering our political climate?

That's the key to what Black children especially need to understand. You are wasting your time doing whatever you're doing if it's not right and if you're not moving in the right direction. Because there are people like this administration, not only the President but the whole shebang, different lawmakers who are going to set laws that are going to continue to set you back. You better have some hope, but you better start thinking about it. We'll be gone, but generations are going to be able to feel this same thing we talking about if all these things stay intact.

If somebody else gets in [as President], it doesn't matter if it is another white man or a Black or white woman, it doesn't make any difference, but if they are the same way [our current President is], you gonna be further behind. And if [our current President] stays in there you gonna be eight years behind already. If somebody just like him gets in after that you gonna be twelve behind and then if that person stays in then that's sixteen years you behind! But if somebody who gets in there and changes some of this stuff and gets us back on the right track, then you benefit. But you better get yourself right and get your house in order. Because you can be set behind so many years if you are not thinking about it now.

But know that [politicians] are working on keeping you down. And while you not thinking, they are working on it 'cause they know you not thinking. They know you not thinking about your insurance and how you gonna raise your children and what college you gonna send your children to. But once those years pass, and we still be in the same predicament or worse and we still be fussing and divided. But you had an opportunity yourself to set yourself right and start to get yourself ready.

Because you see a lot of the stuff he is showing to you . . . he's saying we fixing to send y'all back. If a man can get up anywhere and say "send them back," he won't say directly we gonna send Blacks back to Africa, but that's what he's saying. The man is telling you that. We gonna send you back to slavery time. Back to Jim Crow time. And you still sitting up here not thinking. Not trying to help yourself. So it's a big thing. Now there are people who are working on positive things in all communities. But the main thing is get your own house in order.

One last question. How do you want people to remember you when you are no longer here?

That's not a hard question, but it is a thoughtful question. Over the years I haven't really cared if anybody remembered me about anything. I told my wife that over the past few years I have been to enough funerals where people have remarks [about the deceased]. People get up and say all these things. Sometimes they have to put a time limit on it because it is too long. And I would say to my wife when I leave the funeral, "When I die just put me out on the street and let the cars run over me. Because don't nobody care." Well, not that they don't care, but in essence what I see and what I hear [at funerals], I say this is no good. People just be talking. When I die, don't have no remarks. And if they do and they say the wrong thing, I'm getting up, right there in the church service and the folk would know they lying, 'cause the man never got out of the casket before. So that's what I said.

Years ago, when you told me about writing my memoirs, even though I been saving stuff all my life, I didn't ever think of doing this. But you mentioned it and at the time I said, "Who cares?" Now, I do have a little green book that I carry with me that I always had that I write in. All the time just jotting down things I am thinking about. And then later on, after I thought about it and thought about it and then when we started working on this and I said, "Oh, we really are doing this!" I was surprised that you still wanted to do this.

But now that we are doing this, I want my children and especially my little grandboy to know me. I am blessed to have him. To know that I did live. I want folks to know what I cared about. I don't really care what people think of me, but that I did live a good life and I helped others. As I traveled this journey, I was glad I did the things I did for young people.

I want them to know in Athens that my calling was and is music. I love music. Especially with the Voices, I wanted to expose them to the best in music and all types of music. Not just to be stagnant and boiled down, doing one thing. And that whatever I did, I gave it my best. What has been most important to me is music and serving the Lord. I want people to remember that I was a servant for the Lord. I am not looking for anything. Nobody owes me anything. My funeral should just be music. Don't say nothin'. Just sing.

Appendix I

Testimonials from Family and Friends

From Childhood

James Russell and I have been friends for over 70 years. We were classmates from the first grade throughout high school graduation. It is a privilege to state that he is unquestionably my oldest friend.

Upon graduation from high school, James enrolled in college and I enlisted in the United States Air Force and subsequently pursued a career in retail management. Practically all of my adult life was spent in the Midwest and Northeast. Most of my family remained in Georgia and upon my frequent visits James was always there and made sure that we visited our old classmates and friends. He would drive over to my parents' house and pick me up and we would spend the day reminiscing with friends.

In 2018, I lost my daughter, Ashika, and even though she never resided in Georgia, I made the decision to have her funeral and burial in my hometown of Athens, Georgia. As usual James stepped up and handled practically all of the funeral services. I deeply appreciated the support and brotherly love that was provided by James and his lovely wife, Rosa.

My relationship with James is probably longer than most, but it is not unique. He has been a supporter of numerous individuals in pursuit of their life and/or spiritual goals. This support includes the mentoring of numerous minority students from the University of Georgia and other institutions of higher learning.

—Joe McCurry

From Siblings

My beloved brother James and I grew up as the two worker bees under the direction of Leroy Smith, Sr., our father. Our experiences were gained in a typical Southern segregated environment. We grew up on a farm. Farming from dawn to dusk with a short break for lunch. Warm weather, hot weather, rainy weather, we still worked the farm. Farming was the main occupation of white and Black families [in Clarke County]. In those days, we ploughed with mules, not tractors. The work was hard.

We attended totally segregated elementary, middle, and high schools. In fact, we often crossed paths with white students on the way to our schools as they were going to their schools. In those days, there were few school buses. Most of us walked to school. Discipline at school and at home was strict. Interestingly, there was very little talk about segregation. We accepted our "role." We had plenty of interaction with white residents because we and our parents worked for whites in their homes and businesses to supplement our family incomes.

James was always a gentle, kind soul. He has an amusing sense of humor. He is very smart and energetic. He never let "stuff" get under his skin. That is why he was able to effectively handle the conditions we grew up under.

James and I bonded well even though he is five years younger than me. James loves music. He has excelled as a choir director for many years. He is a great example of the many African Americans that did well in life despite growing up in a segregated environment.

–*Joseph Lee Smith*

The third child of six children, James and I are the closest two. I was born December and he in April a little more than a year later. James has always been very particular. He likes everything in place. He has always washed and ironed his own clothes. He can cook. He knows how to bake cakes–birthday and wedding cakes. They were delicious.

We lived in Virginia for a while. One Sunday we went to church with our Sunday School teacher. She left us! I didn't know the way back but we met up with a gentleman. James told him where we lived and he knew the way home. I got the whipping because we didn't tell our parents we were going to another church.

He has always been smart. We always shared because we were the closest two.

–*Willie Mae Smith*

The most complicated thing to write about my brother James is "Where do I begin?"

I got to know him when I became three years old. From that point on, I looked at him as my bigger brother. Things went along quite smoothly until I became six. At that time, I had to start working.

My job was hoeing cotton with James and our oldest brother Joseph. Turning six started my young working career with my brother James, which lasted about eight years.

Here are a few episodes that are still vivid memories to this day:

On the first day of my job hoeing cotton, I hoed half a row. My brother James told me, "Deddy (this is how we pronounced the name daddy) ain't going for that." Keep in mind the actual size of the rows were about a half of a mile. James was right. Sure enough my daddy whipped my butt. The next day I hoed a row and a half.

We were gathering firewood in the woods one day and somehow the ax broke. When Deddy found the ax and wanted to know who broke it, James and I both denied breaking it. With no one else in the woods but the two of us, Deddy determined that it was I who broke the ax. Because I kept denying that I did it, my daddy began whipping me. He whipped me so long I gave up, and said I broke the ax. He whipped me some more for telling a lie. Of course, you know I really did break the ax.

On very cold mornings when our daddy's 1949 Dynaflow Buick wouldn't crank, Deddy would call on James to hitch the mule to the car and pull it out of the driveway. Once in the street we would push the car down the hill so it would crank. Deddy told James to drive the mule and he told me to whip the mule's butt to make him pull the car.

My brother James bought his first car, which was a Buick. We went out to a nightclub and I slipped out and drove the car without his knowledge. As I was headed down the street a black cat crossed to the left. I politely put the car in reverse and backed it back up the street and took the car back to the club.

I could go on and on, but two things are stopping me. Number one, I don't like to write, and number two, I would fill the whole book.

The episodes I shared are true, but only told for your amusement. I was very much blessed and still am to have a brother like James. He's funny, serious, prompt, hardworking, can be mean, but really full of love. He is well known for his contribution to the community, namely he formed the Athens Voices of Truth Choir, which will celebrate their 40th anniversary this year. I was a member of the choir for several years but James was just like Deddy to me, too strict. I am looking forward to participating in the choir's anniversary celebration. I always admired the way he encouraged students to further their education. May God bless him.

—Frank Smith

———

I am the youngest sister to James. I have always looked at him as my big brother. I don't remember much about him as a child because he is six years older than me. When I was asked to write something about him, I vividly remembered the responsibility he had as a seventh grader when I was in first grade. James was responsible for getting me home from school. We didn't have a bus to ride, so James had to walk me home from East Athens School. Every day when we left school, James would come to my first grade classroom and pick me up. When leaving school, James would play with his friends on the way home and leave me in sight with the crew walking home. One day M. Mapp, a classmate of James, said to me, "Chrissy Pie, you can walk home with me every day." I did, and James would pick me up from her house and walk me the rest of the way home. It must have been a lot for him to be responsible for a six-year-old, but there were no buses for us to ride so we did the best we could.

Thank you, James, for being a big brother to me. Those were the good old days and I would take nothing for them. Love my brother very much. I admire him for all of his accomplishments.

—Christine Smith Jackson

———

With family (extended family as well) being nurtured in the church, it is no wonder that James had a passion for all aspects of its teachings.

Grandfather Charlie Smith was said to be "a preacher" though he may have made a little stronger spirit during the week. Grandmother Betsy Smith, after leaving Oglethorpe County, was a member of Saint Mark A.M.E. Church, pastored much of that period by Minister Johnny Pope. (This is not the same Johnny B. Pope that is mentioned later, but cousins.)

Minister Johnny Pope was first cousin to our maternal grandmother, Josephine Pope Barnes who with her husband Lucius Barnes, a faithful Trustee, were members of First A.M.E. Church. Grandmother was one of the early teachers in the first school for Blacks at First A.M.E.

Most of the Pope family were members of the Friendship Baptist Church, with strong deacons as Will Pope and his wife May Hanna, Deacon Johnny B. Pope and his wife Sarah.

Mother was a faithful member and leader of First A.M.E. Church and frequent attendee, especially during revivals, of Friendship Baptist Church.

Father was a member and deacon of Hills Chapel Baptist Church. The children were members of First A.M.E. Church, where the hymns and spirituals were the highlight of the worship, but it was only when we visited Friendship Baptist, Saint Luke A.M.E., Billups Grove Baptist, and Hill Chapel Baptist, did the real music dimension of the Black experience occur. Many of these visits were to celebrate "Children's Day," where we would perform and of course eat and drink sweet, sweet lemonade.

After the death of our dear great-aunt Lizzie McCambric, "Ain't Sis," as she was affectionately called, it was time to find a place for me to stay during the day. This is approximately early 1956. James is now fifteen and is responsible for me, when my parents can't take or pick me up from Shaw's Day Care (Ramona Shaw Prater). Most days going to school, even if our father was driving, it was James who had to check me in at the kindergarten and to get home James would engage Ms. Ramona to take us to East Athens School where her mother, Ms. Daisy Lee Shaw, was a second-grade teacher. We could then walk from East Athens Elementary home or James would stop by from high school and we would begin our walking journey home from the kindergarten with hopes that an adult known to our parents would happen by for a ride, at least to the end of the pavement of Grove Street Extension.

Later, when I was entering first grade at East Athens, it was the big brother James' time to transfer the safe traveling responsibilities to Frank and Christine, mainly Christine, as Frank and James had heavier home chores that had to be performed. Transportation was still by foot, as the bus ride for Blacks was still not available if you lived within certain mileage parameters.

Before graduating high school and entering Tuskegee, James, during one of these periods, would have a back-breaking job at Alexander Wood Yard. This was a likely place, since our father was working there, but it was the scariest time for me, for him, as I believed he would not survive such hard and labor-intensive work, but he did. While doing this, he was still the best half of the internal dry-cleaning business as he could press (iron) the clothes even better than mother. He ironed clothes for the Kents and we delivered them, particularly when he was working other jobs in anticipation of going away to school. Our parents were on the payroll as James always gave a major portion of his earnings to them first and to others if anything was left. This generosity was evidenced when James worked as a chef in New York and brought home a barrel of coins that he gave to me.

During summer breaks from Tuskegee, there was no fun and frolic for James but hard work to include the tobacco farms and more.

One of the most cherished memories was James coordinating and bringing to Athens one of the best Glee Club Concert groups from Tuskegee, mainly his friends, to the First A.M.E. Church. The first introduction to Athens of the "Vegetable Song" is still a big hit today at many events.

Fast-forward to returning home to work at the high school. The ever-giving spirit continued. Now James resumed his transportation duties with me in tow as we delivered our nephew (Quan Kevin) home safely from the babysitter. Next, he had to make sure I arrived for piano lessons on time and after music lessons many times transport me from Giles Beauty Shop, where big sister was in training and employed. Piano lessons were in walking distance of the shop.

Just a list of all the many imposed and self-imposed duties, jobs, and responsibilities of James R. Smith:

James the emergency driver: When I was mowing the weeds/lawn and a rock pierced the left leg, Mother was frantically trying to assure me that I would be all right, especially since James was on the way. James delivered me to Susan Medical Center, where the doctor who delivered me and Christine into the world, Dr. Green, was trimming hedges and stopped to repair the leg, without anesthesia, and James delivered me back home. I still have a scar to prove it.

James the lead partner (James and Leroy) to serve as janitor of the church, that included a pre-Sunday School cleaning of the pigeon "stuff" from the steps and walkways.

James the spirits store operator, and later owner, would help many voluntarily and many would help themselves to proceeds and inventory. James was not a lender or a borrower, but a giver, and often provided me spending money for college.

Official and unofficial positions at First A.M.E. Church, especially as pertained to music: choir director, building coordinator, building agent, relationship manager, Christian education director, and much more.

These are but a few random thoughts, as I would be writing the entire book if I continue and filling all that was left out here.

–Leroy Smith, Jr.

From the Tuskegee Years

The man I know as James "Smitty" Smith is my friend; no–we are best friends. We both got to know each other as seniors at Athens High and Industrial School, the graduation class of 1959. We attended different elementary schools and did not hook up again until our senior year in high school. We did not get to know each other as fellow athletes. I am guessing that while we were well known as students, neither of us was socially super popular. However, that did not slow us down from showing up where the action was going down.

We both went off to Tuskegee Institute after high school. A number of us went to the student aid office to secure a summer job. We were successful and we ended up at L. B. Haas Tobacco Farm just outside of Hartford, Connecticut in an area called Hazardville. This turned out to be a life changer for those of us as students from Tuskegee. We learned to get along with others from different social and economic backgrounds. Many of the workers were from the streets of the hood from Birmingham, Alabama. On the "Farm" we all were just farm hands. Lessons learned: What you do could have an influence on those who many follow you; we were representing Tuskegee and its reputation of being able to secure summer jobs for deserving students; we had to prove to ourselves that hard work would not turn us into quitters, our word was our bond. Did I tell you that this was the hardest, dirtiest, poorest conditions that we had encountered in our very young work history? When Smitty was asked by the foreman if he planned to return the next season, Smitty told him, hell no–"he would eat rocks before coming back to Hazardville."

The following summer Smitty got a job in the Catskill Mountains in New York. He called to tell me he talked to the owner and he had a job for me as well. He indicated that I should get a bus ticket to New York City and a separate ticket to Woodbourne, NY. He left out the part that I had to get the ticket to Woodbourne from the Port Authority, several blocks from the Greyhound Bus Station. Nor did he indicate that this would take another four-hour bus ride to get to Woodbourne.

The owners, Sally and Harry Friedman, were very hands-on with their employees. Smitty and I had made it from the fields of Connecticut to the kitchen of the SalHara Hotel. Smitty advanced to the position of short order cook and I ended up assisting in the pantry and then assisting the baker. This was a real cultural experience. The chef was Hungarian, the baker was German, the owners were Jewish. Needless to say, all meals were kosher, prepared and served. During our downtime, James talked Harry into allowing us to borrow his car to shop for school clothes and catch shows at Grossinger's Hotel in nearby Monticello, NY. We met a number of students from University of Kentucky and learned what was meant by "mooning" the guests as they drove by.

Lesson learned: Smitty is always looking out for others. Here is a "Smith-ism" for you, "If people just believed just half the way I do this would be a better place to live." James is a man who created his own philosophy of life. We learned quickly, he gravitated to those who could accept him for who he was, as he was not into changing just to make you like him. However, if he liked you, he would give you the shirt off of his back.

During our days at Tuskegee, we both were fortunate to sing in the Tuskegee Choir and in the Men's Glee Club. Smitty's love for music led to the formation of the Voices of Truth. I was always amazed how he was able to pull this off, as he was not a trained musician, but clearly had a real ear for music.

Smitty and I developed a friendship that grew stronger during these work experiences, as we could be very candid with each other. I believed that we both had this inner drive to make our parents proud of us and not to be an embarrassment to them. The kicker was, we had to make it happen on our own merit. Smitty did not want a handout. If you wanted to be his friend, you had to be kind of thick-skinned, because he would not hold any punches. He did not do it in meanness but in pure candor. We have gone through a lot over the years. We have not always seen things eye to eye. We have called each other out when we went through our crazy times. Our disagreements never resulted in us falling out with each other, as that is what friends are expected to do. Friends do not hold back when you are wrong. Lesson learned: We did not focus on the things that made us different. Instead, we celebrated the things that we could appreciate that we liked–about friends, about food, and life in

general. When he said, "Freddy, you are crazy," it was just his way of acknowledging that he did not agree with me. I was not expected to believe
and do things he would or wouldn't do all of the time. We just had to do
it "half of the time" to make it a better place to live.

There is so much more to share about Smitty that could result in a
volume two. The evolution of becoming lifelong friends is filled with low
points in our lives as well, as much as the fun years running the streets of
Athens, adventures to new places, the people in our lives, the bond that
was established between our parents and our families may sound like a
make-believe story. However, it is not–I have only shared a snippet of it,
the things that resulted in us becoming the best of friends based upon a
shared life of the good ole days.

–Marvin F. Billups, Jr.

I met James R. Smith in the fall of 1960, on the campus of Tuskegee Institute (Tuskegee University). I was a bewildered freshman trying
to navigate by new environment. Both James Smith and I decided to join
the famed Tuskegee Institute Choir. I had a background in high school
band and choir. James Smith (Smitty) and I both shared a love of music.

I am not sure of Smitty's musical training at that time but it was
clear that he was devoted and determined to do his best to be one of the
leaders in that choir. He was not skilled at reading musical scores (neither
was I) but, through his determination and pure drive, became a competent music reader and one of the singers chosen for the Tuskegee Institute
Touring Choir.

Our friendship extended beyond the walls of the choir practice
room and he and I became good friends. I found him to be reliable, hon-
orable, and trustworthy. If he committed to an effort, you could depend
on it.

In 1962, Smitty was a member of the Touring Choir that performed at the National Christmas Tree Lighting. At the end of that performance, President Kennedy turned to Dr. Relford Patterson (then choir
director), expressed his appreciation, and said, "I'll see you at my house
tomorrow." That tour required travel through Washington D.C., Ohio,
Michigan, and Illinois. The highlight of this tour was the introduction to
world-renowned gospel singer Mahalia Jackson and an invitation to her
home. The award for more consistent performances during the tour was
given to the bass section, in which Smitty was a member.

Smitty was part of the Tuskegee Male Chorus and later a popular vocal group called The Cliques. Smitty showed his unique organizational skills when he arranged a concert at his home church for The Cliques. This included transportation and dining arrangements. The group was transported from Tuskegee, AL to Athens, GA, presented a concert, and returned to Tuskegee all during the same day. As part of The Cliques, Smitty was instrumental in selecting two Miss Tuskegee winners. The group was a major factor in these selections. The Cliques was enormously popular on campus and in retrospect could be called the precursor to the Commodores (also from Tuskegee!)

I have kept in touch with Smitty during the years since leaving Tuskegee and am therefore not surprised of his success since that time. However, I was surprised to see him conducting the Voices of Truth. Remember, when we met, he did not read music scores but through diligence and determination has been able to rise above all obstacles to organize the group, recruit superior musicians, and instill the discipline necessary to develop the group into a local and national treasure.

–McArthur Fields

From Athens

Just before dawn, I sat in my car waiting on the others to arrive for the beginning of a long day of "getting out the vote" for my brother, who was hoping to make history as the first African American to be elected to the House of Representatives since Reconstruction. We would begin the day with a prayer meeting.

A van drove in the office parking lot. It was still dark, but I could see the silhouette of Mr. James Russell Smith. He was wearing a cap as always. On the side of the van, I could see the words, The Athens Voices of Truth.

Though the choir was not on the van, I could hear from the depth of my spirit the voices of many decades of spiritual songs under the direction of Mr. Smith. His presence was a reminder to me that no matter what, "It was well with my soul."

Many members of the Voices of Truth that he directed are now singing with the heavenly host. However, Mr. Smith continues to carry the royal banner of commitment, dedication, and selflessness. He holds high the cross of Jesus. He realizes that it will not suffer loss as he ministers to souls through spiritual songs.

I love him as my friend, but most of all as my "big brother." His voice will resound eternally through the Athens Voices of Truth.

—*Barbara Thurmond Archibald*

I talked with Mr. James Smith a few days ago. This phone call came after several failed attempts to reach him; he's still a very busy man. The purpose of this call was to see if he remembered how long we've known each other and how our paths had brought us together. Neither of us could remember; I'm fairly sure it was music that played a big role, however. That had to be more than 30 years ago.

I've had a deep appreciation for Mr. Smith's vision to organize and direct the Voices of Truth as long as I have known him. Anyone who has heard this group perform soon comes to realize that it offers a great variety in styles: included are the classics, anthems, spirituals, both contemporary and traditional gospel. Mr. Smith (Smitty) believes, as did William Shakespeare, that he must satisfy the palate of all his audience.

Smitty, thanks much for your leadership, your sense of humor, your unwavering dedication, your wisdom, your straightforwardness, and for being the God-fearing person that you have been and still are. It is a pleasure to have known you for these 30-plus years and for having me as an occasional organist for the Voices.

—*David Bolton*

I believe I first met James Smith in 1989. I moved to Athens to take a job at the University and as I was making my rounds to explore the community, I was fortunate to hear a concert presented by the Athens Voices of Truth. I met Mr. Smith following the concert and we had an exchange in conversation. Later, I got to know him better as my family united in fellowship at Ebenezer Baptist Church, West. I also held a part-time position at First A.M.E. church as a church musician. This is the home church for the Smith family so I was fortunate to meet many more of his relatives.

From my earliest encounters with Mr. Smith he has always presented himself as a confident and secure statesman. His personality was cordial, friendly, compassionate, caring, concerned, and yes, of course, CRAZY, with loads of humor and fun. As I got to know him, I found him to be very genuine and an authentic brother of grave integrity. He could cut up with the best of us, but when it came to the Lord's House, the worship of God, and the presentation of worship music, he was always a man of no nonsense. His perceived ambition was to always do whatever you are going to do at the highest level of excellence possible or don't do it at all.

Mr. Smith is a man with a heart for his community and its constituents. He makes himself available for networking and collaborative projects to enhance the life and living experiences of those with whom he shares the planet. His primary vehicle for these efforts has been the Athens Voices of Truth. In order to achieve his desired goals, I have seen him navigate all necessary avenues to bring together those persons who could enhance the bringing forth of his vision. He very often selects clinicians and facilitators who bring to the table those attributes, gifts, and callings which compliment his own personal areas of strength and weaknesses.

He is at home with statesmen and common people. His heart is for the betterment of all. His commitment to excellence in all things has brought a level of communication across cultural and racial lines in the Athens-Clarke County area. He extends himself beyond these borders at state and national meetings and conventions that he perceived would enhance his vision for the work in Athens.

The impact of his work with music has influenced the entire Athens community. Many local churches have been exposed to the Voices of Truth and their presentations have influenced the music activities at their local settings.

I am proud to call James Russell Smith my friend and brother. We share a passion for Christ, His Church, and a love for the presentation of worshipful music at a level that honors God in every aspect.

–Dr. Gregory S. Broughton,
Associate Professor of Music, University of Georgia

———

I remember like it was yesterday looking up to James Smith as my godfather! Picture this: candy offered every time I went to visit, hearing the jovial laughter of my parents with him and his wife Rose. And then, when sadness struck, he was there for us. His presence alone filled the void in the room where my father once sat. James was there with other friends of my dad and someone said to me, "There's one person missing, your dad." Even to others, it was noticeable how much James was such an important part of our family.

Let's fast-forward. A few years ago I was with my mother attending a class reunion banquet for all who had attended Athens High and Industrial School. The D.J. played one of my favorite songs and before I knew it my godfather had joined me on the dance floor! Talk about discovering new dance moves! He wasn't missing a beat and I was trying to keep up! I could only imagine the high school dances he attended in his day.

I could go on and on because there are truly so many memories in my head. Being a flower girl in his wedding was a beautiful time. I can still see the turquoise ribbon around my white dress.

James is the epitome of leadership, kindness, strength, and compassion. I wouldn't trade him for another godfather in the world. The fact that he is a dear friend and brother to my mother, he is more like an uncle to me and a great uncle to my children. They too know and appreciate the role he plays in our lives. I am honored to share these words with James. I want him to know that he and Rose are loved and appreciated for being in our lives. I wish them nothing but continued happiness as they enjoy life with their now adult children, daughter-in-law, and grandbaby.

James, your meekness is admirable. Your service is commendable. And your spirit is a blessing. But most of all your presence in my life is greatly appreciated and we love you for that.

So, to my godfather, James Russell Smith, congratulations on all of your endeavors and may God continue to bless you!

–Monica Smith Fladger, Kennedy, and Kyle

I met Mr. Smith at Ebenezer Baptist Church when a friend from my doctoral program at UGA brought me there for Sunday morning services. It was around the Fall of 1999, and either that day or soon after, there was an announcement about church families adopting students who were in Athens for school and away from their own families. For some reason, Mr. Smith readily selected me and from that moment on I had a family in Athens. The warmness and kindness of Mr. Smith touched me right away. In an instant, I felt connected to him, that he truly cared about me, and knew he was sincere. All these things were true and more.

For the next three years while I was in school at UGA, through the final fourth year when I went away for internship in Columbia, SC, to when I returned for graduation, Mr. Smith was a constant, positive, and supportive presence in my life. He was the same way with all of my friends that I introduced to him. Mr. Smith often took us to breakfast and lunch, and I cannot count the number of meals I had at his home with Mrs. Smith and their beautiful children. He welcomed me into his family and his home like I belonged there. He made a community for me in Athens, shared the history of the city, and told me stories of his own upbringing. I cherished all of these moments.

What makes Mr. Smith truly extraordinary to me is his energy, his smile, and his special way of making me, and everyone around him, feel special, comfortable, safe, and important. He has a way with people that is connecting and validating. I always knew how much he believed in me and that he hoped and prayed I would have a good life. Mr. Smith was also understanding and not demanding. He would check in with me back then, similar to the way he checks in now, "I just wanted to see how you are doing and to let you know that I am doing well (as an old man:-))." Mr. Smith is the type of older man that I hope to be.

Our most recent time together was when I was in Athens to receive an Alumni Award from the College of Education. Naturally, Mr. and Mrs. Smith came to the ceremony and sat with my advisor when I attended UGA, as well as my family–which included my partner Juliette and our sons, Harper and Sky, all who came along years after Mr. Smith and I formed our relationship. It reminded me of when I graduated from UGA, over 16 years ago, and Mr. Smith was also at the party at my advisor's house, with my mother, father, extended family, and friends.

Since he adopted me at Ebenezer Baptist Church, Mr. Smith has always been there supporting, cheering, and celebrating. Mr. Smith is a blessing to me and my family that I carry in my heart with all of the love he has given to me over the years. I always want to do the same for him. Thank you for who you are, everything you have done, and all that is to come. I love you.

–Marc Anderson Grimmett, Ph.D.
Associate Professor of Counselor Education, NC State University

———

Smitty asked me to write to you regarding our friendship, which spans over forty-five years. I first met Smitty in March of 1974 at our fraternity's alumni chapter monthly meeting. At that time, I had in-laws here in Athens as well as friends from college, but Smitty was the first Athenian I met that didn't fit these two categories. When I moved to Athens in June of 1974, I immediately looked him up and discovered that he owned a popular liquor store. As our friendship blossomed, we hung out on weekends together. These outings involved everything from bar hopping to parties and Georgia football games. Smitty has a religious side as well so he invited me to his church, introduced me to his then very charismatic minister at First A.M.E. church.

I found Smitty to be very community minded as well. In addition to our fraternity, he was very active in a very well-known Black community men's organization, The One Hundred Percenters. I think his most famous accomplishment is the formation of the infamous "Voices of Truth." The best gospel group around. I think he's been involved with this group the entire time I have known him. I attended his wedding to his lovely wife Rose and was also around during the birth of his two children. We're too old to bar hop anymore so our enjoyment now comes from teasing each other twice a month when he services my lawn. Smitty and I will always be friends!!! He's a gentleman and a scholar!

–Ernest Hardaway

———

In February 1979, I relocated from my hometown, Gainesville, GA to Athens. I was 28 years old and found myself in need of a new start. For reasons totally unclear to me at the time, I decided to move to Athens. I knew no one in Athens although I had been told we had family there. I had only been to Athens a couple of times as a child. It was basically a faith move.

I was a single father with a son and a daughter and had no idea how the move would turn out.

Amazingly, on my first day in the city, I was blessed to find a job as a police officer with the UGA Police Department. I found housing and connected with some long-lost cousins.

As a rookie police officer, I had to go through a rigorous training program and for the first time in my life I could not attend church on Sunday. In my whole life I could not remember being anywhere else on Sunday morning. I had served most of my life as a church musician at my home church in Gainesville. Everything that I knew and that I was familiar with came to a halt with my move and my new start.

I attempted to locate a church that had an evening service, but to no avail. I would attend evening programs at various churches just to stay connected. I knew nobody and nobody knew me and that was fine as I truly wanted to work on my new beginning.

My children were in the middle of the school year and it was decided that they would remain in school there for the remainder of the year.

One day while looking for a barber shop, I asked a young man about a church and he pointed me to the Hill First Baptist Church, which was in sight of where we were standing. I left him and drove over there and the pastor, Rev. Ben K. Willis, just happened to be coming out of the building. I met him and started attending there whenever I was off work.

One particular Sunday that April, they were celebrating Men's Day. They had a special men's choir but no music. I felt totally guilty sitting there knowing that maybe I could be of service, so I got up and moved to the organ just to help out if I could.

It was that Sunday that a visitor, there for the program, introduced himself to me after the service was over as James Russell Smith.

He was somewhat overbearing and straightforward, to the extent that he made me a little uncomfortable. "Who are you? Where did you come from? What are you doing here?" I answered very little and kept walking. I had started to sort of enjoy being an unknown and staying to myself. He asked me if he could have a contact number so that he could follow up with me concerning a vision he had for the community. I did give him a contact number and kept moving.

He called me that night and the moment I heard his voice on the phone I knew that I had made a mistake by giving him my number. It was the end of my solitude. He began to share with me his vision of organizing a community choir. I heard him out and then told him that I wasn't interested. I really was not that great of a musician and that when he saw me, I was just filling in because I saw a need. He said I heard you play, and you have the gift I so need, so just think about it. I'll call you in a day or so.

A few days later, my phone rang.

I knew it had to be him. I didn't know anybody else. Again, he began to tell me about this great plan that he had for this choir and how I was going to help him. I honestly thought that I had gotten myself hooked up with a crazy man.

After a few conversations he began to talk in a way that sort of caught my attention. "Whoever you are, I don't believe that God sent you here for nothing, and you can't take a God-given gift and just hide it away. At the very least you are going to have to use that gift somewhere."

I finally said, "OK, I'll try," and that was the beginning of a lifelong friendship.

In the beginning, it was all about the choir, but as time passed, he became more and more inquisitive about me as a person. During that time my children were with me only on weekends and he seemed to be quite impressed with the fact that I took my role as a father so seriously. He, too, was a family man and a new father and seemed excited to share his family. He took me to Lyndon Avenue and introduced me to his wife, Rose and his baby, yet in the crib, Tiara. I remember wondering how in the world is this bold, straightforward, and bossy little fellow married to such a sweet, gentle, and soft-spoken woman. With Tiara it was love at first sight. She reminded me of my own little girl. She already had godparents, but I quickly became a close second.

In Smitty's estimation I lacked exposure, and he set out to make sure that I knew people and that people knew me. He introduced me to Mrs. Neely, who helped me with a place for childcare. Mr. Mitchell, who was a barber, and many others. Little by little my little private world began to crumble, as Smitty knew everybody.

He came by once and took me to a house party to meet some friends. I went, met some wonderful people, but quickly realized I was out of my league. Very nice people, but I could tell I was making them just as uncomfortable as they were making me. I heard one of them ask Smitty, "Why did you bring him here? You can tell he's like a fish out of water." Smitty was kind enough to leave just to get me out of what was obviously not my cup of tea. [The men were drinking.]

As I got to know him better and as we worked on his vision to put together a community choir, he carried me by his job at a liquor store. He got out of the car and went in. I stayed in the car. He came out and told me that I didn't have to sit in the car, I could come in. I said, "No thank you, I'm fine." When he came out and we were leaving, I asked him point blank, "What kind of choir is this we are organizing?" He told me a choir that could do all kinds of sacred music. I challenged him on the spot. The conversation went sort of like this:

"Before I can go any further with you in this endeavor, you have some decisions to make. If we are going to do this, we've got to do our best to represent God well. While I am far from perfect and have more flaws than I care to talk about, I'm serious when it comes to my service to God." We talked about my concerns that we had to try to be the best examples that we could be.

The next time I saw him he told me he had given notice that he was leaving that job. It was then that I realized that this brother is serious about this choir.

As we continued to get to know each other I began to assure him that I, just like everybody else, had more shortcomings than I even wanted to talk about and never ever wanted him to think that I was some "holier than thou" character but I was at a point in my life where I had been given an opportunity for a new start and I refused to blow it. With me it's all about where God has brought me from and where he's trying to get me to. At that point I had no idea where that was.

Smitty had a lot of respect for that and I saw him go out of his way not only to honor that but to hold me accountable for that.

Smitty and Rose met my children and immediately loved them. They would avail themselves to do whatever they needed to do to help me with them. My daughter and my son love them to this day.

That same year, I found that Dr. Winfred Hope had been called as the Pastor of Ebenezer Baptist Church. I knew him from the state convention. My search was over. Soon after he arrived, my son Jayson and I united with Ebenezer Baptist Church. I know that Smitty had a genuine love for God and was a faithful and committed member of his church, but after visiting Ebenezer a few times and hearing Pastor Hope he became quite interested in the direction and ministry of Ebenezer. I was quite surprised that before long Smitty brought his family to Ebenezer.

The Athens Voices of Truth became a reality and Smitty was on cloud nine. I was amazed at how he was able to pull together so many people from so many different walks of life. I was amazed at how his straight talking, direct, and stern manner never changed. I saw God use him just like he is. It brought a discipline to the choir that I had rarely seen anywhere.

I could go on and on but I'll suffice it to say that God can do more than one thing at a time. Not only was this the beginning of the Athens Voices of Truth, which has blessed so many over the years, but it was the beginning of a lifelong brotherhood, and since that time the Haynes family and the Smith family have been inseparable.

From my eventual acceptance to the call to the preaching ministry, which eventually took me away from the choir, to my marriage to Beverly Billups, who was also a lifelong friend of the Smith family, to the many accomplishments of our daughters, to the birth of his son, my godson who bears a portion of my name, to the call of both of our sons to preach the gospel and both now servicing in successful pastorates, the Smiths have been nothing short of family. And always will be. And the Athens Voices of Truth, after 40 years, continue to bless people everywhere.

–Rev. Dr. Richard B. Haynes
Pastor, Salem Missionary Baptist Church, Lilburn, Georgia

Looking back over the years, I realize that I am more aware of who I am and how I got here. My mother and father started it all with love and care. While they were ever vigilant about my whereabouts and "whoabouts," they never worried when I was in the company of James Russell Smith. For some strange reason, this near legendary older brother of my dear friend Leroy seemed like he had automatic trust and supervisory privilege. I am even more amazed to realize that he was not that much older than I, even though he seemed too wise and mature.

Smitty, as we came to call him, arrived on the scene in 1965 and proceeded to win the hearts, minds, and loyalty of a legion of my friends and schoolmates. He commenced to involve us in a Christian youth group based at First A.M.E. Church, a male singing group, and more importantly a group of dedicated, committed friends and future leaders with similar ideals and energies, all of which seemed to radiate from Smitty. It is said that there are no coincidences in God's world. 1965 was a tumultuous year in America and especially unsettling for Black youth. The Malcolm X assassination, the Watts Riots, escalation in the Vietnam War. The arrival of Smitty with his energy and enthusiasm made the world more stable and trustworthy. Fun with a spiritual and value-based twist made a difference in our lives.

We met together, laughed, played, joked, and learned songs and productions, including *God's Trombones*, a pageant. The Youth Group and the E. L. Terrell Male Ensemble, named in honor of Smitty's prematurely deceased dear friend and fraternity brother, traveled to Northeast Georgia churches and schools performing and entertaining, visited the communities and homes, caroling at Christmas, and generally making Athens a better place.

Our earliest mode of transportation was Smitty's 1960 silver grey Pontiac Catalina, "The Grey Ghost," which typically made at least five routes per Saturday transporting the youth group and one or two nights per week transporting the Ensemble to meetings, rehearsals, and performances. "The Ghost" ended up running a top speed of twenty mph with one forward gear in its automatic transmission. It was replaced by a blue-and-white Oldsmobile Cutlass, which Smitty gave unselfishly to the cause. The Ensemble performed on the local live radio show, "The Hour of Sharing," to promote our four-selection record, our very own recording. We raised money and purchased gold, double-breasted blazers and went on an epic trip via U-Haul panel van to see Smitty's beloved Tuskegee Institute. The highlight of the trip–the van burned, the trip proceeded, we ate at one of Smitty's favorite eating places in Tuskegee. We returned to Athens by bus in the wee hours of the morning, went to school the next day. Our parents' only comment was a rhetorical question, "Why didn't you guys call for help?" The answer was obvious: we were with Smitty, we didn't need help.

We lived, we laughed, we played, we worked.

The lessons keep on coming but were disguised as fun. Many of our compatriots are gone but they live in memory. The memories are care of Smitty. How a young man could come home and give of himself so unselfishly to so many youths is a mystery to me.

Smitty's pastor, Rev. C. D. Wilkerson, was the spiritual support and gave of his time and church in Smitty's mission. However, the force that left us with memories was the man, the myth, the legend, the VIP, James Russell Smith.

Fifty years later, Smitty remains a vital force in my life. What is more, he is a dear friend and brother. I am still mystified as to how he could have, and still does, give so much of himself with great humor and humility.

–Dr. Farris Johnson, Jr.

Growing up an only child in a small college town in the 50s and 60s presented challenges for me. There weren't many opportunities to "expand horizons" and because of my parents' choice of school for me, during a large period of high school, my only outlet was selecting band as an elective class. Being a minority, the ability to participate in extra-curricular school-related activities was limited; in fact it was non-existent. If it had not been for my friends at another school, the practice of being "invisible" could very well have consumed me. It just so happened that one of my friends had an older brother who saw a need! That older brother was none other than James Russell Smith, lovingly referred to by his mentees as "Smitty"!

Expanding on an idea for his church's Youth Department and another group which James was already working with, an invitation was extended to other youth in the community to join in and become part of an experience that for me was life-changing. During a span of the next two years this group of teens met each Saturday as Smitty became our "big brother," our director, our coach, our advisor, our chauffeur, our mentor, and our friend. There is a fond memory and inside joke of just how many teens could fit in his car as he would drive around Athens picking up many for our Saturday practices. He developed our oratorical talents and cultural appreciation as some memorized and recited several of the sermons in James Weldon Johnson's *Gods Trombones*. All of us developed or added to our musical gifts as we were directed by Smitty and as we learned and sang numerous Negro spirituals, favorite hymns, and traditional holiday songs. Because of his expectations of aspiring close to perfect, we also acquired the additional discipline to perform as an impressive choir. When we were deemed ready, we traveled the city from church to church presenting our rendition of a much-appreciated musical of *God's Trombones*, adding to our singing abilities that of acting. In addition, our distinguished group, under the direction of James Russell Smith, rendered many concerts and sang in many special programs in the area.

Our exposure to music, acting, and cultural appreciation did not end with just our personal performances; with Smitty and a few parents providing transportation, we traveled to see and hear others share their love of the arts through music, dance, and drama. In fact, I will always remember our not-so-small group traveling to Atlanta, Georgia to see the Reverend William Holmes Borders, Sr.'s portrayal of Jesus Christ in the dramatic production of *Behold the Man*. The opportunity to experience this in the Atlanta-Fulton County Stadium will remain one of the highlights of my high school days.

James Russell Smith saw a need and answered the call to lead a group of teens and provide for them a cultural exposure which many of the group may not have otherwise experienced.

As I think back on those days, I remember not feeling as comfortable as my peers in claiming the part of soprano or alto, and therefore fell into the group of "rattlers." Thank you, Smitty, for your help in developing a social, cultural, and civic opportunity and a fairly decent "soprano"!

Your efforts will be long remembered and deeply appreciated.

—Janet Robinson Jordan

————

Smitty has come to be one of our best friends. It all goes to show that the adage "you can't judge a book by its cover" is TRUTH. The first time I remember having a conversation with Smitty was in the parking lot of Ebenezer Baptist Church, West. I can't recall what the conversation was about, but I DO remember how gruff Smitty was! I thought he was just a mean old man. I was a newcomer to Athens. I didn't know him and I wondered how/why someone could be so unfriendly. As the years have moved on, though, I have come to know and cherish the friendship of the authentic Smitty. He is still a gruff old man (not really, although he would have you think so), but has the kindest, most open heart of anybody! A grandchild pricks his heart in all the tender places and his friends find in him loyalty, generosity, and an extra uncle for our children. We have had lots of fun over the years with Smitty and Rose—at restaurants, musical events, on trips, etc. Smitty's humor and candid revelations make for an interesting time every time. This is my husband's and my testimony.

Rev. Benjamin and Natalie Lett

————

I met James Smith and the Athens Voices of Truth during my freshman year (1979) at the University of Georgia. The choir had given a performance at Hills First Baptist Church and I was invited to attend. The choir rendered several spirituals and gospel selections. As a piano major, I wanted to venture out into the community to experience the various musical facets of the city.

At the concert, "Smitty" directed the group. During one of the selections he jumped way up in the air. I was very startled. At that moment, I knew this group was very special and were very sincere about their ministry.

I began accompanying the group and working with them.

After graduating from UGA, I remained in close touch with them. Over the years, I have served as a music consultant with AVOT and have accompanied them in many concerts. It was without reservation that I submitted Smitty and the AVOT to the Intermountain Music Festival of Spirituals/Salt Lake City, Utah, with a performance at the Mormon Tabernacle Temple.

It is so apparent that Smitty enjoys working with the AVOT. Smitty is a very unique person. His love of God and his love of music is paramount. Smitty is all about helping people, his community, and the church universal. He is a true friend and brother.

−Ron Lowe

It is an honor and a privilege for me to pay tribute to a group of singers whom I have enjoyed, supported, and followed through the years.

There is a popular statement which says that there are three forms of greatness. Some men are born great, some men have greatness thrust upon them, and some men achieve greatness. I think out of these three forms, the greatest one is the achievement of greatness through service. As one writer puts it, "When man reaches out to help his fellow men; when he extends a strong arm to lift the fallen; when he utters a cheery word to encourage others; when he acts as a true friend to the lonely and friendless; it is then he travels the road to true greatness."

The Christian conception of greatness is found in our Lord's teaching to His disciples. Jesus taught that true greatness comes in serving others. He tells us that service is the true path to greatness. The proper way for human beings to live is to be a servant to others, to be used by a great idea, to be used in a great cause of humanitarian uplift. In His teaching of greatness through service, Jesus said to His disciple, "the harvest truly is plenteous but the laborers are few. Pray ye therefore the Lord of the harvest, that He will send forth laborers into His Harvest" (Matthew 9:37-38). Jesus wants us to look out on this world and see the challenges and opportunities for service.

Forty years ago, the Voices of Truth under the leadership of Bro. James Smith accepted the challenge in music ministry and made the choice to serve the Lord by singing and praising His name through song. This choice of service has fulfilled the vision of greatness. I am sure that there have been trials and tribulations, highs and lows, over the years. Nobody achieves greatness by endless daydreaming and inactivity. Nevertheless, through faith and perseverance this gospel train of willing workers for Christ has kept moving and pressing on with commitment, dedication, and hard work for these many years of service. They had to believe that there is no greater privilege or reward than to sing for the King of Kings.

−Ambrose McDow

I can't remember the first time I attended a Voices of Truth concert. What I can remember is that once I witnessed one of their performances I have been hooked since that day. When I want to hear good quality singers performing in harmony—soprano, alto, tenor, and bass—this choir provides the food for my soul. Singers and singing groups come and go, but songs performed by the Voices of Truth will never be outdated and will be enjoyed for many years to come. The mixture of hymns, spirituals, traditional gospel, anthems, and a touch of contemporary gospels are their specialties. The pain and struggles from slavery performed in songs can only be done by people who know and understand what our ancestors have been through. This choir understands and hasn't forgotten our heritage. The uniqueness of the Voices of Truth can also be seen within the group itself. In this world of unrest and racial tension it is good to see a group that is all inclusive. It doesn't matter if you are young or old, black or white. The members are also from different denominations.

The person who helped to organize the choir is Mr. James Russell Smith, the director. He had a vision of putting together a choir that could touch the souls of everyone with their performances. He demands perfection and accepts nothing less than the best. This may explain why the choir has performed out of state and at programs like the Dr. Martin Luther King, Jr. services at the State Capitol. Whether you are rich or poor, young or old, Mr. Smith and the choir try to include everyone. The selection of songs to be performed are also relatable to all. One song that I think showcases the real talents of the choir is an arrangement by V. Michael McKay called "Oh Jesus." Who would have ever thought that these two words could bring out such raw emotions when sung the right way? This song reminds me of something my grandmother said years ago, "Baby, you have to have been through some stuff in order to sing some songs." "Oh Jesus" is one of those songs and it brings tears to my eyes every time I hear it.

Forty years have passed since this choir performed their first concert at Hill First Baptist Church. I know some of the members are weary and consider leaving the choir. For forty years of extraordinary performances, I say thank you. I am hoping that the Voices of Truth will continue performing even if it's just a couple of times a year. Please don't pass the torch on to the next generation. I really don't want to hear the rap version of "Oh Jesus."

—Janice Murray

James Russell Smith has been and is a special person in my life. Since I was a very young child, I remember my family would visit his family mostly Sunday afternoons, after church. He had a proud family steeped in solid core family values. His mother Mrs. Vallie stressed the importance of education to all of her children.

It was several years later when I was in high school that I was re-acquainted with my long-lost cousin. He was a substitute teacher and I had the pleasure of being in the classes he taught. He was rather unique in the fact that he could be honestly brutal and insanely hilarious simultaneously. You would feel chastised one second and encouraged by his humor the next.

A couple of years after that ('70-'71) I learned more about James, his college career and how he worked to attain funds for his tuition, his being a businessman, mentor, church and civic servant, encourager, motivator, and friend.

I remember when I was in high school and college, James would mentor us (by us, I'm referring to my close circle of classmates—Michael Thurmond, Horace King, Richard Appleby, myself, and many others). We respected and gravitated to James. We saw that he was trustworthy and really cared about us properly navigating our teen years successfully. He demonstrated and spoke to us about good stewardship, patience in pursuit of worthwhile endeavors, to associate with persons of common goals (positive and uplifting), and if you fall, get up and never give up!

I thank God that James is still in my life. Each time I see him, my heart leaps with joy!

—Rev. Clarence Pope

During the early eighties, my wife Pearl and I first heard about a vocal group known as the Athens Voices of Truth, and attended a concert which was held at Hill First Baptist Church under the directorship of Mr. Smith. Beginning with this initial experience and subsequent attendance at other locations to witness this glorious ministry, I also began to more closely observe the caliber of leadership which he consistently demonstrates as it become more apparent over the years.

Therefore, without reservation, I can attest to the fact that the following indicators exemplify the high quality of leadership which he exhibits with this singing group. Thus, Mr. Smith reveals a keen sense of purposeful mission and direction as God's chosen one to lead this ministry. He, of course, knows with obvious strength of conviction, what he wants to accomplish with this group and where he wants to go. Moreover, he displays clarity and precision as he directs the choir with dynamic emotion, abounding enthusiasm, friendliness, and faith in the Almighty God. Considering the foregoing indicators, I have often heard him say or lead the congregational song of assurance, "It Is Well With My Soul," and to me, this infers that Mr. Smith is satisfied and comfortable with whatever he is doing to ultimately please God through his leadership ministry with the Voices of Truth.

In addition, I directly experienced his dedicated leadership when I was once an invited guest singer for the tenor section of this group in the presentation of an Annual Fall Concert at Ebenezer Baptist Church, West. His dedication of time, talent, and interests to the work and ministry of our Lord are also synonymous with the foregoing paragraph. Furthermore, he has been a sterling example of love for his work, choir members, and our Lord, Jesus Christ, along with enjoying and encouraging choir members to make singing a sustaining activity that infuses and uplifts their own lives as well as those of the concert audience. To this extent, one can believe that people's lives are being transformed, and that God is speaking to them through the mingling of worship and performance.

Finally, I contend that the history of Mr. Smith's conductorship is leaving an indelible mark in the sand of time, while members of the Athens Voices of Truth come to feel it was part of their own destiny. It is my prayer that God will continue to bless and keep this ministry.

—Jack V. Powell, Ph.D.
Professor Emeritus, College of Education, University of Georgia

———

When I think about Mr. James Smith, this word comes to mind: commitment. See, when I was a young teenager, he came to pick up others and myself for choir rehearsal at First A.M.E. Church. Now I went with them just to ride in his nice car. Who could have known it could have lasted this long? But when you are committed and trust in the Lord there is nothing impossible for you. May God continue to bless and keep you, Mr. Smith.

—Haree Robinson

———

I met James in 1965 or 1966. His brother Leroy is my friend. We were high school freshmen. When he returned to Athens, he heard me, Leroy, Farris Johnson, Michael Holmes (pianist), James Campbell, Prentice Jewell, and Harry Sims sing. He gathered all of us and formed a male ensemble, later named the E. L. Terrell Ensemble. We sang for church programs and community programs. We sang together through high school. James also directed the church choir at First A.M.E. Church. He invited me to sing with that group. I learned many things about organizing and directing a choir.

I went to college and earned a degree in music education. When I returned to Athens, James discussed the possibility of forming a community choir. He had a lot of community contacts and influence. Out of those discussions, the Athens Voices of Truth was formed. We performed at primarily church functions, because our repertoire was mostly sacred music.

I owe James a lot. He was a counselor, teacher, friend, and encourager.

—Johnny Sims

James Russell Smith and I met our freshman year in high school and have been friends to this day. After we left for college, time slipped away and we lost track of each other. Soon after I married my late husband, Richard, we were back in touch and we were all close friends. So much so that after the birth of our baby girl, Monica, we asked James to be her godfather. He graciously accepted and Richard and I never questioned our decision. To this day I have the fondest memories of that time. James has remained a dedicated and thoughtful godfather to Monica and my grandchildren.

My husband passed away in 2000, and shortly after that James started to take care of my lawn. He knew how much Richard loved keeping his yard up, and that I would have no clue or desire to do the same. James also looks out for my house when I am gone to visit Monica and my grandchildren. He collects my mail, newspapers, and pulls the trash cans up for me.

I treasure the friendship we have along with his lovely wife, Rose. God has truly blessed me by placing them in my life. I love James like a brother, and I am very proud of all his successes in life. I pray that God will continue to keep him in his loving care.

—Mrs. Audrey Milner Smith

I have known James Russell Smith ("Uncle Smitty") since my birth. He is part of the village that gave me the support (spiritual, emotional, financial, etc.) I needed in my upbringing. He was one of those steady hands that guided me throughout my childhood and taught me many of life's lessons.

Many of those lessons were taught by his mere presence and the example that he set as a man. His Godliness, passion, and dedication to gospel music, his vision and commitment to his family and friends are just some of his core values that stand out to me when I think of my uncle. It is amazing how God places certain people in your life that affect who you become as an adult. Uncle Smitty was one of those people.

He is the role model who took me to my very first University of Georgia football game when I was five years old (1972). I remember arriving at Sanford Stadium early enough to hang out on the field and take photos with some of the football players during their pre-game warmups. As a five-year-old boy, it was one of the best days of my life. I did not realize at the time that those football players were pioneers who would go on to become historical figures in Bulldog Football lore. It was not until I was much older that I realized that my uncle had a lot to do with those young men being the first black football players to sign at the University of Georgia. This is one of the many stories that I share with my two sons ad nauseum. I find it only fitting that I write about this experience during Black History Month.

Uncle Smitty has touched many people through his activism and his music. He is definitely one of the pillars of his community. I am truly blessed to have him in my life as one of the folks that looked out for me. May God continue to bless him and his beautiful family.

–Tony Smith

Smitty is an amazing person who has always mentored and supported young people in Athens. What he has been able to do with the Voices of Truth is nothing short of inspiring and uplifting for Athens and the state. He has been a valuable friend, mentor, and advisor. He's my brother and I'm proud of him and all he has been able to accomplish.

–Michael Thurmond
C.E.O., Dekalb County, GA

As I reflect on my time in Athens, Georgia, my affiliation with the Voices of Truth was pivotal to my journey in the Classic City. Affiliation with the group was a big part of my introduction to Athens. I met James R. Smith a week or two after I arrived in Athens. I visited First A.M.E. Church, which I eventually joined, and Smitty happened to be sitting on the row behind me. When I introduced myself as a visitor, he realized that I was a friend of Don Weston's and was the same new professor at UGA that Don had told him about.

Smitty introduced me to his family at First A.M.E. Church, his family at home, and told me about the Athens Voices of Truth. He probably invited me to join. I don't remember my response. However, I must have mentioned to him that I was a musician (pianist, to be specific). Before I knew it, he was sharing AVOT music with me and I was a member of the team, along with Joelene and Bruce and eventually Tom. As many would say, the rest is history.

The Voices are stellar musical ambassadors and were key members of my Athens, Georgia village. Even as I eventually departed from Athens as a resident, the AVOT will always be an important part of my experience. It was indeed a privilege to be a musician for this group. It sometimes challenged me, but it made me a better musician (even though I was sometimes reluctant). Smitty does not really take no for an answer. I needed that spirit in my life during my time in Athens. Thank you, James Smith, for having confidence in my abilities and for the friend that you have been to me for all these years.

Congratulations to James Russell Smith and to the Voices of Truth on this celebration of 40 years. I wish you many more as you sing and continue to bless your community.

–Dr. F. Carl Walton

As we sit on the periphery of forty years of the Athens Voices of Truth's existence, I'm confident that James Russell Smith had no idea of the impact, the influence, or the wide-reach that this musical formation would have. He had faith and just did it!

As I pause, ponder, and peruse the pages of my life with James Russell Smith (aka "Smitty"), my mind immediately takes me back to the summer of 1985. I'd just completed my undergraduate studies at the University of Georgia and was beginning a career with Ford Motor Credit Company there in Athens.

While I'd heard my cousin and roommate, Ron Lowe, talk about Smitty, it wasn't until one evening that he and several choir members stopped by Ron's and my apartment after an evening of choir practice. Needless to say, he and the other members were in the kitchen laughing loud and having a good time fellowshipping with each other.

Upon hearing this roaring chatter, I immediately closed my bedroom door so as to not disturb them or to be disturbed. I guess a closed door didn't mean anything to Smitty, because he burst through my door while saying, "Don't you hear us out here talking? You need to come out of this room and come talk with people!" Well, needless to say, this was my formal, yet informal introduction to Smitty–an introduction which has forged a lasting friendship of close to thirty-five years.

As one might imagine, these three-plus decades have been filled with many memorable moments, lively and lovable laughter, silence and sadness, hope and optimism, and this list goes on. It mattered not the state or the moment that Smitty was in, he knew his abiding faith would sustain him through anything.

It is his strength and his faith that have richly impacted me! I have witnessed his caring, his giving, his sharing, his living, his courage, his boldness, his truthfulness, his directness, his honesty, and his modesty–and it's from these things I have grown to the man I am today!

In closing, a wise man once said, "We live in deeds, not years; in thoughts, not breaths; in feelings, not in figures." Believe me, James Russell Smith is a sterling example of this wise man's proclamation–he just does it!

–*Don Weston*

From Choir Members

Years ago, we were singing for a "state dinner" in Atlanta. Just after grace was said over the food, we were asked to do another selection. Mr. Smith had us to perform a "novelty" song. The words were:

"Black eyed peas, my Lord, those good old black-eyed peas! Black eyed peas, my Lord, those good old black-eyed peas! First you put them in a pot and eat them good and hot . . . Um, um! Um, um! Those good old black eyed-peas!"

So, Mr. Smith had a bag of black-eyed peas and proceeded to throw them around gently as we were singing. Then, the next verse was "collard greens," etc. To our surprise, Mr. Smith had a fresh bunch of collards! He proceeded to tear the bunch apart and direct with the collard stalks! Needless to say, the whole choir lost it! The audience just broke out in laughter and it was never the same after that!

—Brenda L. Bellinger

I will start this off by saying congratulations to a brother in Christ, a dear friend, and a classmate who I call "Smitty." And to one that had a vision to start a community choir in the Athens area and to have worked with this group for forty years. To me, he is a person who is kindhearted and is willing to help in any kind of way, but very straightforward in being honest and frank when talking to him. I will close with one of his sayings: Proverbs: 24:18. "Where there is no vision, the people perish."

—Gloria Bizzle

James Russell Smith ("Smitty") is a well-known, much respected man of integrity. He is a Christian, mentor, and a friend who I highly respect.

I joined the Voices of Truth around 1988-89. My first impression was that Smitty, the choir director, was loud and rude. I soon learned that he had a kind, caring heart. He cared about the choir and wanted us to do our best. He would yell at us one minute and within a few minutes, he would make us smile. If he said or did anything to offend anyone, he would quickly apologize. His devotion to the choir always stood out.

Smitty loves music and wants everything to be done right. He has high expectations of the choir and he holds us to that standard and level of performance. He would often say, "If you can't get it right, then we're not going to do it." His strong, firm attitude is what the choir needed in order to accomplish the success which we have had for the last forty years.

Smitty has served the Athens community and other areas well, as he directed the singing of the Voices of Truth. His service is greatly appreciated and will always be remembered.

—Willimenia L. Haynes

Working with James Russell Smith, as I address him, has truly helped me learn the importance of commitment. When we started with the Athens Voices of Truth, we made the commitment of setting aside each Tuesday night as our rehearsal night. My mother would say, "Lord, don't let me get sick on a Tuesday night," because Smitty said we had to be in rehearsal. This is the commitment I made forty years ago and I have always planned work schedules and meetings around this time.

I must say that we have had some joyous times in rehearsal, but the one incident I will never forget is the one night we were in rehearsal at First A.M.E. Church and Smitty was directing a song, someone was not watching his directions and came in too soon. Smitty jumped up and down in the aisle about five times and he was yelling, "Watch me! Watch me!" I couldn't stop laughing. Every time I looked at him and then at one of our members, J. C. Maddox, I couldn't sing because all I could see was Smitty jumping up and down in the aisle. I actually thought my sides were going to burst from trying to hold my laughter inside. Tears were rolling down my cheeks. Believe it or not, that scene is embedded in my mind.

I have always been terrified of singing out in the wrong place so my eyes are always fixed on Smitty. This is the one thing I learned from him, always watch your director when singing in a choir because you must be focused.

Through the years, I have witnessed that this choir is a ministry and it is not about Smitty, but the Lord. I can truly say that this choir has helped me in my religious training because I've learned to listen to the message within the song and that our expressions, when singing, help set the tone of how the audience receives you and how much they get involved in the program.

Being a member of the Voices is like a family. Under Smitty's leadership, we have learned to embrace each other, support each other in all of our endeavors. As we know, a group is only as strong as its leader, so things like this just don't happen but they are taught and it comes from the leadership.

James Russell Smith doesn't just talk the talk, but he walks the walk. When he says commitment, he sets the example by being there, full of energy (Lord knows I don't see how he does it after working in the heat all day), being prepared for our rehearsal and giving us his all. I can't remember a time, in these forty years, that we came to rehearsal and he was not prepared, even when he was sick or going through something. He doesn't believe in excuses. This commitment exemplifies that this is his passion and that God is truly in this plan.

I feel blessed to have been a part of this group for forty years. The experiences of singing in various places for various occasions, the friendships that have developed from the group are invaluable and have helped me to become the person I am today.

I thank God for giving Smitty the vision of organizing this choir, along with others like Rev. Richard Haynes and Johnny Sims; the stamina and commitment to keep it going in a successful manner and not becoming stagnant; and introducing me to the various genres of music.

–Shelia Neely-Norman

APPENDIX 2

James' Mentees through the Years

From Burney-Harris High School: 1965-1970

Richard Appleby
James Campbell
Laurine Daniel
Pamela Favors
Terry Green
Milton Jordan
Horace King
Josephine Morton
Leslie Morton
Diane Neely
Garfield Neely
Clarence Pope
Haree Robinson
Anthony Sims
Rosetta Terrell
Michael Thurmond
Joyce Williams
Reba Williams

From First A.M.E. Youth Group

Cherly Harris
Valere Harris
Willimenia Harris
Sandra Hawkins
Janet Jordan
Michael Smith

Michelle Smith
Thomasene Smith
Tony Smith
Brenda Taylor

From the E. L. Terrell Ensemble

Andy Hill
Michael Hill
Michael Holmes
Bruce Holt
Ricky Hudson
Farris Johnson, Jr.
Reginald McBride
Harry Sims
Johnny Sims
Leroy Smith, Jr.

From the University of Georgia

Chuck Kinnebrew
Ronnie Swoopes
Gene Washington
Larry West
Rayfield Williams

From Ebenezer Baptist Church, West

Dr. Marc Grimmett
Ron Lowe
Don Weston

Appendix 3

Athens Voices of Truth Members and Musicians

Current 2019 Members

Brenda Bellinger*
Angela Billups
Gloria Bizzle*
Tom Broadnax
Henry Brown
Shirley Butler*
Joelene Cherry*
Fredric Creamer
Tiffany Drayton
Jo Ann Handy
Willimenia Haynes
Brook L. Johnson
Eric Johnson
Larry Johnson*
Hortense Lee
Mildred Lyle
David Mack
Donald Maxey
Michael Moore
Ada Mosley
Shelia Neely-Norman*
Hazel Roach
Raleigh Robinson
Janice Roundtree
Aurelia Scott
Beverly Smith
Frank Smith
Tiara Smith

Homer Thurman
Sylvanus Turner*
Reginald Willis
Connie Woodall*

original members in 1979

Members through the Years

James Alford
Linda Allen
Beth Alvarado
Alfreda Ballard
Janice Barnes
Jonetta Barnett
Willie Billups
Larry Blount
Doris Bostic
Al Brown
Lynn Camp
James Campbell
Teklia Cannon
Martha Carol
Jackie Chester
Calvin Clark
Wayne Cole
Harriet Collins
Lucille Cooper+
Carrie Cox
Nancy Cox
Alma Darden

Linda Darden
Debra Davenport
Howard Davenport
Margaret Davis
Georgia Dillard
Horace Dunn+
Luther Durham
Richard Dye
Isiah Eberhart+
Yvonne Eberhart
Joyce Echols
Derrick Ellis
Linda Fair
Donna Ford
Lynsey Gardner
Cecilia Woods Grant
Erin Green
Erwin Green
Harold Green
Duchess Goss
Cornell Grimes
Sharon Heard
Alegra Henderson
Monique Henderson
Bessie Hill
Doris Hood-Bostic
Joann Huff+
Patricia Huff
Joyce L. Jackson
Alzena Johnson
Earlene Johnson+
Larry Johnson
Ralph Johnson
Dorothy Jones
Michelle Jones
Dewayne Law
Joyce Little
J. C. Maddox

Renee McDade
Thomas Mitchell+
Minnie Moore
Wilbertine Morton+
Michelle Jones Pace
Patricia Pelham-Harris+
Tikica Platt
Stephanie Watson Rackard
Bertha Rambeau
Melvin Rambeau+
Angie Roberts
Raymond Roundtree
Deliah Sally
Pauletta Scotland
Johnny Sims
Georgette Spann
Catrina Stevens
Edwina Theresa Stevens+
Westervelt Stevens
Bessie Thomas
Valencia Thornton
Bernard Turner
Etheline Tyree
Anna Uhde
Ellen Walker
Kenneth Walton+
Betty White
Tekelia White
Samuel Wicks
Reba Williams
Carolyn Willis
Kelvin Willis
Martha Carol Wilson
Susie Wise
Cecelia Artis Woods
Vennie Lee Simmons Yancey+

+deceased

Current Musicians

Joelene Cherry
Tom Broadnax
Eric Johnson
Ron Lowe

Musicians through the Years

David Bolton
Ron Campbell
Rev. Richard Haynes
Rev. Lonnie Johnson
Judy Sikes
Johnny Sims
Dr. F. Carl Walton
Bruce Ware

APPENDIX 4

Partial List of Athens Voices of Truth Performances

1980s

- UGA Law School Awards Event, 1980
- State Congress of Christian Education, Albany, Georgia, 1980
- Classic Clarke Jubilee in connection with Georgia's 250th birthday, 1983
- Dr. Martin Luther King, Jr. services at Ebenezer Baptist Church, West, 1985
- Atlanta Coalition on Hunger, 1985
- Winners of Athens Cultural Award, 1987
- Historical Morton Vaudeville Theater, Athens, Georgia
- State meeting of Alpha Phi Alpha Fraternity, Inc.
- State of Georgia Legislative Black Caucus
- State of Georgia Masonic Lodge
- Hosts of First Community Gospel Workshop
- Hosts of Second Community Gospel Workshop

1990s

- Dedication of ACC Library, 1992
- McDonald's Gospelfest Competition (semi-finalists), 1994
- Official opening of the Athens Classic Center, 1995
- Performance for CBS telecast, 1995
- Dedication at the "Spirit of Athens" sculpture, 1996
- Torch festivities for the 1996 Olympic Games, Athens, Georgia, 1996
- Australian Olympic delegation, Athens, Georgia, 1996
- Pre-Christmas concert tour with country singer Kenny Rogers, 1997

- Hosts of Third Community Gospel Workshop
- Hosts of Fourth Community Gospel Workshop, 1998
- Baugh Heritage Music Festival, Keysville, Georgia, 1999
- Kiwanis convention, 1999
- Concert with the Athens Master Chorale, 1999
- "Celebrate 2000" concert at The Classic Center, Athens, Georgia, 1999
- Boggs Academy concert
- Concert with the Afro-American Choral Ensemble at UGA

2000s

- Eighth Annual William Levi Dawson Institute for Classical and Folk Music, Tuskegee University, 2000
- UGA Presbyterian Center for MLK Week celebration, 2000
- Dr. Martin Luther King, Jr. Week Gospelfest at the University of Georgia, 2000
- Walton County Music Guild's American Heritage Concert, Monroe, GA, 2000
- Hosts of "Learn, Sing, Do" community workshop, 2000
- State Meeting of Kappa Alpha Psi, 2000
- Intermountain Choral Festival at the Mormon Tabernacle in Salt Lake City, Utah, 2002
- Dr. Martin Luther King, Jr. services at the State Capitol in Atlanta, 2002
- Veteran's Day ceremony

2010s

- Prayer breakfasts for Athens civic and community groups, 2017, 2019
- First Presbyterian Church for Martin Luther King, Jr. holiday, 2017, 2018

Regular and Annual Concerts over the Years:

- Annual Fall Concert
- Black History Month performances
- Local church revival services
- Performances at various churches throughout the Northeast Georgia region

Appendix 5

James' Favorite Scripture and Sacred Music

Scripture

Psalm 23
Psalm 27
Psalm 118
Psalm 121
Psalm 150
Isaiah 43:19
John 3:16
Romans 8:28
Colossians 3:15
I Thessalonians 5:17-18

James' Favorite Hymns and Other Sacred Songs

Blessed Assurance
Come Unto Jesus
Great Is Thy Faithfulness
Hear My Prayer
Holy Is He
In Me
It Is Well With My Soul
Just Tell Jesus
Keep Me Everyday
O How I Love Jesus
O Jesus
Only What You Do for Christ
Solid Rock
Sweet Hour of Prayer
The Invitation
There's Not a Friend

Appendix 6

History of the Hymn, "It Is Well With My Soul"

The title of this book is taken from James' favorite hymn, "It Is Well With My Soul." The hymn was written in 1873 by Horatio Spafford, a prominent lawyer and real estate investor in Chicago. Life was good for the Spafford family for many years, but their luck took a turn for the worse in 1871 when the Spaffords' infant son died. In the same year, the Great Chicago Fire destroyed many of the properties Spafford owned. In the midst of this financial and emotional struggle, the recession of 1873 further depleted Stafford's financial resources.

Despite this string of misfortunes, in November 1873 Spafford planned to accompany his wife and four daughters on a long-anticipated trip to Europe on the SS Ville du Havre. At the last minute, he sent his family on ahead while he tended to some business. Tragically, while crossing the Atlantic, the ship collided with another vessel and quickly sank. All four of Stafford's daughters drowned, but his wife was mercifully and miraculously spared. Setting off to meet his heartbroken wife in Europe, he penned a poem as his ship passed the area where he assumed his children had perished.

The Spaffords returned from Europe hoping to rebuild their lives. Tragically, the family suffered a further loss when another son, born after their return, died at a young age. Unfortunately and perhaps unbelievably, their church deemed this string of tragedies

The Spafford children. The four daughters across the top of the album were lost in the shipwreck. (Photo from the Library of Congress.)

The Sinking of the Steamship Ville du Havre. Courier & Ives; Library of Congress.

divine punishment and ostracized the family. As a result, Spafford, his wife Anna, and their two remaining children (daughters also born after the accident at sea) created their own Messianic sect, which they named "the Overcomers."

Deeming it necessary to leave the U.S. to escape the harsh judgement of their community, the family moved to Palestine and settled in Jerusalem. While there, the Spaffords formed a group called the "American Colony." The members of this group performed charitable work among the various religious communities but did not proselytize. Because of this and their selfless acts, this small group gained the trust of the Jewish, Christian, and Muslim communities. The family spent the rest of their lives overseas. Spafford died on October 16, 1888 and was buried in Jerusalem.

When a noted composer of the time, Philip Bliss, read Spafford's poem, he was inspired to write music to accompany it. He intended this composition to be a hymn and it was subsequently published in *Gospel Songs No. 2* in 1876. It quickly became a popular piece, frequently performed in a variety of Christian churches. It was sung by choirs and appeared in hymnals of all denominations.

The Athens Voices of Truth have sung this hymn many times. It is clear that when James directs it, it is transformational for him, for the choir, and for the audience.

APPENDIX 7

The Petition, 1950

Leading up to the consolidation of the city and county school districts, movement toward equalizing African American and white schools in Athens was glacially slow. Discrepancies in the facilities, teacher pay, teaching staff loads, equipment, and supplies were indisputable, and especially disturbing to those in the African American community. In May 1950, the spring of James' fourth grade year, a group of (African American) "interested citizens" delivered a petition to the Athens Board of Education highlighting the many inequalities in the district. This petition sparked debate and some fear among the members of the Board, the mayor, and the city council. The district responded but did not address most of the issues the petition raised. Nor would these concerns be fully addressed for another 20 years, until the district finally completely desegregated. Even then, the remedies that the Board proposed for these inequities had limited success as far as the African American community was concerned.

Superintendent Ayers presented the petition to the Board and its content was recorded in the meeting minutes. The petition read as follows:

Athens, Georgia

To: The Superintendent of Schools and the Board of Education of Athens, Georgia.

This petition shows:

1.   That your petitioners are Citizens of Athens, many being patrons of the public schools of Athens and all are interested in the education of our youth, without regard to race or religion.

2.   Your petitioners show that there are 86 teachers employed to instruct 2,833 children who attend the white schools or a

teacher for 32.8 students. In the Negro schools, 39 teachers are employed to teach 1,507 children which is a teacher for 38.6 pupils. The teacher load in the Negro schools is 17.6 percent greater than in the white schools.

3.   This petition also shows that the 86 teachers in the white schools receive a total salary of $271,651.76 or an average annual salary of $3,158.85. The Negro teacher with a greater pupil load than the white teacher receives $1,370.57 less per year than the teacher in white schools, thus the salary of the Negro teacher is only 56.6 percent of that of the white teacher.

4.   Your petitioners show that there are 29,642 volumes in the libraries of the white schools, having a value of $30,935.55 or 10.4 volumes per pupil in the white schools. In the Negro schools, there are 4,524 library books, or 3 volumes per pupil with a per pupil value of $3.14 or less than one third of that per pupil in the white schools.

5.   It is shown that there are 10 brick and 1 cement buildings for the white children, making all of their buildings of permanent structure, while for Negroes, there are two brick and six frame.

6.   Your petitioners show that there is invested in school plants for white children $1,145,392.56 or $481.48 per pupil in average daily attendance. On the other hand, the value of the school plant for Negro children is only $128,241.21 or a pittance of $96.28 per pupil in average daily attendance. Thus, the Board of Education of Athens has a plant investment of five times as much per white child as per Negro child. This fact is all the more significant when we take into consideration that if the present plans of constructing a million dollar plant for a white high school and only approximately $100,000 for a Negro elementary school materializes [sic], the Athens Board of Education will have a plant investment of almost 10 times as much per white child as per Negro child.

7.   Your petitioners show that the curriculum of the white schools include special teachers for art, band instruction, commercial training, and physical education; while none of these

are offered in the Negro schools.

8. We show that these gross discriminations in school facilities in the public schools of Athens are unfair, unjust, unchristian and illegal since they are based wholly on race.

9. Your petitioners pray that the Board of Education remove these inequalities in educational facilities based on race and color, forthwith, and pray further:

a. That the Board invite the Superintendent of State Schools to make a study of school needs in Athens, such a survey to be used as the basis for correcting the existing inequalities in education in the public schools of Athens.

b. That the Board of Education provide additional teachers in the Negro schools, thus making the teacher-pupil load in the Negro schools approximately the same as that in the other schools and also provide for the same type of enriched curriculum.

c. That the Board of Education will also put into operation only one salary scale for all teachers provided the white teachers to suffer no loss in this readjustment.

d. We petition the Board to provide library facilities, teaching aids, science and vocational equipment and other equipment and facilities in the Negro schools equal to those in white schools.

e. We further petition the Board of Education of Athens to provide from funds now available from the recent bond sales, a modern school plant for the Negro high school, the school to have all modern facilities such as library, cafeteria, auditorium, ample rest rooms, teachers' lounges, gymnasium, etc., and the building to be fire resistant throughout. The present high school plant is outmoded, a fire hazard, overcrowded, and in no wise does it meet the standards of modern education.

To correct this ratio of these wide inequalities which this petition shows and which any casual observer will verify upon a visit to the Negro plants, is a challenge to your Christian statesmanship which we pray you may meet with courage and with a sense of fair play. Georgia and America expect of the Negro boy the same intellectual strength and moral character and patriotism that they expect of other citizens. We appeal to you then, to prepare the Negro child as you prepare other children so that he may meet the challenge of his community, his State and his Country. He cannot do this when he receives only one-tenth of his share.

He can and will if he is given a full chance such as the law exacts, Democracy demands and Christianity requires. We urgently beg you for a formal reply at a very early date.

Most respectfully yours,

Interested Citizens of Athens

I was not able to find the names of any of the "Interested Citizens" who wrote or contributed to this petition. I believe, based on notes in the school district papers at the time, that several were prominent African Americans in Athens, perhaps including teachers, business executives, and pastors. This may be one explanation for why they did not sign their names. It would be very difficult and even dangerous to sign one's name to such a petition if one depended on the school system or the community for their livelihood. Another possibility is that they *did* sign their names but they were omitted from the record. I could not locate the original petition in the archives.

After discussing the petition, the BOE voted unanimously to write a letter acknowledging its receipt and informing the citizens that the matter would be referred to a special committee for study. A detailed reply was to be sent as soon as possible.

On June 15, 1950, the special "committee," made up of Mr. Howard McWhorter and Mr. H. G. Callahan, met with Mayor Jack Wells and Superintendent Fred Ayers. The committee announced that it would make "specific recommendations concerning the petition submitted by Negro citizens after contracts for projects, already approved, have been let." In other words, current projects, for which a bond fund had been approved and was substantially allocated, must be completed before the BOE would let the "Interested Citizens" know of its intentions.

At the July 27, 1950 BOE meeting, Mayor Wells presented the following response that the committee would send to the "Interested Citizens of Athens":

———

July 27, 1950

From: Athens City Board of Education

To: Interested Citizens of Athens

Re: Petition submitted to the Athens Board of Education; May 25, 1950

This is to acknowledge receipt of your petition which was read in full to the Athens Board of Education at its regular monthly meeting held May 25, 1950.

A special committee was appointed to make a study of your petition. This study has been completed and this committee has made recommendations to the Board concerning the items mentioned in your petition.

At the regular monthly meeting of the Athens Board of Education, held on July 27, 1950, the Athens Board of Education passed the following resolution concerning a new high school plant for Negroes:

> That all funds remaining in the school bond account, after the contracts have been awarded for the new Athens High School building, the gymnasium and the East Athens Elementary School, be applied on the cost of a new Athens High and Industrial School.

> We recommend that, should additional funds be needed to complete a new Athens High and Industrial School plant, the Athens Board of Education ask the Mayor and Council of the City of Athens to call a bond election for the purpose of securing funds to complete this plant, and that the Board of Education pledges its wholehearted support in carrying such a bond election to a successful conclusion.

> We recommend that land be secured for the erection of a new Athens High and Industrial School and that the Board of Education authorize the preparation of plans and

specifications.

This summer the Athens Board of Education is spending between $12,000.00 and $15,000.00 on painting, repairs and renovations to existing buildings. More than two-thirds of this amount is being spent on buildings provided for Negro pupils. We have either completed or will have completed before the summer is over the following work on buildings provided for Negro pupils:

1. Painting interior of Newtown School
2. Painting exterior and roof of Newtown School.
3. Painting interior of Reese Street School.
4. Painting exterior and roof of Reese Street School.
5. Painting interior of Athens High and Industrial School.
6. Painting roof and gymnasium at Athens High and Industrial School.
7. Painting interior and exterior lunchroom and Home Economics Building at the Athens High and Industrial School.
8. Installing new floor in lunchroom at Athens High and Industrial School.
9. Doing all needed repairs at the Reese Street School and the High and Industrial School.

We have made a careful study of the building facilities provided for both White and Negro children and we contend that–when the painting, repairs and renovations listed above have been completed–when the East Athens Elementary School has been completed–and when a new high school plant has been provided for Negro pupils, building facilities for White and Negro pupils will be equal in every respect.

We recognize the fact that there is a difference in the salary schedule for White and Negro teachers. This is true on both the local level and the state level. If you will check with the officials in the State Department of Education, Atlanta, Georgia, you will find that the City of Athens is one of only a few systems in the state providing local supplements for Negro teachers.

On January 1, 1948 every Negro teacher in the Athens System was given a $240.00 annual supplement from local funds. On

January 1, 1950 this supplement was increased by $100.00, making the annual supplement to every Negro teacher $340.00 per year from local funds.

It is our intention to continue additions to this local supplement each year until Negro salaries have been made equal to that paid to White teachers insofar as the local supplement is concerned.

The Minimum Foundation Program, which has already been passed by the Georgia Legislature, provides equal pay for both Whites and Negroes as far as the state is concerned. When this program is financed salaries for Whites and Negroes will be equal as far as the state schedule is concerned.

It is our hope to equalize the local supplement by the time the Minimum Foundation Program is financed.

Two years ago the Athens Board of Education started a Kindergarten program for Negro pupils. This program is financed entirely from local funds. If you will investigate you will find very few, if any, school systems in the state providing Kindergarten facilities for Negro pupils.

In your petition you referred to inequalities in the library facilities as provided for Whites and Negroes. We recognize the fact that our library facilities in all schools are not what we desire but it is our intention to provide library facilities for all children on a fair and equal basis in all schools when our building program has been completed.

In your petition you referred to the inequalities in per pupil investment in school plants based on average daily attendance. We contend that when the work on buildings, outlined above, has been completed the per pupil investment for Whites and Negroes for school plant facilities will be equal in every respect.

You mention in your petition certain differences in curriculum offerings in the schools provided for Whites and Negroes. You mention special teachers for art, band instruction, commercial training and physical education. It is our intention to correct these curriculum deficiencies as rapidly as possible after our building program has been completed.

It is the desire of your Board of Education to deal fairly with all the citizens of Athens in administering the affairs of the Athens City Schools. We recognize and believe you will also recognize that certain conditions which have developed over a long period of time cannot be corrected in one year or two years. We believe we have shown you, from the action we have taken, that it is our intention to provide equal facilities in every respect for all the children of the City of Athens.

Yours very truly,
Athens City Board of Education
By Howard H. McWhorter, Chairman

Mayor Wells made a motion that this communication be approved. The motion was seconded and approved unanimously.

Nevertheless, the petition and its response made the school board and the city government nervous. They knew an increasing number of cases had been brought before local courts alleging discriminatory practices in the distribution of resources in segregated school districts. These lawsuits were, by and large, brought before county courts by African American plaintiffs who were often represented by NAACP lawyers.

Moreover, case law was beginning to be settled in favor of equalizing all resources for physical plants, equipment, teacher pay, and number of pupils per teacher. Although this was prior to the historic *Brown v. Board of Education* decision, Athens officials were nervous enough that the mayor and Superintendent asked the city attorney, James Barrow, to weigh in on the respective responsibilities of the city and school district, so they would be prepared in the event that they were sued over the inequalities. Consequently, at this same July 27, 1950 BOE meeting, Mayor Wells read the following letter from the city attorney, Mr. James Barrow (I have condensed the letter to its salient points):

Dear Mr. Wells:

I am in receipt of your letter requesting an opinion as to the obligations and responsibilities of the City of Athens with respect to the petition for equalization of white and colored school facilities which has been filed with the Board of Education.

In my opinion, the proceeds of the bonds issued by the City of

Athens for school purposes have been properly turned over by
the City Officials to the Treasurer of the Board of Education
for administration by the Board; and there is no direct and
immediate responsibility on the City of Athens for the administration of these funds. . . . It seems obvious [from various
enactments] that it was the intention of the General Assembly that the City of Athens should furnish adequate financial
support to the Board of Education through appropriations; and
that the Board of Education should have sold [sic] responsibility for the administration of the funds raised and turned over to
it by the City.

In an indirect way, however, the City is quite vitally interested
in the conflict over equalization of white and colored school
facilities in Athens; and for that reason I would like to give you
my opinion with respect to the situation.

Article VII, Section 1, Paragraph I of the Constitution of Georgia provides, "Separate schools shall be provided for the white
and colored races." In accordance with this provision, the act of
the General Assembly creating the Board of Education requires
that separate schools be provided for white and colored children in the City by the Board. . . . The Fourteenth Amendment
to the Constitution of the United States provides "nor shall
any State . . . deny to any person within its jurisdiction equal
protection of the law." It has been held by the Federal Courts
that this provision of the Fourteenth Amendment to the Constitution of the United States does not prohibit separation of
white and colored races by a State or by a State instrumentality
provided that there is equality of treatment and of privileges
accorded to the separated groups. . . . If there is discrimination
in regard to the treatment or privileges accorded to segregated
races by a State or State instrumentality, such discrimination
violates the quoted provision of the Fourteenth Amendment.
With respect to schools, discrimination which is unlawful may
exist with respect to the distribution of textbooks; the enforcement of laws providing for compulsory school attendance; the
length of the school year; the curricula made available to the
study body; standards of promotion; events on the school cal-

endar; teacher qualifications; or physical facilities. . . . It is my understanding that the complaint in the instant case is based on the ground of inequality of facilities which will exist when funds now in the hands of the Board of Education have been expended in enlarging the physical equipment of the school system in accordance with plans which have been made public by the Board.

Mr. Ayers has given me the following information:

> The number of children in the colored schools–1,508
>
> The number of children in the white schools–2,565
>
> The present value of the physical equipment of the colored schools - $406,467.45
>
> The present value of the physical equipment of the white schools - $1,309,491.90
>
> The amount proposed to be spent on physical equipment for the colored schools - $281,295.77
>
> The amount proposed to be spent on physical equipment for the white schools - $1,000,000.00

From these figures it can be seen that 37 percent of the students in the Athens Public Schools are colored; that 24 percent of the value of the physical equipment of the public school system is now being used to educate this 37 percent of the school body, and that if the improvements as now proposed by the Board of Education are made, only 17 percent of the value of the physical equipment in the public school system in Athens will be devoted to the education of the 37 percent of the student body who are colored. Even if these figures are not strictly accurate and if they require some readjustment on account of the retirement of the present white high school from active use, **it is obvious that the proposed plan will result in substantial discrimination against the colored students insofar as the value of the physical facilities is concerned** [*emphasis added*]. While it is true that the rights accorded by the Fourteenth Amendment are personal to the individual and are not conferred upon a class as such, nevertheless, evidence of class discrimination of the sort indicated in the figures set out above has been accepted by the Courts as proof of a discrimination against the individual student in the school system. . . . If there is any doubt in your mind as to what the Federal Courts mean by their requirement of equal facilities, I strongly urge that you read the decision of the Supreme Court of the United States in the case of Sweat [sic] vs. Painter, decided June 5, 1950, a copy of which is enclosed herewith. While this decision deals with education at the college level, the principle is equally applicable to all levels of the Federal Courts; and this we must be prepared to furnish if we expect to maintain segregated school systems. **It is my opinion that the proposed action of the Board of Education will discriminate against the colored students in a manner and to an extent forbidden by the Fourteenth Amendment to the Constitution of the United States, and that it is consequently illegal** *[emphasis added]*.

When unlawful discrimination in the granting of school facilities exists, the Federal Courts can correct the situation by declaratory judgment and injunction. . . . For the reasons set out above it is my opinion that the expenditures of funds as now proposed by the Board of Education is illegal; and that there exists in the Federal Courts an effective judicial remedy to correct or prevent this illegal expenditure of funds. In the event that the Board should proceed with its present plans, and the complaining parties should bring suit in the Federal Courts, it seems to me most likely that there would be three possible results to such a suit. First, the Board might be compelled under Court supervision to equalize facilities by allocating to the colored school system physical facilities now intended to be used for white children. Second, the Board might be required to expend such additional amount of money as may be necessary to equalize facilities. Third, the expenditure of the funds now in the hands of the Board might be tied up by injunction and be allowed only in the event the expenditures were supervised by the Court to ensure that they were spent in such a way to equalize facilities. Any one of these three possible outcomes of such a suit would require the expenditure of additional funds by the Board of Education to comply with the judgment and at

the same time satisfy the demands of the public for school facilities. In as much as the City has the duty imposed upon it by
law to furnish the Board of Education with funds adequate to
enable the Board to carry out its responsibilities, this requirement of additional funds would have to be met by the City.

For these reasons it is my opinion that the City has a very substantial interest in forestalling litigation which may lead to such
unexpected financial burdens being imposed upon the City.

> Sincerely yours,
> (signed) James Barrow

Immediately following the reading of the letter from James Barrow, the minutes of the BOE meeting are recorded as follows:

> Mr. Wells proposed the idea that since there was
> $1,281,000.00 in the bond fund when this fund was turned
> over to the Board of Education, and since, by previous action
> of this board, we are already on record to keep the expenditure
> of the Athens High School within a million dollars, that, by
> adding approximately $119,000.00 to the $281,000.00 in the
> bond fund in excess of the million dollars, this would give a
> total of $00,000.00 [*sic*] for Negro school purposes which is
> the amount that had been requested by interested citizens who
> had previously appeared before the Board. Several members of
> the Board asked questions concerning how this action, if passed
> by the Board, would affect the opening of bids [on building
> projects already in the works] to be held on September 6. After
> discussing the matter at length Mr. Wells made a motion that
> the Board of Education allocate $400,000.00 of the bond
> funds for Negro school purposes. Motion seconded by Mr.
> Driftmier, who, at the same time, made a motion that this
> motion be tabled until after the opening of bids on September
> 6. Mrs. Thurmond seconded Mr. Driftmier's motion. Motion
> carried with a majority voting an affirmative vote and Mr.
> Wells voting No.

This second motion had the effect of postponing the decision as to
whether the Board would allocate additional funds for the African Amer-

ican schools. Mayor Wells' original motion was never considered again.

While James Barrow's letter emphasizes the financial risk to the city and the legal risk to the Board of Education, he is clearly stating that given the current state of affairs, the Athens City Schools were skating on thin ice with regard to equal treatment under the law for Black students. The only thing that might save them from a lawsuit was to show intentional and purposeful equal allocation of funds for the African American students in the district. However, after the September 6 opening of bids for the remaining school district projects, there is no further mention of the petition or its response in the Athens City School Board meeting minutes for the remainder of 1950. While the Board did build two new schools for Black students over the next six years, these schools were never funded at a level equal to the white schools. The Athens City School Board gambled that the "Interested Citizens" would not pursue their complaint in the courts . . . and won.

APPENDIX 8

Model Cities Program:
Priorities, Successes, and Legacy

In 1980, Walter Denero, the director of Athens' Model Cities Program, wrote his doctoral dissertation in Public Administration at the University of Georgia. His topic was whether the Model Cities Program had "resulted in a new service delivery system and institutional change in the ways that city governments operated with respect to the administration and implementation of large-scale federally funded anti-poverty programs" (Denero Abstract). In particular, Denero analyzed "the processes of comprehensive planning, coordination, citizen participation, and decision-making by local elected officials to see whether support can be found indicating that these processes and procedures became institutionalized in Athens" (Denero 99). Denero served as the director of the Model Cities Program from September 1970 to November 1973, when he became director of the newly created Division of Housing and Community Development in Athens.

In his dissertation, Denero asserted that before the Model Cities Program was adopted, most city and county planning dealt with zoning and land use, with very little focus on social or economic planning. Model Cities planning represented a completely new approach to tackling poverty, and the comprehensive community plan it required was a complete departure from previous programs. The five-year program encompassed a variety of ambitious and far-reaching goals. Some of these came to fruition and their results are still evident in Athens, while other projects withered on the vine for lack of continued funding or lack of leadership after the program ended.

This appendix will outline, based on existing records, the priorities, proposed projects, evidence of effectiveness, and outcomes of the Model Cities Program in Athens. I begin by providing data on the area and discussing how the major issues identified in the Model Neighborhood Area (see map on page 160) were addressed.

Some 1969 data on the Model Neighborhood Area (MNA)

- Population of Athens in 1970: 44,342
- Number of residents in the MNA: 13,500
- Median income in MNA: $3,607
- Athens median income: $6,079
- 76% of the unpaved streets in the city were in the MNA
- 71.9% of all structures on unpaved streets in the MNA were dilapidated
- 96.4% of all structures in the MNA were either deteriorated or dilapidated
- 423 lots had only outdoor toilets
- 639 acres had no sewerage

Original Goals of the Model Cities Program

When the Model Cities Program began, the administrators acknowledged that the problem of unemployment and underemployment in the MNA was due to "lack of basic education and/or usable work habits" (Davis). As a result, job training was a priority, but the program administrators recognized that this was not the only issue residents faced. They also understood that citizen involvement was key to making any real change. So their first task was to conduct surveys of the MNA residents to ascertain their needs and wants.

The following 16 goals were established as a result of that survey data (Denero 103):

1. To develop and distribute ideas, methods, and techniques by which private investors can obtain fair returns by investing in the low-income housing market.
2. To provide housing for all economic classes by providing new housing and rehabilitating existing housing.
3. To provide a mass transportation system between home and job for all residents of the model neighborhood area.
4. To eliminate at least 50 percent of the flow of heavy traffic to the model neighborhood area, one of the major contributing factors to urban blight.
5. To provide a plan for traffic management in the model neighborhood area.
6. To provide by improving at least by 100 percent the quality and

quantity of recreational and cultural facilities and programs for residents of the MNA.

7. To provide for neighborhood health facilities and programs which meet the needs of the people in the model area.

8. To provide for an educational enrichment program which will, after five years, have elevated the educationally disadvantaged to the same level of achievement as other children in the community.

9. To provide more training, particularly in human relations, for police personnel, and to develop a probation and correctional program for the city's misdemeanor prisoners including juveniles.

10. To provide more and better social services in the model neighborhood area. This includes a broad range of services such as family counseling, child care centers, family financial planning instructions, and alcoholic rehabilitation.

11. To develop and implement programs in the model area which are consistent with the needs of model neighborhood residents and which residents have had a major role in developing.

12. To upgrade the skills and knowledge of the existing labor force so that underemployment, defined as those gainfully employed full-time but not earning a sum equivalent to their potential with additional skills and training, will be substantially reduced.

13. To have strong neighborhood organizations within the model neighborhoods which can provide a means by which the attitudes and needs of the area residents can be effectively expressed.

14. To provide a cost-benefit analysis on all program components.

15. To provide legal aid to everyone requiring legal assistance in the model neighborhood area but who are unable to pay the full cost of the service.

16. To develop the older downtown business area as shopping, service, and employment center for residents of the model neighborhood area. (Denero 103-104)

According to Denero, the strategy was to encourage as much MNA resident involvement as possible. It was deemed critical to the success of the program that citizens be involved in all phases of the process and all decision making. Another major goal of the Model Cities Program was to engage city officials more actively in the workings of the government.

The guidelines for the program also deemed it essential to establish public and private partnerships to ensure that projects were implemented and administered in the most effective and efficient manner possible and to avoid duplication or overlap of services. The following agencies had at least one representative working on Model City administration and planning:

- Action, Inc.
- Athens-Clarke County Health Department
- Athens-Clarke County Planning Commission
- Athens Community Council on Aging
- Athens Housing Authority
- Citizen Participation Council for Action, Inc.
- Clarke County Bar Association
- Clarke County Department of Family and Children Services
- Clarke County School District
- Georgia Department of Labor
- Mayor and City Council of Athens
- University of Georgia

There was one major glitch just before the program was to begin that could have kept Athens from participating in the program. Athens had already been chosen as a Model City when HUD realized, very late in the process, that the city had not completely desegregated its public schools. School districts were required to be in compliance with all federal education standards, including desegregation, for cities to be eligible to receive Model Cities funds. As noted previously in this book, Athens struggled to finalize and implement a desegregation plan that was deemed acceptable by both its citizens and the courts. The federal government eventually approved Athens' desegregation plan even as it continued to wind its way through the courts, and HUD released the Model Cities funds.

Thirty-eight individual projects were identified for the first year of the Model Cities Program. During this first year, fifty-nine percent of the funds awarded were spent on physical improvement projects such as paving roads or providing water and sewer services, while the remainder supported health care, child care, services for senior citizens and the blind, paraprofessional training, a tutoring center, and a youth employment project.

Summary

In his dissertation, Walter Denero asserts that the Model Cities Program achieved numerous successes that transcended the actual physical and social programs that were implemented. Many of the programs would continue and become a part of the fabric of Athens. However, Denero was most interested in whether the processes and procedures established through the Model Cities Program would also become integrated into the ways the city did business, involved citizens, and made decisions.

Denero's findings may be summarized as follows:

Comprehensive planning: As a result of the Model Cities Program, Denero asserts, a much broader and more comprehensive planning program was institutionalized in Athens. This planning included providing for the social, economic, educational, and physical welfare of its citizens.

Coordination: As a result of Model Cities, Athens recognized that coordinating efforts and programs between and among private and public service agencies would more effectively and efficiently utilize available resources and personnel.

Citizen participation: The enormous increase in citizen input and involvement represented the most dramatic change in the city's approach to making decisions and implementing initiatives in the MC years. Unfortunately, Denero reports, the level of citizen engagement decreased after the Citizen Advisory Committee for Model Cities disbanded. Denero concluded that citizen involvement had not been institutionalized as the other components had been.

I would argue, however, that citizen engagement did ultimately change as a result of this program. Citizen participation is a vibrant element of contemporary Athens, and I would venture to say that without the Model Cities Program, we would perhaps not have reached the magnitude of citizen engagement present in today's city government. The vibrant public participation that characterizes Athens today leads me to believe the program did have a significant and lasting impact.

Involvement of elected officials: As a result of the Model Cities Program, the city council absolutely became more involved in decision-making in relation to federal grants. City council members began to sit on committees and task forces. They met with constituents more frequently and were consulted about decisions that previously rested entirely with the mayor.

A Final Analysis

In December 1975, Mayor Julius F. Bishop presented his "State of the City" message at a meeting of the mayor and city council, in which he reviewed the accomplishments of the previous year. Mayor Bishop was about to step down after serving as mayor for twelve years (1963-1975). His speech focused on the projects and programs initiated by the Model Cities Program, which had just completed its fifth and final year.

Physical Programs

The Model Cities Program produced numerous improvements in the water and sewer systems throughout the city. A new water filter plant was built and named in honor of Jack G. Beachman, former city engineer. Downtown streets and sidewalks were upgraded.

Housing continued to be improved throughout the city. The widening of Oak/Oconee Street was almost completed, with a new four-lane bridge over the Oconee River, while other bridges were constructed in connection with the bypass expansion. Three community centers opened in 1975: Lyndon House, East Athens, and Bishop Park. Public transportation was due to begin in mid-1976 with sixteen diesel, air-conditioned buses on nine routes covering sixty-two miles of city streets. The new transportation system was expected to create forty-five new jobs.

Social Programs

The Athens Information and Referral Service [or "Helpline"–which evolved into Community Connection 211], which took calls, made referrals, and performed outreach services, reported a total of 13,637 client contacts. Child care was provided for 461 children at eight local child care facilities. Employment at these centers provided 125 jobs.

As a part of the five-year Model Cities Program, HUD provided a total of $9,479,500 to Athens, while another $6,150,000 in matching state and federal funds helped complete numerous projects. The newly formed Community Development Department, which would replace Model Cities, had a grant of $3.4 million to continue the work begun under Model Cities. A new police chief was hired, as was the city's first female police officer, and a major reorganization was underway in the Police Department.

The City Recreation Department opened five new parks and renovated the seven existing parks. Park acreage increased from 78 to 203 acres. The city and county parks departments merged so all city and county residents had access to all facilities. Bishop Park opened, and more parks and recreation programs for children and adults were created.

Political Action

Through public ballot initiatives, the citizens of Athens approved the creation of a Chief Administrative Officer for the city, established a Local Option Sales Tax (now SPLOST), and elected the mayor and city council members. The city also held numerous public hearings for zoning, transportation, community development, an employee merit system, the budget, etc. The November 1976 ballot was to have an initiative asking citizens to approve the creation of a Downtown Athens Development Authority.

Administrative

A major housing analysis was completed by the Athens Housing Authority to determine future housing needs. The city established a group insurance program along with a new pension plan for all city employees. It also established an incentive plan for police officers to continue their education, whether through a college degree or advanced training. The city tax office was completely computerized.

Many of the programs begun under Model Cities were continued under the Community Development Grants, also funded by HUD. Athens received $9.3 million dollars for three years after the Model Cities funding ended, which helped sustain the health center, tutoring center, paraprofessional training, child care, senior citizen services, youth services, police services, and the Helpline.

Reflections

The Model Cities Program represented the largest infusion of federal funding to help impoverished neighborhoods in American history. While not all of the programs or initiatives continued, a great deal of good came out of those five years, not the least of which was increased citizen engagement. In addition, Model Cities funded major programs, initiatives, services, and projects that absolutely uplifted large parts of the Model Neighborhood Area during that time period and beyond.

However, fixing the root causes of and attendant issues surrounding poverty was and remains challenging. While streets may be paved, piped water provided, child care centers opened, public bus systems created, and health centers established, there is still a deep cultural bedrock in our country that was built upon discrimination and the perpetuation of an underclass of citizens. If the ultimate goal of the Model Cities Program was to end poverty in Athens, it fell short. But no one program and no infusion of funds, no matter how sizable, can accomplish such a huge task.

Ending poverty is extremely complicated, but I still want to believe it is possible. However, I am not sure we have the political, moral, or economic will to do it. And while I do not presume to know what the solution is, I suspect that many of the problems of poverty in Athens arise from a long legacy of racism and discrimination. Federal, state, and local governments have implemented many programs over the years to address poverty and diminish its effects on people's lives, but money alone cannot undo centuries of relegating an entire segment of our society to second-class status.

Nearly forty-five years after the Model Cities Program ended, the poverty rate in Athens remains unconscionably high, belying any gains by this program. And while no single program, no one-time infusion of cash, and no one system can undo the effects of centuries of our history, the ugly truth is that the legacy of slavery, discrimination, racism, and inequality remains a yoke around the neck of our city and this country.

James' Acknowledgments

I am grateful to Ms. Ellen L. Walker, author of *It Is Well: The Life and Times of James Russell Smith*. Thank you for your consistency, research, dedication, hard work, and perseverance to this project. Thank you for taking on this work. I am honored and humbled to have had the chance to work with you from the beginning to the completion. You will always be remembered by my family and myself.

Thanks to Rosa, my wife, for your help and cooperation.

This writing will be cherished by us and it will serve as a lasting history for my children, Tiara, J. Ricardo, Rhondolyn, and my grandson, Jameson.

Thanks to my siblings, Joseph, Willie Mae, Frank, Christine, and Leroy, Jr. for your contributions.

Thanks to family, friends, mentees, and choir members who contributed to this work.

Thanks to all who shared testimonies. You are awesome!

–James R. Smith

AUTHOR'S ACKNOWLEDGMENTS

I would first and foremost like to thank Smitty for allowing me to write his biography. I am grateful that he was willing to share his life, his story, his friendship.

Thanks also to Smitty's family, who endured many Saturdays when he and I would sit for hours in his den talking about his life. I hope they are happy with the result of our conversations.

I am forever indebted to Diane Miller, who edited this manuscript with precision and expertise. She has been a friend for many years, but is also a professional editor. When I asked if she would be willing to read and edit my writing, she very graciously said yes. What resulted is a much better, clearer, and more concise story and I am so grateful for her immeasurable contribution.

Many thanks to the entire staff of the Hargrett Rare Book & Manuscript Library at the University of Georgia for going above and beyond to assist in the research for this book. They were always very patient, kind, and helpful.

Boundless thanks, appreciation, and love to Daisy, who lived through the many months in which I was completely absorbed by this project. She kept me buoyed with her usual patience, understanding, nourishment, and endless words of encouragement. She also read each chapter as I finished it and gave invaluable advice about how to make the story flow.

And while all three of my sons live over one thousand miles away in three different directions, I am grateful for their long-distance encouragement, love, and support. I am enormously proud of each of them and love them more than words can express. Thank you, Zach, Alexander, and Rad for being the most wonderful young men a mother could ever hope for.

–Ellen L. Walker

BIBLIOGRAPHY

Adair, David James. *An Inventory and Analysis of Extant County Training School Buildings in Georgia Originally Established with Philanthropic Funds Devoted to African American Education (1911-1937)*. 2006. University of Georgia, Master's thesis.

Aderhold, O.C., Ira E. Aaron, Joseph C. Bledsoe, Fannie Lee Boyd, J. L. Dickerson, J. A. Williams. *A Survey of Public Education in Clarke County, Georgia*. The Bureau of Educational Studies and Field Services, College of Education, University of Georgia, Athens, GA, 1950.

Aerial photograph of Athens. The Abrams Aerial Survey Corporation, Rochester, MI, 1946.

Alkan-Ga. "The Price of Cotton 1800-2000: A Table." *Google Answers*, Google, 26 June 2002, http://answers.google.com/answers/threadview/id/33770.html.

"Amendment No. 4 Seems to Have Been Voted In." *Athens Banner-Herald*, Nov. 3, 1954.

Athens. *Negro Settlement Areas in Athens, Georgia*. 1959. [Publisher unknown]

Athens Banner-Herald, April 28, 1941. [Front section]

Athens City Directory Company. "City Directory of Athens [1920-1921]." University of Georgia. Map and Government Information Library, 1920/1921.

Athens, Georgia City Directory (including Bogart, Hull, Watkinsville, Crawford, Lexington, Winterville), 1977. Johnson Publishing Company, 1977.

Athens, Georgia City Records, 1860-1970. MS 1633. Hargrett Rare Book & Manuscript Library, The University of Georgia Libraries.

Athens High and Industrial School, Aeck Associates, 29p, May 15, 1954. [Blueprints]

Athens Model Cities Program, MS 879, Hargrett Rare Book & Manuscript Library, The University of Georgia Libraries.

Athens Office of the City Engineer. *Athens, Georgia: June 1955*. Rev. ed, 1957.

Athens Public Schools. *School Plant Survey: Negro Schools*, Athens, Georgia, April 1952.

Aued, Blake. "Watch This Documentary about the Civil Rights Movement in Athens." *Flagpole Magazine | Athens, GA. News, Music, Arts, Restaurants*, 3 July 2014, flagpole.com/blogs/culture-briefs/posts/

watch-this-documentary-about-the-civil-rights-movement-in-athens.

Baldwin Directory Company, Inc.. "Baldwin and Chamber of Commerce's Athens Georgia City Directory [1938]." University of Georgia. Map and Government Information Library, 1938.

Baldwin Directory Company, Inc.. "Baldwin's Athens Georgia City Directory [1940]." University of Georgia. Map and Government Information Library, 1940.

Baldwin Directory Company, Inc.. "Baldwin's Athens Georgia City Directory [1942]." University of Georgia. Map and Government Information Library, 1942.

Baldwin Directory Company, Inc.. "Baldwin's Athens Georgia City Directory [1947]." University of Georgia. Map and Government Information Library, 1947.

Baldwin Directory Company, Inc.. "Baldwin's Athens Georgia City Directory [1949]." University of Georgia. Map and Government Information Library, 1949.

Ballanco, Julius. "The Plumbing Census." *Plumbing Mechanical RSS*, Plumbing & Mechanical, 14 Jan. 2013, https://www.pmmag.com/articles/93671-the-plumbing-census.

"Bathrooms of the Early 20th Century." *Bathrooms - Vintage Homes - 1900 to 1950 - Old Houses*, Antique Home Style. http://www.antiquehomestyle.com/inside/bathrooms/index.htm.

Beacham, J. G. *Map of City of Athens, Georgia Jan. 1944*. Athens, Ga, 1946.

Beacham, J. G. *Map of City of Athens, Georgia*. The McGregor, 1952.

Berry, Riley M. Fletcher. "The Black Mammy Memorial Institute and Its Founder." *Table Talk,* The Arthur H. Crist Co., January 1912, https://play.google.com/books/reader?id=UQFBAQAAMAAJ&hl=en&pg=GBS.PA1.

Berry, Riley M. Fletcher. "The Black Mammy Memorial Institute: How a Southern School is Training Colored Women in the Household Arts," *Good Housekeeping Magazine*, October 1911, pp. 562-563.

Bill, Jill. "The Black Mammy Memorial Institute." *Prezi.com*, 5 Dec. 2017, https://prezi.com/sovsec6myrtt/the-black-mammy-memorial-institute/.

"Black History Month: UGA Timeline." *UGA Online*, https://online.uga.edu/node/5346.

Bledsoe, Madison. "Cornering History–A Look at the Hot Corner of Athens." *Georgia Political Review,* Spring 2017, http://georgiapoliticalreview.com/cornering-history/.

"Boll Weevil in Georgia." *Todayingeorgiahistory.org/*, 12 Aug. 1970, https://www.todayingeorgiahistory.org/content/boll-weevil-georgia.

"Brown v. Board of Education." Wikipedia: The Free Encyclopedia, Wikimedia Foundation, 13 Aug. 2019, en.wikipedia.org/wiki/Brown_v._Board_of_Education.

Bryan, Mary Givens (comp.). *Georgia's Official Register: 1953-1954*. State of Georgia Department of Archives and History, Longino & Porter, Inc., 1954, http://dlg.galileo.usg.edu/statreg-images/pdfs/1953.pdf

Bureau of Labor Statistics and National Urban League. *The Economic Situation of Negroes in the United States*. U.S. Dept. of Labor, 1961.

"Cases Adjudged in the Supreme Court of the United States at October Term, 1970." *Swann et al. v. Charlotte-Mecklenburg Board of Education et al.* Certiorari to the United States Court of Appeals for the Fourth Circuit, No. 281. Argued October 12, 1970. Decided April 20, 1971.

Champion Map Corporation. *Map of Athens and Clarke County*. Champion Map, 1960.

Ciomek, Summer Anne. *The History, Architecture, and Preservation of Rosenwald Schools in Georgia*. 2007. University of Georgia, Master's thesis.

City of Athens, Georgia . Western States, 1957. [Map]

Clarke County Board of Education papers, 1871-1983. MS 3179. Hargrett Rare Book and Manuscript Library, The University of Georgia Libraries.

"Clarke Voters Favor School Consolidation." *Athens Banner Herald*, Nov. 3, 1954.

Collins, Jan. "Replies Given to Grievances," *Athens Banner-Herald*, April 30, 1970.

Collins, William J., and Katharine L. Shester. "Slum Clearance and Urban Renewal in the United States," *American Economic Journal: Applied Economics*, vol. 5, no. 1, January 2013, pp. 239-273, https://www.jstor.org/stable/43189425

Currier & Ives. "The Sinking of the Steamship Ville du Havre" [lithograph]. Library of Congress, New York, c. 1873, http://loc.gov/pictures/resource/ppmsca.07650/

Dartt, Rebecca H. *Women Activists in the Fight for Georgia School Desegregation, 1958-1961*, McFarland & Co, Inc., 2012

Davis, Mike. "Unemployment A Key MNA Problem," *Athens Daily News*, April 30, 1969.

Denero, Walter Alexander. *The Model Cities Experience: A Transfer of Processes and Procedures*. 1980. University of Georgia, Ph.D. dissertation.

Ellett, Ashton, G. "Not Another Little Rock: Massive Resistance, Desegregation, and the Athens White Business Establishment, 1960-61." *The Georgia Historical Quarterly*, vol. 97, no. 2, Summer 2013, pp. 176-216.

Ellis, Marion, Bamby Ray, and Lynn Speno. "Public Elementary and Secondary Schools in Georgia, 1868-1971," National Register of Historic Places, U.S. Department of the Interior, https://georgiashpo.org/sites/default/files/hpd/pdf/Historic_Schools_Context_0.pdf

"Enlisted Pay Chart 1940-1941." *1940-1941 Military Pay Chart*, www.navycs. com/charts/1940-military-pay-chart.html.

Fairclough, Adam. "Being in the Field of Education and also Being a Negro . . . Seems . . . Tragic: Black Teachers in the Jim Crow South," *The Journal of American History*, vol. 87, no. 1, June 2000, pp. 65-91, http://www.jstor. org/stable/2567916.

"Fair Deal." *Wikipedia: The Free Encyclopedia*, Wikimedia Foundation, 16 August 2019, en.wikipedia.org/wiki/Fair_Deal.

"Federal Writers' Project." *Wikipedia: The Free Encyclopedia*, Wikimedia Foundation, 17 March 2019, en.wikipedia.org/wiki/Federal_Writers'_ Project.

Fetter, Donnie. "Breaking Bethel, Part 1: What the Future Might Hold for Athens' Most Notorious Neighborhood." *Athens Banner-Herald*, 23 June 2018, https://www.onlineathens.com/article/20150922/ NEWS/180629476.

Flynn, George Q. "Selective Service and American Blacks During World War II," *The Journal of Negro History*, vol. 69, no. 1, Winter 1984, pp. 14-25.

Foote, Joseph. "As They Saw It: HUD's Secretaries Reminisce about Carrying Out the Mission"
Cityscape: A Journal of Policy Development and Research, vol. 1, no. 3, September 1995, pp. 71-92.

Forstall, Richard L. "Population of States and Counties of the United States, 1790-1990," Department of Commerce, U.S. Bureau of the Census Population Division, Washington, D.C., March 1996.

Franklin D. Roosevelt Presidential Library and Museum. *Our Documents: Executive Order 8802 - Prohibition of Discrimination in the Defense Industry, June 25, 1941*, http://docs.fdrlibrary.marist.edu/odex8802.html.

"Friedman's Lake View Hotel, View of Hotel from the Lake" [digital image]. *Catskills Institute*, Brown Digital Repository, Brown University Library, 1941, https://repository.library.brown.edu/studio/item/bdr:46948/

"Georgia Census Data: Link to Census Report of U.S. Population for States and Counties, 1790-1990." http://earlyushistory.net/georgia-census-data/#TOP.

Georgia Department of Education. *School Plant Survey.* Athens Public Schools, 1952.

"God's Trombones." *Wikipedia: The Free Encyclopedia*, Wikimedia Foundation, 11 June 2019. en.wikipedia.org/wiki/God's_Trombones.

"*Gomillion v. Lightfoot.*" *Wikipedia: The Free Encyclopedia*, Wikimedia Foundation, 7 May 2019. en.wikipedia.org/wiki/Gomillion_v._Lightfoot.

Graham, Vince. "Urban Renewal...Means Negro Removal. ~ James Baldwin (1963)." *YouTube*, YouTube, 3 June 2015, https://www.youtube.com/ watch?v=T8Abhj17kYU.

"Great Migration (African American)." *Wikipedia: The Free Encyclopedia*, Wikimedia Foundation, 30 July 2019. en.wikipedia.org/wiki/Great_Migration_(African_American).

Harris, Tene A., *Value, Networks, Desegregation, and Displacement at One of Georgia's Black High Schools, Athens High and Industrial School/Burney-Harris High School, 1913-1970*. 2012. Georgia State University, Ph.D. dissertation, https://scholarworks.gsu.edu/eps_diss/95

Harrison, Dr. Robert Edward. *First African Methodist Episcopal Church, Athens, GA 1866-2016*. Athens, Georgia, 2016.

"History." *The Yellow Jacket*, http://www.theyellowjacket.com/history.html.

"History of Athens Regional Library." *The Georgia Librarian*, South Carolina History Project, University of South Carolina, Fall 1997, pp. 19-21.

Hi-Y and Tri-Hi-Y Clubs, http://www.vintagekidstuff.com/hiy/hiy.html.

"Hopeforathens.net." *Hopeforathens.net*.

"Horatio Spafford." *Wikipedia: The Free Encyclopedia*, Wikimedia Foundation, 8 Aug. 2019, en.wikipedia.org/wiki/Horatio_Spafford.

"Housing Act of 1949." *Wikipedia: The Free Encyclopedia*, Wikimedia Foundation, 16 Apr. 2019, en.wikipedia.org/wiki/Housing_Act_of_1949.

Howalt, Robert. *Central District, Athens, Georgia* , 1951. [Map.]

Howard B. Stroud Sr. Memorial Page, http://www.bandecrafts.com/Howard B. Stroud Sr. Memorial Page 03-31-08.htm

Hribal, Sean. "History of the Dunbar Branch Library," Athens Regional Library System, www.athenslibrary.org/athens/departments/heritage/services/blogs/colophons-annotations/315-history-of-the-dunbar-branch-library.

"If We So Choose." *Vimeo*, 10 July 2019, vimeo.com/99725662.

Insurance Maps of Athens, Clark County, Georgia, Dec. 1913. Sanborn Map Company, 1914.

Insurance Maps of Athens, Clark County, Georgia, 1918. Sanborn Map Company, 1918.

Insurance Maps of Athens, Clark County, Georgia, 1926. Sanborn Map Company, 1926.

"It Is Well With My Soul." *Wikipedia: The Free Encyclopedia*, Wikimedia Foundation, 24 June 2019, en.wikipedia.org/wiki/It_Is_Well_with_My_Soul.

"It Is Well With My Soul - Lyrics, Hymn Meaning and Story." *GodTube*, https://www.godtube.com/popular-hymns/it-is-well-with-my-soul/.

"James R. Smith in Music Recital." *Highlight*, Athens High and Industrial School, October 1958, p. 3.

"Jaycees Name Smith Young Layman of Year." *Athens Banner Herald*, November 22, 1972.

"John Lewis (Civil Rights Leader)." *Wikipedia: The Free Encyclopedia*, Wikimedia Foundation, 9 July 2019, en.wikipedia.org/wiki/John_Lewis_(civil_rights_leader).

Johnson, James Weldon. *God's Trombones*. Penguin Books, Random House, 1976, www.penguinrandomhouse.com/books/321969/gods-trombones-by-james-weldon-johnson/9780143105411/.

Jones, Brian P., *The Tuskegee Revolt: Student Activism, Black Power, and the Legacy of Booker T. Washington*. 2018. City University of New York, Ph.D. dissertation, https://academicworks.cuny.edu/gc_etds/2675.

Kilpatrick, William H. "The Beginnings of the Public School System in Georgia." *The Georgia Historical Quarterly*, vol. 5, no. 3, 1921, pp. 3-19, www.jstor.org/stable/40575679.

Kline, J. Anthony, and Richard Le Gates. "Citizen Participation in the Model Cities Program—Toward a Theory of Collective Bargaining for the Poor." *National Black Law Journal*, vol. 1, no. 1, 1971. https://escholarship.org/uc/item/0fx0k3r8

Knight, Monica Dellenberger. *Seeking Education for Liberation: The Development of Black Schools in Athens, Georgia from Emancipation through Desegregation*. 2007. University of Georgia, Ph.D. dissertation.

Lutz, James D. "Lest We Forget, a Short History of Housing in the United States." American Council for an Energy Efficient Economy (ACEEE) Summer Study on Energy Efficiency in Buildings, 2004, https://ees.lbl.gov/sites/all/files/lest_we_forget_a_short_history_of_housing_in_the_united_states_lbnl-4751e.pdf

Map of the City of Athens, Georgia. Georgia Drafting Company, 1949.

McAdams, Jewell. "Students of the Quarter," *Highlight*, Athens High and Industrial School, March 1957, p. 3.

"Model Cities Program." *Wikipedia: The Free Encyclopedia*, Wikimedia Foundation, 24 June 2019, en.wikipedia.org/wiki/Model_Cities_Program.

Moffson, Steven. *Equalization Schools in Georgia's African-American Communities, 1951-1970*. Historic Preservation Division, Georgia Department of Natural Resources, Atlanta, GA, September 20, 2010.

Morales, Kristen. "Bethel: Affordable Housing or Mismanaged Cash Cow?" *Flagpole Magazine,* 5 June 2013, https://flagpole.com/news/news-features/2013/06/05/bethel-midtown-village-affordable-housing-or-mismanaged-cash-cow.

Morales, Kristen. "Beyond Bethel: Residents and City Officials Urge Redevelopment." *Flagpole Magazine*, 17 Feb. 2016, https://flagpole.com/news/news-features/2016/02/17/beyond-bethel-residents-and-city-officials-urge-redevelopment.

Moss, Mrs. John D. "The Black Mammy Memorial or Peace Monument." *Black Mammy Memorial Institute*, Athens, Georgia, 1910.

"Murder of Lemuel Penn." *Wikipedia: The Free Encyclopedia*, Wikimedia Foundation, 13 May 2019, en.wikipedia.org/wiki/Murder_of_Lemuel_Penn.

National Baptist Convention - Envisioning the Future Exceptionally - Membership & Ministries FAQs, http://www.nationalbaptist.com/resources/church-faqs/membership--ministries-faqs.html.

Neier, Aryeh. "Brown v. Board of Ed: Key Cold War Weapon." *Reuters*, 14 May 2014, http://blogs.reuters.com/great-debate/2014/05/14/brown-v-board-of-ed-key-cold-war-weapon/.

Nelsons' Baldwin Directory Company, Inc. "Nelsons' Baldwin's Athens Georgia City Directory [1952]." University of Georgia. Map and Government Information Library, 1952.

Nelsons' Baldwin Directory Company, Inc.. "Nelsons' Baldwin's Athens Georgia City Directory [1954]." University of Georgia. Map and Government Information Library, 1954.

Nelsons' Directory Company, Inc.. "Nelsons' Athens Georgia City Directory [1956]." University of Georgia. Map and Government Information Library, 1956.

Nelsons' Directory Company, Inc.. "Nelsons' Athens Georgia City Directory [1958]." University of Georgia. Map and Government Information Library, 1958.

Nelsons' Directory Company, Inc.. "Nelsons' Athens Georgia City Directory [1962]." University of Georgia. Map and Government Information Library, 1962.

Nelsons' Directory Company, Inc.. "Nelsons' Athens Georgia City Directory [1964]." University of Georgia. Map and Government Information Library, 1964.

"New Deal." *Wikipedia: The Free Encyclopedia*, Wikimedia Foundation, 7 Aug. 2019, en.wikipedia.org/wiki/New_Deal.

Olken, Charles E. "Economic Development in the Model Cities Program," *Law and Contemporary Problems*, vol. 36, Spring 1971, pp. 205-226, https://scholarship.law.duke.edu/lcp/vol36/iss2/5.

"Our History." *First A.M.E. Church*, www.firstame.org/our-history/.

Parker, Dan. "Coroner Investigating Fatal Shooting of Policeman Here." *Athens Banner-Herald*, Nov. 4, 1963.

Patton, June O., J. Strickland, and E. J. Crawford. "Moonlight and Magnolias in Southern Education: The Black Mammy Memorial Institute." *The Journal of Negro History*, vol. 65, no. 2, 1980, pp. 149-155, www.jstor.org/stable/2717053.

Piedmont Directory Company. "Athens, Georgia City Directory [1914-1915]." University of Georgia Map and Government Information Library, 1914/1915.

Piedmont Directory Company. "Athens, Georgia City Directory [1923-1924]." University of Georgia Map and Government Information Library, 1923/1924.

Piedmont Directory Company. "Athens, Georgia City Directory [1926-1927]." University of Georgia Map and Government Information Library, 1926/1927.

Piedmont Directory Company. "Miller's Athens, Georgia City Directory [1928-1929]." University of Georgia Map and Government Information Library, 1928/1929.

Piedmont Directory Company. "Piedmont Directory Co.'s Athens (Georgia) city directory [1931]." University of Georgia Map and Government Information Library, 1931.

Pressly, Paul M. "Educating the Daughters of Savannah's Elite: The Pape School, the Girl Scouts, and the Progressive Movement." *The Georgia Historical Quarterly*, vol. 80, no. 2, 1996, pp. 246-275, www.jstor.org/stable/40583435.

Pulver, Matthew. "Southern Apartheid and Urban Renewal in East Athens." *Flagpole Magazine*, 25 Feb. 2015, https://flagpole.com/news/news-features/2015/02/25/southern-apartheid-and-urban-renewal-in-east-athens.

Publishers Press (Atlanta, Ga.). "City Directory of Athens [1916-1917]." University of Georgia Map and Government Information Library, 1916/1917.

Reap, James K. *Athens, A Pictorial History, 1801-2001*. The Donning Co. Publishers, 1982/2001.

"Report of Hon. Herman Myers, Mayor, Together with the Reports of the City Officers of the City of Savannah, Georgia, for the Year Ending December 31, 1903." *The Morning News,* Savannah, GA, 1904, http://dlg.galileo.usg.edu/savannahmayor/pdf/1903.pdf

R.L. Polk & Co. "Polk's Athens (Clarke County, Ga.) City Directory [1935]." University of Georgia Map and Government Information Library, 1935.

R.L. Polk & Co. "Polk's Athens (Clarke County, Ga.) City Directory [1937]." University of Georgia Map and Government Information Library, 1937.

Ross, Jayson, Lyric Maze, and Justin Maloney, "A Short History of Black Athens." *Death and Human History in Athens,* https://digilab.libs.uga.edu/cemetery/exhibits/show/brooklyn/short-history-of-black-athens

"Rural Survey of Clarke County, Georgia, with Special Reference to the Negroes." Phelps-Stokes Fellowship Studies No. 2, *Bulletin of the University of Georgia*, vol. XV, no. 3, March 1915.

Schechter, Jody H. *An Empirical Evaluation of the Model Cities Program*. 2011. University of Michigan, Master's thesis.

Schwab, Katharine. "The Racist Roots of 'Urban Renewal' and How It Made
    Cities Less Equal." *Fast Company*, 9 July 2018,
    https://www.fastcompany.com/90155955/the-racist-roots-of-urban-
    renewal-and-how-it-made-cities-less-equal.

Scruggs, Yvonne. "HUD's Stewardship of National Urban Policy: A
    Retrospective View."
    Cityscape: A Journal of Policy Development and Research, vol. 1, no. 3,
    September 1995.

Selective Service System. *History and Records: Induction Statistics*.
    https://www.sss.gov/About/History-And-Records/Induction-Statistics.

Selective Service System. *Return to the Draft: Postponements, Deferments,
    Exemptions*. https://www.sss.gov/About/Return-to-the-Draft/
    Postponements-Deferments-Exemptions.

Sharpless, Rebecca. *Cooking in Other Women's Kitchens*. The University of
    North Carolina Press, 2010.

Smith, Florence B. *State Minimum Wage Laws and Orders: 1940*. U.S.
    Department of Labor, 1941.

"Strikes in 1941." U.S. Department of Labor, Bureau of Labor Statistics,
    Bulletin no. 711, 1942. https://www.bls.gov/wsp/1941_strikes.pdf.

Sutton, Philip. "A History of City Directories in the United States and New
    York City." The New York Public Library, 30 Sept. 2016, https://www.
    nypl.org/blog/2012/06/08/direct-me-1786-history-city-directories-US-
    NYC.

"*Swann v. Charlotte-Mecklenburg Board of Education*." *Wikipedia: The Free
    Encyclopedia*, Wikimedia Foundation, 17 May 2019, en.wikipedia.org/
    wiki/Swann_v._Charlotte-Mecklenburg_Board_of_Education.

Tanner, Laurel N., and Daniel Tanner. "Unanticipated Effects of Federal
    Policy: The Kindergarten," *Journal of Educational Leadership*, October
    1973.

Taylor, Nicole. "Lt. Col. Lemuel Penn: The Hero Who Changed Athens,
    Georgia, and the Nation." *The Bitter Southerner*, 27 Mar. 2017, www.
    bittersoutherner.com/from-the-southern-perspective/lemuel-penn-hero-
    athens-georgia.

"The A.H.I.S. Chorus." *Highlight*, Athens High and Industrial School, March
    1957, p. 1.

Thomas, Francis Taliaferro. *A Portrait of Historic Athens & Clarke County*.
    University of Georgia Press, 1992.

Thompson, Jim. "Killian Remembered as Tireless and Fearless Crusader
    for Justice and Fairness." *Athens Banner-Herald*, 1 Nov. 2016, www.
    onlineathens.com/local-news/2016-11-01/killian-remembered-tireless-
    and-fearless-crusader-justice-and-fairness.

Thurmond, Michael L. *A Story Untold: Black Men and Women in Athens
    History*. 1978. Deeds Publishing, 2019.

Thurmond, Michael L. "Black Educators and Their Schools Quenching the Thirst for Knowledge." *Athens Historian*, Athens Historical Society, https://www.athenshistorical.org/athens-historian-volume4-article2.

"Tuskegee, Alabama." *Wikipedia: The Free Encyclopedia*, Wikimedia Foundation, 7 June 2019, en.wikipedia.org/wiki/Tuskegee,_Alabama.

"Tuskegee University." *Encyclopedia of Alabama*, http://www.encyclopediaofalabama.org/article/h-1583.

Tuskegee University: History and Mission. www.tuskegee.edu/about-us/history-and-mission.

Tuskegee University: History of the Tuskegee University Choir. https://www.tuskegee.edu/student-life/join-a-student-organization/choir/choir-history.

"Tuskegee Veterans Administration Medical Center." *Wikipedia: The Free Encyclopedia*, Wikimedia Foundation, 5 Apr. 2018, en.wikipedia.org/wiki/Tuskegee_Veterans_Administration_Medical_Center.

Urban Renewal Directory. U.S. Department of Housing and Urban Development, 1958-1974.

U.S. Dept. of Labor Wage and Hour Division. "History of Federal Minimum Wage Rates under the Fair Labor Standards Act, 1938-2009." www.dol.gov/whd/minwage/chart.htm.

Venator-Santiago, Charles R. "Are Puerto Ricans Really American Citizens?" *The Conversation*, 2 March 2017 http://theconversation.com/are-puerto-ricans-really-american-citizens-73723.

"War on Poverty." *Wikipedia: The Free Encyclopedia*, Wikimedia Foundation, 2 Aug. 2019, en.wikipedia.org/wiki/War_on_Poverty.

"William J.J. Chase." *Wikipedia: The Free Encyclopedia*, Wikimedia Foundation, 23 Apr. 2019, en.wikipedia.org/wiki/William_J.J._Chase.

Wright, Natalie. "Reflecting, Sharing, Learning." *Rev. A.R. Killian Interviewed by Earnest Thompson*, www.athenslibrary.org/rslathens/video/childhood-memories/3595-rev-a-r-killian-interviewed-by-earnest-thompson.

Young, John Todd. "Model Cities Program." Center for the Study of Federalism, 2006, http://encyclopedia.federalism.org/index.php/Model_Cities_Program

About the Author

Ellen L. Walker is a graphic designer living in Athens, Georgia. Born and raised in St. Louis, Missouri, she earned her B.A. in Art and Elementary Education from Grinnell College in Iowa. She has worked as a professional graphic designer for over 40 years in Ann Arbor, Michigan, upstate New York, and now Athens. She also lived for two years in a small village in Malaysia, where she taught in the local school and assisted with anthropological research. She earned her M.A. in Design from Syracuse University and taught elementary school in Athens for several years. She continues to do freelance graphic design work. She has always loved to write. This is her first book.

Made in the USA
Columbia, SC
24 June 2020